STUDIES IN GERMAN LITERATURE,
LINGUISTICS, AND CULTURE

VOL. 18

STUDIES IN GERMAN LITERATURE,
LINGUISTICS, AND CULTURE

VOL. 18

Editorial Board

Managing Editors

CAMDEN HOUSE
Columbia, South Carolina

THE WELLSPRINGS OF
LITERARY CREATION

a. die Nase.
b. die Stirn
c. die Augen
d. Dallas'sche Beefsteck u Portwein
e. der Ironische Zug oder die Mährchen-Muskel
f. das lange Kinn misgrathe. ne Schauspiele (Blandina etc
g. Neuaptirte Haare oder Geistererscheinungen
h Ein Halstuch
i Ein Kragen.

k. Ein Rokaermel mit willkührlichen Faben
l. Der Backenbart oder übernachtige Gedanken eines Mondsüchtigen.
m. die Mephistophelesmusk. oder Rachgier u Mordlust Elixiere des Teufels.
n. fehlt.
o. Das Ohr oder Kreislers Lehrbrief der weder gehört noch verstanden word
p. Und so weiter

E. T. A. Hoffmann, Self-Portrait with physiognomic detail.

THE WELLSPRINGS OF LITERARY CREATION:

An Analysis of Male and Female "Artist Stories"
from the German Romantics to
American Writers of the Present

Ursula R. Mahlendorf

CAMDEN HOUSE

The text of this book was typeset at
the University of California, Santa Barbara,
by means of a laser printer.

Printed on acid-free Glatfelder paper.

CONTENTS

ACKNOWLEDGEMENTS

Several of the studies of individual authors in this book were printed in earlier, less comprehensive versions. These are the essays on Hoffmann and Mörike which appeared in *American Imago* (vol. 32, 3 [1975], 217-239; vol. 33, 3 [1976], 304-327 respectively) and the essay on Kafka which appeared in *Modern Austrian Literature* (vol. XI, 3/4 [1978], 199-242). I wish to acknowledge my gratitude for permission to reprint the revised and enlarged versions here.

I am grateful to the following for permission to reproduce the illustrations for this book: to the Bildarchiv Preußischer Kulturbesitz Berlin for E.T.A. Hoffmann's self-portrait (frontispiece); to the Gerstenberg Buchverlag, Hildesheim for E.T.A. Hoffmann's drawing to *The Sandman* (Illustration I); to the Adalbert Stifter-Gesellschaft, Wien for the tracing of *die Bewegung,* (Illustration II), and the painting of *die Bewegung,* (Illustration III).

My thanks go to my students who responded so sensitively and enthusiastically to the works discussed here; and to the University of California, Santa Barbara, for giving me the opportunity to teach in my area of interest, and several sabbatical leaves. I further wish to thank Harry Slochower, Editor in Chief, *American Imago,* whose *Mythopoesis* stimulated my early studies, and whose encouragement enabled me to persevere. My thanks go also to Harry Steinhauer, Professor Emeritus, U.C.S.B., whose critical comments were invaluable and to Constance Gagnon who devotedly helped with editing. Finally, my gratitude to members of the Psychiatric Foundation of Santa Barbara, and to John L. Carleton, M.D., Director of the Santa Barbara Psychiatric Medical Group. Over the past ten years, from their psychotherapy sessions, workshops, study groups, and art therapy groups, I have gained such knowledge as I have of psychodynamics, clinical practice, emotional illness and health. We have discussed these stories and writers as if they were real, still-living people. To my surprise, the stories were completely understandable without benefit of a long introduction to the German literary heritage. This is why I feel that these essays, with short plot summaries provided, can speak to a general audience interested in literary creation and its relationship to sanity and madness. What emotional truth these studies may have is due to my day-to-day involvement with the Psychiatric Foundation, and the support of its members.

UM
Santa Barbara, May, 1984

ILLUSTRATIONS

---

*To John L. Carleton, M.D. and to the Members of
the Santa Barbara Psychiatric Foundation.*

INTRODUCTION

A *Künstlernovelle* and *Künstlerroman* (artist story and artist novel) contains the creation of a work of art as a central event of its plot. Based on the creative work and psychology of a fictitious sculptor, painter, poet or musician, "artist stories" have fascinated German authors and readers continuously since the Romantics of the early 19th century.[1] Under German Romantic influence, American writers, beginning with Hawthorne in *The Artist of the Beautiful* (1844) have shared this fascination. Despite Günther Grass's devastating parody in *The Tin Drum* (1959) the genre in German letters is far from exhausted, as Christa Wolf's sensitive *A Model Childhood* (1977) has shown. Recent evidence of the continuing vogue in American letters are Philip Roth's novella *The Ghost Writer* published in the *New Yorker* (June/July, 1979) with allusions to Thomas Mann's artists and John Irving's best-seller *The World According to Garp* (1976) with direct echoes of so unlikely (and misunderstood) a work as Franz Grillparzer's artist story *The Poor Fiddler* (1842).

Why does the artist figure appeal even to a non-literary audience? Fictionalized artist biographies like Irving Stone's *The Agony and the Ecstasy* provide participation in a richer life, insight into works of genius and the mysteries of their conception and birth. Biographies of well-known artists also cater to popular hunger for access to the secret of greatness, always enthralling to the imagination. Artist stories, though less sensational, appeal to similar curiosities. But they usually deal with imaginary or little-known artists and their plot accords with the writer's personal vision of the meaning of artistic existence and the origins of artistic achievement.

In the following chapters, I will analyze seven artist stories in depth. Throughout this study, I will use the words art and artist as generic terms and as equivalents for the German words *Kunst* and *Künstler*. This usage reflects a central thesis of this book: that early childhood creativity expresses itself in many ways, and is not limited to a specific gift, medium, or activity. In the course of development, the future artist may come to prefer a specific medium, art form, or sense modality. But an artist may retain the flexibility of childhood. Some of the writers we will discuss practiced two, or even three arts, although they became celebrated for only one; several settled on writing late in life. E.g., Hoffmann was a musician until his mid thirties though he had been sketching and writing since boyhood. He turned to writing because it paid him better than music and he used his sketches to illustrate his tales.

The studies comprising this volume began more than ten years ago from two entirely different points. When I read Freud's essay *Das Unheimliche (The Uncanny,* 1919), it struck me that Freud's interpretation of Hoffmann's *The Sandman* did not consider the fact that the hero was an artist. To my mind, Hoffmann's making his hero a poet was crucially important. This led me to look at Hoffmann's theory of artistic creation and its reflection in his work as a whole. Further study of *The Sandman* brought up general questions about creativity. What function, for example, did Hoffmann attribute to literary creation in an artist's life, in theorizing (letters, essays, autobiographical accounts) and in his fiction? What emotional, psychosocial and intellectual development did he ascribe to his artist protagonist between childhood and maturity? When and why did his creative career begin?

An essay of mine on Mann's *Doctor Faustus* arose from curiosity about the psychological meaning of music to Mann's protagonist. As I worked on these and other studies on the artist figure,[2] I began reading widely on theories of creativity. It seemed to me that, in general, social scientists (psychologists, psychoanalysts, psychiatrists, sociologists, philosophers) distrust, and therefore dismiss, attempts by writers and artists to explain the creative process. Nietzsche's half-joking comment in *Zarathustra* best summarizes the attitude:

"...poets lie too much." Writers and artists, in their turn, distrust the scientists, fearing that psychological questions may trivialize or invalidate their work, and meet inquiries with derision and obfuscation. Hence Shaw's reply to a psychologist who asked what had done the most for him as a writer, "My father's pocketbook." As literary scholars we have modestly insisted since the beginning of our discipline in the 1880s that our work is valid only if it is restricted to gathering and ordering data, keeping records (for instance, the admirable task, now finally appreciated, of compiling editions and concordances),[3] and to saying "Words about Words about Words."[4] This purism has led to exclusion of our inquiries into artistic and literary creativity from the growing body of such research by social scientists. The result has been neglect of the area of our expertise and sensitivity: matters of style and form. I see my work as a part of the recent interdisciplinary endeavor to end the separation of the study of literature from the study of the natural, physical and social sciences[5] and to make works concerned with man's emotions and thoughts accessible and useful to the other sciences of man.

For an overall view of a writer's insights into creation, we must turn to his essays on aesthetics, autobiographical fragments, and his stories about artists. In fiction about artists, writers tend to use the hero to portray aspects of their own creative struggle. Each work reveals crucial facts about the writer's own psyche. The assumption underlying my study is that when an author composes a story about another artist, he lays bare the psychological roots of his own creativity and illustrates what makes it flourish and grow. In addition to giving us conscious views about the creative process, these stories reveal aspects of which the writers are unconscious. This supplies us with another dimension of the creative process. Combined with other autobiographical material, these works provide a comprehensive picture of the artist's psyche during the creative process. In studying artist stories and their writers, I found a remarkable consistency between their theory and fiction. I have therefore become convinced that the insight of writers into the wellsprings of literary creation deserves serious psychological as well as literary investigation.

When we study the creative process of a writer and examine how it was acquired and how it operates, we must include consideration of the medium — language, imagery, narrative forms and techniques. In the following analyses we shall therefore investigate the relationship between psychology and style. The in-depth look at a writer's development yields information about origins of stylistic and formal patterns. I believe that close study of the connection between psychology and style can lead to a new understanding of a writer's work, especially as to underlying meaning and form. In turn, this understanding can provide a tool for evaluating literary quality.

When I began, I wanted to include a historical dimension, and therefore I chose stories from different literary movements, from Hoffmann's *The Sandman* (1816) to Thomas Mann's *Doctor Faustus* (1947). I thought this diachronic approach would enable me to observe changes in the way writers viewed the creative process, and possible changes in the process itself. But historical factors proved less important than early environment, family composition, the degree of comfort, encouragement of individual development within, and the pressures on the childhood family. If early learning was so crucial, then there had to be significant differences in the origins of creativity in males and females. When I looked for artist stories by German women writers, I found none until Christa Wolf's *A Model Childhood* of 1977. Looking at other Western literatures, I found that the genre, a story about a female artist written by a woman, did not exist until the turn of the century, that the earliest and finest examples came from American literature and that differences between men and women (disregarding biology and literary tradition) were indeed greater than those between Hoffmann and Kafka one hundred years later. Since this is so, I assume that the results of my study are not affected by the neat but accidental distribution into male German writers and female American writers. We might say that the creative process is a basic musical theme, on which every artist plays his own variation, its pattern depending on person and background. The woman artist's theme, however, besides being an individual variation, reverses the male artist's theme.

The reader can see from my continuous attraction to these stories and their authors that I experienced a strong countertransference (usually of the positive kind) to them.[6] This had the advantage of a strong identification with the protagonists and hence an empathy for their dilemmas. It had the disadvantage of wanting to protect myself against feeling the impact of their failures and therefore being tempted to superimpose explanatory, intellectualized frameworks on the stories for my safety (the usual hazard of the psychological interpreter). It carried with it the danger of identifying all too closely with the protagonists and hence being blind to the complexities of the text and to my own historical and biographical contexts. Interpretation involved constantly keeping a rein on my expectations of the text, checking my perceptions against the author's contexts, questioning myself why I was asking a given question, checking other interpretations, other hermeneutical frameworks and psychological theories to find out what questions I was not and should perhaps be asking, and sensitizing myself, again and again, to minimal clues in the web of the text.

My psychological orientation has undergone considerable modifications during the investigation, modifications which, I recognize in retrospect, reflect some of the important changes in psychoanalytic psychology over the last fifty years. Every author presented a variation on creative difficulties, which was not always accessible to analysis by the same psychological models or theories. For example, the schizophrenia of Büchner's poet could not be understood in terms of Freudian oedipal psychology, which in turn was useful to the study of Hoffmann's artist. The only adequate frameworks for Büchner's work were theories of schizophrenia dealing with double-binding, and communicational and personal failure. Even the oedipal dilemmas of Hoffmann's story, so well discussed by Freud, are greatly modified by pre-oedipal development. Hence I had to include the entire recent study and theory of infantile psychosocial and cognitive development. In addition, I had to look at the post-Freudian authors' areas of agreement and disagreement with Freud in terms of theoretical frameworks differing from the Freudian. British psychoanalysis (Spitz, Anna Freud, Winnicott, Balint — to name a few), the self psychology of Heinz Kohut and the Chicago school, and recent psychiatric, psychological, and psychoanalytic studies on transitional objects and child development provided concepts necessary to study aspects of creativity rooted in earliest mother-child relationships and inaccessible to the oedipal Freudian framework. From early on, I wanted to include women writers, because they contribute to understanding the minimal conditions required for artistic development and how creation can be frustrated. Freudian oedipal theory was of little help here; conceptual frameworks extending to the mother-child symbiosis and the social group were more useful.

Late in my undertaking, I became dissatisfied with reliance on the drive energy model provided by classical Freudian analysis. Surveying my authors, I could see sources of creative energy other than instinct, than libidinal and aggressive psychic energies which were sublimated by creative labor. In many of the stories I analyzed, I found that psychic energy for the creative process came from the social environment. This was energy internalized in the early primary group, restimulated by later encounters and companions. For my authors, creation was social and personal. Thus I found helpful the explanatory frameworks of Kohut, Balint, and Ammon, which locate creative energy in the earliest mother-child relationship and the primary social group.

No single theory accounts for all the facets presented by my authors. Consequently, I took from each theoretical framework what was necessary to understand the creative process as seen by the writer himself. The scholar not acquainted with psychoanalytical inquiry will find that I also examine the creative process and its depiction in works of literature by the traditional methods of literary biography and criticism. The first chapter discussion of the psychological meaning of form and of major psychological and psychoanalytic theories of creativity is intended to acquaint readers with psychological issues and approaches to the study of the creative process so that later discussions may be more readily understood. For the benefit of the reader not readily conversant with the various schools of psychoanalytic theory, a glossary of terms as used in this study is appended.

Through many years of psychological and psychoanalytic inquiry and introspection I have become convinced that psychoanalytical methods and theories have an important place in literary study. I have explored the dynamics of interpersonal relationships portrayed in literature in various psychiatric and academic settings and feel that the interdisciplinary approach is true to the tradition of subjectivity which produced Freud, Jung, and the beginnings of psychoanalysis. And since Freud and early psychoanalysis, as Bruno Bettelheim recently reminded us,[7] are very much rooted in the German language and its literature, I considered that I was reclaiming for literary study a heritage which we Germanists had sorely mis-used.

Of course, much in psychoanalysis has changed since Freud's time. As a sub-specialty of psychiatry, it has been enriched during the last fifty years by an enormous mass of clinical data from research by clinics, teaching hospitals, child care institutions, and private facilities. And it has been modified by other theories of human behavior; most significantly, for our purposes, by those of interpersonal dynamics and infant development. From this rich array of data and theories, literary scholars can formulate new questions concerning the writer's problems with his craft, their relationship to his life history (early life history especially) and the psychological function of a writer's creative process in his life. Ignorance of this wealth of theories and supportive data has led even respected monthlies such as *The Atlantic* or publishing houses like Farrar, Strauss and Giroux to take seriously such confused, ill-informed attacks on psychoanalysis and Freud as Jeffrey Masson's *The Assault on Truth: Freud's Suppression of the Seduction Theory*.[8] Reading these strange accusations and claims, I felt tempted to join with Paul Robinson in bewailing "the dilapidated state into which [Freud's] legacy has fallen," and blaming it on "the decline of intellectual and literary standards" since Freud's day.[9] More convincing motivation for such attacks, and the alacrity with which they are adopted, is what Freud identified as "the narcissistic blow" psychoanalysis continues to deal to man's pride by asserting that man is not master of his own thoughts.[10]

More serious to psychoanalysis and to all introspective and empathic psychologies are the challenges coming from the growing neurosciences. Freud himself felt that one day many mysteries of mind and soul would be understood as biological processes. Indeed, advances in neurobiology, neurochemistry, neurolinguistics, immunology, systems and living systems theory have generated the popular belief that biochemical solutions to psychological problems are so near that psychological insight and working-through in therapy are fast approaching obsolescence. Such optimism (or pessimism, if one fears abuse of such knowledge) rests on error: great as the advances in the neurosciences have been, they are far from resolving the mysteries of the human mind. Only isolated processes have been made comprehensible (for instance, the workings of a given neurotransmitter, analogous to one brick in a whole building). The vast complexity of many simultaneous, ever-changing brain processes in interactions with the many matter, energy and information processes of the environment are far from being understood. But even if they are comprehended, human understanding of other human beings through introspection and empathy cannot be replaced. It seems more likely that psychoanalysis, "the science of complex mental states, the science of man's experiences," as Heinz Kohut described it, will pose "the ultimate challenge to scientific thought: to be objective *and (in its explanations) phenomenon–distant in the area of the subject,* the human soul, the human experience itself."[11]

I
ISSUES IN THE STUDY OF THE CREATIVE PROCESS

Function and Psychological Meaning of Form

For all our writers, creation is something sensuous and real. In Mörike's *Mozart* the creative process begins with sight, touch, and smell of an orange; for Chopin's woman artist Edna it begins with the music of a prelude which arouses "the very passions ... within her soul, swaying it, lashing it, as the waves daily beat upon her splendid body."[1] Writers embody thoughts, feelings, insights about the creative process in events, symbols, characters, rhetorical figures, syntactical forms and relationships.[2] These forms continue to reverberate with the sensuousness in which they originate, and therefore reflect the history and vicissitudes of the artist's existence in the here and now. An artist's style and form is the accretion of life experiences which have been integrated into the innermost being. As Rilke says concerning the poet's feelings, and the memories which flow into his work, "Not till they have turned to blood within us, to glance and gesture, nameless and no longer to be distinguished from ourselves — not till then can it happen that... the first word of a verse arises in their midst and goes forth from them."[3]

Contemporary psychoanalytic theory of creativity agrees with the Romantic view that the artist is a person different from other men. "The creative person maintains and has maintained an alternative to his normal identity structure at each level of his psychogenic development."[4] The artist therefore always has two identities, and by this fact is an exception and likely to be a problematic existence. Jochen Schmidt, in a brief history of the artist novella from Hoffmann to Kafka, connects "something particularly novella-like" with the very "structure of the artist's problem. Ever since the Storm and Stress and its concept of genius the artist has been a figure of exception and crisis. Goethe in his *Tasso* was the first to realize this. And when, in early Romanticism, artistic man was elevated to the sphere of the marvelous, the theme of the poet as the representative of ideality was transposed to the sphere of the extraordinary and marvelous as well."[5] The novella form compresses many aspects of existence into one extraordinary, marvelous event. In the *Künstlernovelle,* this event is always related to the creation of a work of art. Because the creative process is different from other ego processes and the creator an extraordinary man, the novella is a particularly suitable vehicle for the portrayal of creator and process alike. It is dramatic and predicated on conflict. Unlike the drama, the novella depicts inner rather than outer conflict. Its structure is tight and symbolic, the central object symbol relates to artistic creation. Because of the multivalence and the abundance of its symbols, the novella can, in compact space, render admirably the complexity of literary creation and its attendant impulses and processes, both conscious and unconscious. But precisely because of its compression, the novella needs much elucidation. The artist novel being longer, less compressed, more explicit in stating motives and artistic theories needs less interpretation. It covers the artist's entire life with much detail. But unlike the *Bildungsroman* of which it is a sub-genre, the *Künstlerroman* deals specifically with the dilemmas of a man as artist, with his feelings and thoughts, his work habits and relationships with others and his audiences as they affect his creation. It traces these back to patterns of infancy and childhood.

Both artist novel and novella are well suited to an analysis of a writer's creative process because both deal with an artist and the creation of a work of art in the context of a total life and environment. Both forms allow us to understand the creative process as the author envisages it from all perspectives, conscious and unconscious. In the following chapters on individual works, we will trace the relationship between an author's or a character's direct statements about the function of art and the latent meanings of forms and content. We will observe that direct statements about the function of art, and overt and covert meanings of forms and symbols referring to creation, supplement rather than contradict each other. Form and symbol for our authors stand in the service not of defense but of change of ego boundaries through a new synthesis of unconscious and conscious materials. In artist stories we get to know the creative process as a protagonist's continuous dynamic interaction with the world and as an integrated, total response to a sequence of internal and external, past and present, experiential and developmental stimuli. We discover the relative importance given by a writer to various impulses, as well as the different functions and results of the creator's responses in the social universe of the story.

An author's total message about the creative process does not lie in any one statement about it in his writings. In the artist novel and novella, it lies in what the author says, through which character, at what point in the character's development, at what point in the narrative, by whom, to whom, in what way, in what situation, by what images, by what rhetorical figures, through what form, syntax, rhythm. Only by such formal means, analogous to the forms and mechanisms of dream work, can the author render the complex differentiations and integrations which go into the creative process.

Because psychological messages are keyed into different forms, and different forms have definite psychological values, aesthetic form and its analysis are of key importance to our study. The emotional and communicative values of verse forms, for example, are a part of well-established tradition. The elegiac meter has become associated with mourning and grief. The novella likewise has history, tradition, and requirements. The novella serves to study a creative process from beginning to end because, as a form, it tries to encapsulate a total universe in one plot, and to mediate universality by portraying one extraordinary, marvelous event. It therefore gives us all the information we need to understand an author's view of his creative process. Yet, because the novella can compress its universality into symbols, and especially into the central *Dingsymbol* (object symbol), these must be carefully scrutinized and interpreted as rich sources of unconscious and conscious knowledge about creation. They must be seen in the context of the story and the writer's personal history and psychology. They must also be seen in the mythical and historical meanings he assigns them. For instance, the orange which plays such a crucial role as *Dingsymbol* in Mörike's *Mozart,* represents to the hero a childhood idyll, and to the author, the luxurious court of Louis XIV and pre-revolutionary European culture. Furthermore, the author has his hero transform the orange into a gift of the muse and a song. In addition to these conscious historical and mythical meanings, the orange symbol has various unconscious meanings. On this level, it represents sensuous existence and the mother's breast, it brings back an experience of mystical union with the maternal element.

The creative writer's most essential capacity, to visualize the co-existence of opposites in one object, one place, at the same time, finds memorable expression in the orange symbol.[6] In our study we will return many times to the dialectics of primary process and secondary process which writers compress into form, symbol, and metaphor.[7] The writer's art consists in externalizing the complex web of relationships existing between abstract mytho-historical, conscious meanings, and unconscious archaic meanings, between allegory and symbol and their concrete sensual manifestations.

Psychological meanings attach also to what happens to symbols in the course of the story. Psychological meanings are likewise mediated by narrative devices such as encapsulated letters or poems, story within story, editorial comment, allusion, repetition, the role of the narrator, sequencing (beginning in *mediis rebus,* flashbacks, foreshadowing), the relative weight given different characters or events, and finally, by the roles which the characters assume toward each other. We will discover that any formal symbolic element has one or more psychological functions and meanings within the narrative context in addition to its historical, traditional literary meaning. The writer can be aware of the historical tradition and its psychological meaning, or he can be blind to either or both.

Regardless of the writer's degree of awareness, every formal device has a secondary process component (clearly thought out, with deliberate historical, logical, causal antecedents) and a primary process component (intuited, global, multivalent and associative). Primary and secondary process components may have intended and unintended meanings. The secondary process is not the only process capable of complexity. As our dreams demonstrate, the primary process is capable of finely differentiated meanings.[8] All our authors deliberately and skillfully structure for aesthetic and psychological effect. They place their heroes in definite historical periods and give them conscious philosophies, and they are aware of their literary predecessors. Interested as they are in probing psychic processes, they are alert to the complexities of the primary process and intuit many of its meanings, operations, devices and significance. Post-Freudian writers especially portray underlying primary process meanings. To understand the creative process in its totality as presented by the author, we readers must be sensitive to abstract meanings of the secondary process and underlying primary process meanings.

Let me give one example of the use of a formal device in an author's rendering of the creative process. E.T.A. Hoffmann begins *The Sandman* with his hero Nathanael's letter to a friend. Later in the story, the narrator ironically comments on this formal device, claiming he used it because other beginnings were unsuitable, and giving examples of discarded beginnings. He mentions the relative advantage of the letter as an introduction, its capacity to arrest the reader's attention by seeming authenticity. Both devices — claiming authenticity for one's story (it is a letter, it must be true) — and ironic comment on choices (these were the options I had, this is what I chose, my reasons are these) are characteristic of late 18th and early 19th century narrative art. Hoffmann places himself in this tradition and assumes superiority to it. The letter form itself has another important psychological meaning. It tells the reader immediately that communication and subjectivity are important issues. A mis-communication (the hero addresses his letter to the wrong person) confirms the importance of communications. And indeed, communication is central to Hoffmann's ideas about the creative process. Moreover, the letter form directly mediates the hero's reflections to the reader and puts the reader in the middle of highly charged events which he does not understand, events intended to arouse anxiety. Like the hero, the reader comes to fathom them only gradually. This last use of the letter form effectively mediates to the reader an important characteristic of the creative process stressed by all our writers, though in many different ways — that an artist is overcome by stimuli and feelings which he does not understand and which initiate the creative process. He comes to understand these feelings only as he tries to work them through by symbolizations in his medium, and by his actions. The letter form forces the reader to experience a similar triggering stimulus and begin to work it out with the hero. A reader does not consciously grasp the complexity of response to the letter form. Hoffmann hides from the reader, by irony and play on devices and conventions, the important psychological functions these devices have. Yet his pointing to the importance of the letter form does make us aware that formal considerations have psychological meanings for him. With Hoffmann, the form has the function of both revealing *and* hiding.

The novella genre itself has multiple functions and advantages. The secrecy of writers about the creative process testifies that it is a delicate matter for them; easily upset or interfered with. It needs, so to speak, a protected space to be played out. A well-defined, circumscribed, traditional form like the novella can provide such a safe play space, within which writers can reveal the unfolding process even while they shield it from unsympathetic scrutiny and gross oversimplification.

Our writers use additional safeguards. Kafka, for instance, creates distance between himself and his reader by telling his story through the perspective of a mouse. Protected by this device, Kafka can safely play out various splits of his own self against each other. The humorous animal perspective disarms the reader's defenses, cancels the risk of losing his sympathy and also distances Kafka's own emotional involvement. The double safeguard expresses Kafka's need and yearning for containment. Into the safe narrative space, as into a crucible, he can project conflicting aspects of himself involved in the creative process. He can freely experiment, dissolve and recombine them, and work out new integrations. Confinement in the novella form allows dissolution and blending, struggle and dissonance, but its structure (one main event, one to two high points, few characters, length of about 100 pages) helps to compress and organize material into comprehensible, sensuous segments.

The novella's most important characteristic, condensation of its key concern into the *Dingsymbol,* provides a center around which segments revolve and group according to relative importance. The novella aids the writer in achieving condensation and clarification of thought, and helps him to integrate, resolve, and master the problems raised. In addition to the prescribed formal elements, every writer uses characteristic devices to achieve safety and mastery, letting go and control, disintegration and reintegration. Because this safe, structured play space exists in the artist story as a psychic reality between writer and reader, we can discover more about the creative process from analyzing the artist novella than from studying a writer's theoretical, non-fiction statements, which are more one-dimensional and guarded.

A discussion of form would be incomplete without mention of two complementary formal devices employed by all authors — splitting and synthesizing.[9] Characters in an artist story reveal themselves as splits of a few basic psychic types: parents, peers, or parts of the self. Each type can appear in sub-types; a mother figure, for example, can be good/bad mother, oral mother, oedipal mother, latency mother. The patterns in which these split-off parts interact can be characteristic of other and sometimes all works of the same writer. We can and will trace these to autobiographical childhood patterns. A common way to split the author's self is between hero and narrator. This allows the author to project aspects of himself into the hero who, if he proves too much of a psychic liability, can be eliminated. E.T.A. Hoffmann and Kate Chopin deal with their protagonists this way. Another common form of splitting is to counterpoise split-off aspects of the self against each other. Kafka in *Josephine the Singer* projects part of himself into the narrator, another part into the singer, and a third into the mouse folk. Following their inter-relationship, the reader learns the importance and role of each in Kafka's creative task. Both kinds of splitting (hero as segment of omniscient self, or several protagonists as segments of a single, conflicted self) convey an essential function of the creative process: to allow parts of the self to struggle against each other or parent figures or peer figures, to free and differentiate themselves from old selves and to establish new constellations in resolution of the conflict.

An important aspect of the creative process is the artist's capacity to split off feeling from thought, sensation from feeling, feeling from action, fantasy from reality, here from there, new from old. Splitting can be projected into objects, symbols, locales, actions, and events. Splitting can establish and resolve whole series of oppositions. In Mörike's *Mozart on the Way to Prague,* when the women separate from the men for a stroll in the park, Mozart's wife relates a house-hold incident concerning her husband. This part of the story is

clearly separate in locale and time from the main plot and presents
Mozart as householder and father, a view incongruous with the Mozart
of the rest of the story. He yearns to be a good father and householder, but is a failure. The split-off section shows what an artist
cannot be, defining him by negation.[10]

In Stifter's *Progeny,* the painter-protagonist's ancestral family
split into two branches several generations past. During intervening
years, the families expanded and then contracted geographically
(North/South), aesthetically (poetry/painting), and numerically
(several/two). The remaining families are mirror images of one
another: father/mother, unmarried son/unmarried daughter. Since
sexes and arts are complementary, intermarriage resolves the split,
reconciles branches and arts, enriches each by the other, and ensures
continuance. Splitting generates diversity, establishes distinctions
and differentiations, enriches plot, scope and action.

Stifter's kind of splitting contains its own integrative pattern. The
synthesizing devices our authors use to resolve splitting and conflict
reflect their psychic development and are related to the function of
the finished work in their psychic economy. Synthesizing devices
depend on and affect the mastery intended and achieved —
intellectual/emotional working through, intellectualized rationalization, emotional abreaction, or formal-mechanical defense. Lastly, the
synthesizing device determines the work's aesthetic quality. Psychological analysis therefore gives us a basis for judgment of aesthetic
quality. A few examples will illustrate this.

Hoffmann's *The Sandman* is weighted down with *leitmotifs,* structuring devices and synthesizing strategies.[11] Its key symbol, the sandman, appears six times, with three appearances grouped together and
contrasted against the next three. The first three are given in letters,
hence from the subjective perspective; in content, they are reports of
mastery of the apparition. The last three, in narrator's, hence objective perspective are reports of failure to master the appearances.
The story is therefore structured as a rising and falling line of the
protagonist's fortunes. At the apex of the two lines, in the middle of
the story, the narrator addresses the reader in a subjective, ironic
reflection on his narrative method. His discourse is immediately jux-
taposed to his subsequent objective report on the protagonist's abortive poetic process. The outer story line juxtaposition of sandman
appearances is paralleled by the inner juxtaposition of the two poetic

processes and focuses the reader's attention on the discourses on poetic process: here is the core of the matter. Looked at more closely, however, the two poetic processes merely repeat the earlier juxtaposition in the story line: subjectively reported mastery stands against objectively reported failure. The expectations raised by the focal placing of the poetic discourses lead to no new insight and the reader feels teased. The juxtapositions appear contrived and mechanical. The narrator's address to the reader too shrilly disrupts the story line (variations on "dearest reader" are repeated six times in the space of two pages) for the reader not to feel Hoffmann's struggle with the subject of the uncanny. Yet the strategy of defense, because of its mechanical repetition is hauntingly, uncannily appropriate to its subject.

Many of our authors use parallels and contrasts as synthesizing methods. Motivation, purpose and successes greatly vary. Sylvia Plath in *Bell Jar,* written to exorcize her suicidal urge, contrasts and parallels an old against a new self, by using the perspective of an *I* narrator. The encounters with violence and madness of the old self make sensational reading. Emotional appeal is immediate, the satire assures punch, and the simple language and personal perspective guarantee wide impact. Nevertheless, Plath fails in terms of the integrative device she set up (present/past self). The device presupposes that the writer understands underlying relationships between past and present self and is able to show this. Plath fails to make clear who the present self is, and how the past self became the present one. An accomplished craftswoman, she understood that something in her heroine needed changing to explain her emergence at the novel's end from insanity. As a post-Freudian with some knowledge of psychotherapy, she eliminated two segments of the sick self by splitting them off from the heroine. She also had her heroine undergo the sexual initiation ritual associated by popular psychology with adult normalcy. These are mechanical, defensive resolutions of her heroine's deadly dilemmas. They trivialize some symptoms and leave real problems unresolved. A few weeks after publication of the novel, failure to understand her own anger led Sylvia Plath to suicide.

A different, richly allusive integration maneuver dominates Mörike's *Mozart on the Way to Prague.* Rather than establish a dialectical structure like Hoffmann, Mörike creates a series of symbolical, allegorical transfigurations, all radiating from one simple concrete object, an orange. The composer transforms the orange into a song, the song into an opera. Orange and opera link historical and classical precedents and psychological issues of infancy and childhood. Each symbol and allegory refers back to the central object. The beauty of the concrete, symbolical, and allegorical worlds and the richness of their interrelations mediate an insightful psychology of the creative process. But the linkages to history and myth are too learned, the aesthetic values too aristocratic, and the emotional tones too delicate. The novella's subtlety demands a very discerning reader. Our examination of different formal patterns in the following essays elucidates the multiple aesthetic and psychological functions of devices and techniques in the artist story and clarifies their relationship to each author's psychology.[12] To attune the reader to these issues in the study of the creative process which we need to watch for, let us first survey some major approaches to and theories of creativity.

Theories of Creativity

Definitions of creativity are legion. Lawrence Kubie defines it pithily as ability "to sort out bits of experience and to put them together in new combinations."[13] K.R. Eissler speaks of "ability to give existence to unusual, original values."[14] A common concern of these and many other definitions[15] appears to be ability to discern what is valuable and produce it in new, original ways. These brief definitions are useful in making judgments about creativity in fields where the originality and worth of an idea, and the width of its application, can be shown by objective criteria. One need only glance at the list of Nobel prizes for literature to realize how difficult it is for a writer's contemporaries to measure his value. Many winners during the first fifty years are totally forgotten. Not only are judgments by peers often misleading or unjust (any Goethe student knows about his gross, tragic misjudgment of Hölderlin and Kleist), but appraisal by scholars and critics can be equally unreliable, as demonstrated in the history of literature. Taste is subject to personal factors, shifts in society, philosophy, politics, changes in personal relations, and discoveries in other fields. Even if critics could avoid the Scylla of personal bias, they could not escape the Charybdis of historical and social limitations. Recent revisionism in all the humanities has drawn attention to the capriciousness of literary repute. Kate Chopin is a good example of a writer whose work would have been lost but for revision of the Victorians.

Because judgments of artistic creativity are necessarily unreliable, theory, definitions, and research cannot help being arbitrary. Studies of the great, like Eissler's of Goethe, for instance, may generalize what is particular to Goethe's creativity, and therefore include purely personal characteristics not necessarily related to creativity.[16] Frank Barron's valuable studies of contemporary authors, who were selected on the basis of recognition by critics and scholars, may omit the true genius unrecognized by his age, who may, like Kafka, make every effort to hide from it, and whose unusualness has an important bearing on his creativity.[17] It is amusing to speculate which of our authors might have been included in a study like Barron's and at what age. It is illuminating that the first kind of study, of genius and the creative exception, pessimistically links creativity to pathology, whereas studies of the second type, statistical samples of creative persons, optimistically link creativity and mental health.

Theories of creativity, and research on creative persons, despite their numbers and scope, can be classified into three major approaches, two of which, at least, date back to the dawn of civilization and are reflected in myth and legend. The pessimistic (I) and the optimistic (II) traditions are concerned with the creator as person, and the relative degree of happiness experienced or expressed. A third way of viewing the creative process (III) disregards the personal, and concerns itself with actual production of a work, mental functions used, and the sequence in which they operate during the process.

The mythic prototype of the pessimistic, tragic tradition is the poet marked by the gods, inspired by divine madness, tabu to his fellows — blind Homer, Orpheus killed by Maenads, Empedocles the outcast throwing himself into Mount Etna, rejected Sappho casting herself from the Leucadian rock into the sea. Today's psychoanalytic studies of the artist's pathology, and the presently unfashionable psychiatric pathography based on 19th century antecedents (e.g. Lombroso's *Genius and Madness,* 1863) are based on this tradition. Over the past two centuries creative diseases have had their fashions and theorists. Consumption, syphilis, epilepsy have had their day, and so have drug addiction, alcoholism, schizophrenia, manic-depression, and various deformities and inferiorities. Many of our authors were afflicted or said to be afflicted. Yet not one attributes creativity to illness or disease — not even the Romantic Hoffmann. On the contrary, they all connect failure of their creativity with illness.

Literary critics lean toward the tragic tradition as their very titles proclaim, for example Edmund Wilson's *The Wound and the Bow*[18] and Alvarez' *The Savage God*.[19] On the whole, psychoanalytic theory has decidedly preferred the tragic view. Freud himself set the pattern with his writing on art ("Creative Writers and Daydreaming" [1908], "Leonardo da Vinci and a Memory of Childhood" [1910], "The Moses of Michelangelo" [1914]).[20] Freud's thought was divided on the matter, and subsequent analytic writing allowed the tragic theory two forms; art is

  (a) escape from reality, flight into fantasy, oceanic states, narcissistic gratification resulting in alienation, maladjustment or madness.

However, looking at the life of an artist like Michelangelo (or a thinker like Freud), psychoanalysts can regard art as

  (b) heroic overcoming, transformation of conflict, anger, aggression, or libidinal energy into culturally useful achievement.[21] By extension, art could be viewed as sublimation of oedipal love, atonement for oedipal guilt, or a quest for the pre- or post-oedipal parent.

The common feature of (b) theories is that symbolic transformation requires renunciation, shouldering special hardships and responsibilities, the triumph of ego and superego over instinctual gratification.[22]

Intrapsychic issues and the origin of the work are in the foreground of theories (a) and (b). Marxist-analytic theories (Ernst Bloch, Harry Slochower)[23] add interpersonal, historical issues, and concern for social function in the future of man. In these theories

  (c) the artist is aware of his historical situation and in conflict with it, and explores the symbolic potential of the present world as a model for a future world. The artist's counterworld undermines the *status quo* but is not prescription for change. The artist is the perennial misfit who sabotages the present to form the future.

The optimistic tradition is rooted in Greek science and mythology. The protagonist is immortal — he is Hermes, the divine child, who stole the cattle of his brother Apollo on the first day of his life, invented the lyre, and gave it to the physician-god in atonement.[24] Art

as invention and healing power, the artist as radiantly healthy, youngest, luckiest child and immortal trickster: these views come from
myth and appear in optimistic views of creativity. The artist's childhood, and his likeness to a child, have dominated theories and
research in psychoanalytic developmental psychology. Researchers
have tried to trace factors contributing to the special health displayed
by the creative child, the kind of parents[25] and the position in the
sibling sequence[26] that foster development of creativity. Following
Freud, psychoanalysts connected creativity with the child's special-
ness to the mother,[27] with specific mother/child interactions, and
family constellations[28] with primary group dynamics during the symbiotic phase[29] and with early primary group communications and
their revival in narcissistic transferences during intense creativity.[30]
The artist's spontaneity and flexibility have been stressed, and similar measurable personality traits have been inventoried and tested in
Frank Barron's research on creativity[31] in which living writers were
questioned about their creative process, observed in life situations,
and tested to assess their thought, memory and feelings, conscious
and unconscious. If we compare ours to the writers Frank Barron
tested, we can attribute to our writers and their heroes all the
descriptions to which Barron gives statistical significance.[32] They
would be like his highly creative subjects during periods of writing,
but at periods when their creativity failed they would share the
characteristics of Barron's intelligent but low creative subjects. All
optimistic psychological and psychoanalytic researchers and theorists
emphasize the mastery displayed by the creative person. It is traits
acquired through nurture that they study.

An optimistic theory subgroup views creative activity as therapeutic. In the problems of life, all symbolic activity, and especially all
imaginative, creative activity, makes flexible approaches and salutary
resolution possible. Once again, the theories go back to Greek antiquity (Aristotle's catharsis) and number many useful conceptualizations ranging from Schiller's *Spieltrieb* in *Letters on the Aesthetic
Education of Mankind* (1795) to Huizinga's *Homo Ludens* (1939).
The voluminous literature on the role of symbol, play, and playthings
(transitional objects)[33] now encompasses studies as diverse as one on
noise as a transitional object in adolescence[34] to the role of fairy
tales at various developmental stages.[35] Jungian contributions, beginning with Jung's use of active imagination[36] have been insightful in

their view of the function of symbolism in therapeutic art. Finally, following researches of the Tavistock Institute and R.D. Laing, theorists, clinicians and literary scholars[37] have been occupied with re-evaluation of psychotic experience and the creative potential of communication in such illnesses as schizophrenia.

From the Kabala and the Christian mystical tradition comes another subgroup (IId): the view of moments of creation as moments of self-realization, unity with the divine, peak experience. Nietzsche in *Thus Spake Zarathustra* describes the personal growth of the philosopher by peak experience and relates it to creation of values. Whereas Freud saw creative "oceanic" experiences[38] as regressive Jungians see them as conducive to growth. In general, a proclivity to mysticism has been found characteristic of creative persons.[39] A writer rather than a psychologist or analyst, Arthur Koestler in *The Act of Creation* (1964) undertook the framing of a theory of creativity as expansion of consciousness at a time when Guilford[40] had just coined the word to designate a special ability of genius distinct from intellectual capacities. Koestler described it as a special gift for "bisociative" thinking[41] ("The bisociative act connects previously unconnected matrices of experience.") and rooted this ability in a spectrum of distinct emotions from aggressive, assertive (humor) to exploratory (science) to participatory and self-transcending emotions (art). The connection between tears, tragedy and art Koestler makes much of agrees with the formulations of the writers discussed in the study. The optimistic orientation tends to associate consciousness expansion with growth; the tragic orientation views it as resulting from pathology. All authors dealt with in this study either describe such mystical experiences, or attribute them to their heroes, but their view of the mystical varies.

The last major approach of research to artistic creativity considers the process itself, its distinct phases, and the human capacities at work. Psychologists have done the most work on cognitive capacities employed, and psychoanalytic ego psychology has broken the process down into various sub-phases and delineated the relative importance of primary and secondary process, and of the systems unconscious and preconscious in the process.[42] The various capacities of the ego during the creative process have been widely discussed, and such concepts as "regression in the service of the ego," "the dissociative function of the ego,"[43] and the tertiary process[44] were defined to distinguish adaptive from pathological regression. More recently, the parallel and co-existent function of the primary and secondary process in all phases of the creative process has been hypothesized to bring psychoanalytic cognitive psychology into concordance with advances in neurophysiology, especially with split brain research.[45] The different types of mental and neurological activity involved in symbolic and imaginative functions have provided useful distinctions.[46] Similarly, theories based on summaries of contemporary psychological, neurophysiological-psychiatric research have favored clearer separation between pathological and creative capacities. Conceptualizations such as the Janus function (ability to hold two opposing ideas at the same time) and the homospatial process (capacity to imagine two things occupying the same space) have been suggested to account for the special alogical capacities possessed by the creative person.[47]

Theorists and researchers may cross from one orientation to another, but on the whole those psychologists concerned with childhood take an optimistic view of the creator, his experience, capacities and rewards. Researchers concerned with the adult artist stress deprivation, hardship, alienation, negative capacities, and pathological potential. A mixture of both is true of our authors. In fact, an important characteristic of writers and heroes in the throes of creation is ability to function simultaneously on many different emotional and intellectual levels: they can be both child and mature man/woman, they can open themselves to their most archaic emotions and pathological ideations and integrate them into present feeling and thought. In other words, their primary process ranges from early archaic/primitive to present levels of psychosocial development. The primitive/mature spectrum of the primary process is paralleled by a similar secondary process spectrum:[48] the writer can be aware of, and command, the most sophisticated cultural tradition and its most archaic aspects simultaneously. In some areas of their lives, our authors are as pathological as the heroes they present as failures. In other aspects, especially those related to their literary career at its peak, they are supremely healthy. Let us now turn to them and their work on the creative process.

II
E.T.A. HOFFMANN'S *THE SANDMAN*:
THE PSYCHO-BIOGRAPHY OF A ROMANTIC POET[1]

When Freud considered *The Sandman* in *The Uncanny* (1919), he
did not dismiss the protagonist's experiences and fantasies as "products of a madman's imagination,"[2] but showed that the hero's fear of
losing his eyes represents the oedipal level of the "bad" father. Freud
concentrated on showing the reader how the hero's feelings, desires,
and infantile beliefs were transformed into the plot and images of a
work of literature. He was also interested in showing what motivates
a reader's aesthetic response to images and plot. Considering his fascination with art, and artists, it is odd that he disregarded the crucial
fact that the hero was an artist. As early as 1908 *(Creative Writers
and Daydreaming)* Freud expressed the desire for an "explanation of
the creative work of writers" *(St. Ed.,* IX, 143). Discussing daydreaming, he developed many ideas about the role of creative activity
in life and most of the basic theory needed to understand Hoffmann,
his characteristic Romantic view of the genesis and development of
artistic activity, and its function in the life of an artist. In *The
Sandman,* Hoffmann links the creativity of his protagonist, the young
poet Nathanael, to childhood development. By a fictional biography,
he provides many details for a psychoanalytic, developmental view of
the function of art in a life history. Furthermore, in portraying the
dynamics which enter the creative process, Nathanael's ambivalent

relationship to his fiancée and his family, Hoffmann provides insight into reasons for success or failure of the creative function.

Form and Plot

In a brief narrative of some thirty pages, this novella covers an entire life, from early childhood to death at twenty. The events of this life are not related chronologically, but telescoped into two episodes and one extraordinary central event: the appearance of the eyeglass dealer Coppola, who is identical with the fateful sandman figure of the title. The first episode begins with the eyeglass seller visiting the hero, who is studying physics at a university. Nathanael reports the visit by a letter to his fiancée and foster-sister Klara and her brother Lothar. He connects his fear of the visitor to his resemblance to a lawyer, Coppelius, whom Nathanael holds responsible for his father's violent death. To explain his fear, he describes his childhood and the growth of the Coppelius/Sandman figure in his mind. In an answering letter, Klara tries to dispel his fear, but only angers and alienates him. To overcome their estrangement, Nathanael visits her. Their reunion briefly dispels his apprehensions about the sandman and his future with Klara, but soon he is again preoccupied with the sandman and their quarrel is renewed. Nathanael tries to resolve his fear and doubts by writing a poem about the sandman, Klara, and death. When he reads it to her, Klara is understandably annoyed by a poem portraying her as a death-bringer. The quarrel flares up again, Lothar takes his sister's part, and the two young men face each other in a duel. Klara pleads, they do not fight, and the quarrel is forgotten.

Nathanael's return to the university begins the second episode. The eyeglass seller returns, and Nathanael buys a pair of binoculars and begins to observe the home of his teacher, Professor Spalanzani, and his daughter Olimpia. He falls in love and courts her, but when he goes there to propose, finds her being torn to pieces by Spalanzani and Coppola. She is an automaton. Nathanael attacks Spalanzani in a fit of madness. After a stay in an asylum, he returns to his family, that is, to his mother, Klara, and Lothar. The lovers plan to marry and live on a country estate with Nathanael's mother and Klara's brother Lothar. Shortly before the marriage, Nathanael attacks Klara while they are on a tower. She is rescued by Lothar and Nathanael throws himself from the height.

There are six appearances of a sandman figure in the story. Two occur during Nathanael's childhood; the third opens the novella, and the fourth, fifth and sixth appearances comprise the second part of the tale. In various guises (Coppola, Coppelius, Spalanzani, father) the sandman is the *Dingsymbol* which embodies the central idea of the novella.[3] The sandman is an external reality independent of Nathanael (his father, for instance) and an internal, psychic reality projected by Nathanael on father figures such as Coppola. In the sandman figure, internal and external reality are inextricably mixed.

Throughout the first part, Nathanael responds creatively to the sandman and grows as person and poet; in the second part, he reacts submissively or violently, lives in fantasy, ceases to grow, and becomes insane. The central idea of the novella is the making and un-making of a poet, in whom a crucial change occurs. Although Freud sees Nathanael as static and passive throughout, Hoffmann's emphasis is on the dynamic growth of a poet and his dramatic struggle for sanity. The narrator twice draws attention to Nathanael's active ambition to be "a zealous and cheerful cultivator of the fields of science and art."[4]

Development

Before dealing with the reasons for the change in Nathanael, let us consider his account of what made him a poet. Once again, communication or failure of communication are crucial. The failure of the lovers' letter-exchange repeats a misunderstanding between Nathanael, the child, and his all-too-rational mother. This misunderstanding is inherent in the discrepancy between child and adult in awareness, knowledge, experience, capacity for abstraction, and mastery. Nathanael claims that the early failure in communication led to his interest in poetry. The child's situation and the creative process are directly linked in his perceptive, detailed history of the development of an artist.[5] Explaining his fear of Coppelius, Nathanael recounts the measures he learned to deal with fear, emotions and impulses. This history covers four distinct stages, corresponding to significant psycho-sexual stages as Erikson develops them and finding some parallel in Piaget's scheme of intellectual development.

The first stage begins long before Nathanael is ten years old and extends over three to five years. He occupies the nursery with his siblings, is comfortable with father and mother on evenings when his father tells stories to the children. In his mind comfort and storytelling come to be associated. When the entertainment is interrupted by noises on the stairs, his parents seem uneasy and melancholy. The air is oppressive from the smoke of his father's pipe. The mother sends the children to bed, saying "The Sandman is come" (184). At this point, Nathanael is mystified by his parents' behavior and only occasionally afraid of noises at night. He is entirely dependent on auditory perceptions and associates his parents' discomfort with the arrival of the sandman about whom he knows nothing except that he "sends us away from papa" (184).

His curiosity grows gradually and at the next stage, he asks his mother what the sandman looks like. His question betrays the wish to see. His mother gives a rational explanation: "There is no sandman...when I say the sandman is come, I only mean that you were sleepy and can't keep your eyes open, as if somebody had put sand in them" (184). Nathanael doesn't believe her because his perceptions belie his mother's words: he hears noises on the stairs. Furthermore, because of his parents' unease he feels that something is happening, and suspects the noises must portend something terrible, if his mother denies them. His sister's nurse provides, by a story of the terrible sandman, an explanation which fits Nathanael's perceptions and feelings. This terrible, sadistic story gives him a framework by which he can order his perceptions, feelings, his life: he needs it. "Then I ran into my bedroom, and the whole night through tormented myself with the terrible apparition of the sandman" (185).

A young child's orientation in the world is given by his parents. In Nathanael's account, the sandman disrupts the harmony between child and parents during the early pre-oedipal stages, represented by the happy, storytelling evenings. As Nathanael gradually moves into the oedipal stage, the sandman comes to represent feelings of discomfort, resentment for being sent to bed, uneasiness at his parents' strange behavior. His feelings about their behavior are based on a complex of unconscious, infantile ideas about their sexual life and the origin of his siblings. He wants to see what he has earlier heard, is afraid to see, feels guilty for wanting to see, fears punishment for his wish to see and participate. Wishes and fears are reflected in the actions his imagination attributes to his father and Coppelius/Sandman. We witness the establishment of a rich store of primal images concerning the origin of life through alchemical means, in homosexual parentage, primal images of mechanical homunculi, splits into good and bad fathers, explosive childbirths, parental giants of immense power, and omnipotence. The sandman figure gradually alienates Nathanael from his parents. He never asks his mother another similar question, and he is restrained from asking his father "by an unconquerable shyness" (185). The sandman causes and represents the child's inevitable alienation from his parents which cannot be remedied once it has occurred. Though originating earlier, the sandman complex during the oedipal phase becomes the focal point of the child's life. All feelings and thoughts are organized around it. That the sandman fulfills Nathanael's vital need for a unifying symbol appears in his holding to the fiction even after he is old enough to realize that the old woman's tale "couldn't be altogether true" (185).

As latency approaches, the sandman attains a different function. The story becomes a regular feature of his play. "He had been the means of disclosing to me the path of the wonderful and adventurous,...I liked nothing better than to hear or read horrible stories of goblins, witches, dwarfs,...but always at the head of them all stood the sandman, whose picture I scribbled ... everywhere" (185). The fiction of the sandman, like the father's earlier stories, gives comfort to the child who learns to play with fiction and thus achieve ego mastery. He holds to the fiction because it has acquired a new function in his life, allowing him to externalize fear and wishes as socially acceptable symbols (note his drawing the figure everywhere). He can play with the symbol, give it whatever meaning and importance he wants. Through this play, the threat is experienced as a pleasant thrill. At this point, he merely leaves his scribblings around. Later, he entertains others with his stories. The sandman thus provides the transitions from the preoedipal to oedipal phase to latency. The same fiction which once mystified, then frightened him, teaches him a way out. Realizing that what scares him is a symbol, he learns to project feelings into symbols. In Piaget's terms, during the oedipal and latency stages Nathanael holds on to intuitive, symbolic thought, and does not yet use operations. Notwithstanding romantic theories about the originality of children, Nathanael does not make up his own stories. He learns symbols from fairy tales, from his nurse, from picture books, and then uses them to work out the discrepancies he experiences between his feelings and perceptions and a reality which he often misunderstands. He resolves differences between fact and fiction in favor of fiction. He is not yet interested in causal explanation. This disinterest in operations in Piaget's sense, in observation and theory, which characterizes Nathanael at this stage of his childhood, corresponds to the romantic ideal of the child dominated by symbol and fiction.

Not by chance is "ten years old" (185) the first exact figure Nathanael provides. The child has his own room, is at the end of latency and the beginning of a precocious puberty. In Piaget's terms, he has become capable of concrete operations. He is now willing to discard symbols altogether and investigate the real sandman. To find out what goes on, he plans to hide in the study, first observing his parents carefully to judge from their actions when to hide. Both the plan for future action and the causal connections made through observation are concrete operations. However, like the earlier symbolizations, the "scientific" investigation is rooted in the oedipal complex. Artistic activity and scientific interest come from Nathanael's wish to master his fear and resolve the discrepancy between feeling and reality.

Up to this point in the child's life, auditory perceptions dominate. When he is hiding in the study, sound predominates at first. For Nathanael and for Hoffmann, the wish to see is obviously the wish to understand, but Nathanael's desire to understand his father's mysterious activities is, of course, also a desire to master through understanding. Because of the way Nathanael earlier used symbolization, the attempt to understand the father merges with the attempt to gain mastery over him. Consequently, the effort to see what his father and Coppelius are doing arouses guilt and is immediately followed by Coppelius' threat to pluck out his eyes as punishment for the transgression. During this episode, auditory perceptions disappear and Nathanael is now so overwhelmed by visual perception that he loses consciousness. The faint is followed by relapse into an earlier psychosexual stage, represented by illness. Nathanael awakens in his mother's arms, a child warmed by her breath (188).

A year or so later, the sandman makes a surprise visit. This means that puberty overtakes the adolescent, while the killing of the father by Coppelius in an experiment means that Nathanael has indeed overcome the father, since he is dead while Nathanael remains with his mother. Mastery and a precocious adulthood have been gained at the cost of his father's life. This is the guilt Nathanael takes on as he moves from latency into adolescence, into the fourth phase of his intellectual and emotional development. He projects this guilt on his dead father, whose face appears to him "burned black and fearfully distorted" (189) so that he is afraid that his father's association with the "diabolical Coppelius could...have ended in his everlasting ruin" (190). At the funeral, the signs of guilt have disappeared; Nathanael represses knowledge and guilt. But they remain to be called forth at the next stage, young adulthood, when he desires sexual maturity, independence, and marriage. In early adolescence, according to Piaget, formal operations are added to and complete man's intellectual development. In Hoffmann's text, Nathanael is not present at the appearance of the sandman which results in his father's death, but imagines it. This seems to mean that he can perform formal operations independently of perceptions. His parents' saying that the sandman is coming for the last time signifies that he is a child for the last time: he has gained full understanding of the relationship between his parents' life and procreation. The new formal operations also appear in the religious-philosophical dimension the sandman acquires. Before this incident, Coppelius was a frightening man and a threatening spook; as the incident unfolds, he becomes, to Nathanael, "the Evil Principle" (198), and in this capacity dominates Nathanael's young adulthood.

In the young poet and scientist, artistic and scientific activities have become independent of their origins in the preoedipal and oedipal situations. As the story opens he responds to reawakened childhood fears by healthy artistic activity. However, in his eagerness to assure ego mastery in the conflict, Nathanael is ruthless. Though he knows that his poetry torments Klara with "dreadful pictures" of "a terrible and ruinous end to her affection" (200) he must read the poem to her. The drive toward demonstration of mastery has become an end in itself; art has taken on its own life. Therefore, even when Coppelius had "faded considerably in his fancy," even when it "cost him great pains" to present him in vivid colors in his literary efforts (199) Nathanael clings to his misery. Tragically, he no longer wants to break through the conflict between wishes, fears, and reality. Rather, he wants to stay in conflict, so he can use it as incitement to creation, as occasion to prove mastery. The mastery he then feels takes on erotic significance, because he hopes the poem will "enkindle Klara's cold temperament" (200). Consciously, Nathanael wants to achieve greater closeness to Klara; unconsciously, he wants distance from her. By writing the poem and reading it to her, he uses her, creating at her expense, and keeps them both in the dilemma.[6]

In portraying Nathanael's development, Hoffmann provides important insight into the growth of a poetic metaphor. Throughout Nathanael's life, the sandman takes on ever richer, more varied meanings. Originally furnished by a mother figure, the nurse, the metaphor is associated with the very early mother and the oral phase of development. It serves as a favored play fantasy, a transitional object, a manipulable substitute for the mother, on which Nathanael can project feelings which he can then control. He can smear the sandman's figure on walls and fences, and thus externalize his anger over the nightly discomfort with his parents; he can draw it small or large, make many figures or few. All these acts give him a sense of mastery. Into the transitional object, he projects the fears and feelings appropriate to his stage of development, which it would be dangerous or impossible to express (his shyness about his father's changes in mood). The metaphor reaches from its root in the oral phase all the way to young adulthood and his relationship with Klara. It is deeply embedded in his inner life and he encounters it constantly in the external world. It provides him with a center around which present conflicts organize themselves and challenge him. In Nathanael's poem, Hoffmann presents a key fantasy and several peripheral ones (eyes, glasses, Klara as muse-bride). Hoffmann himself had many more (e.g., the doll, the double) and could combine them in different ways. The central metaphors can appear as images or as structural devices. For instance, the eye/eyeglass can also be a device to organize the narrative point of view. In *My Cousin's Corner Window* the window directs the eye and establishes distance, as well as the sequence of events. For Hoffmann, metaphors and formal devices originate in the transitional object. All transitional objects/fantasies are split-off aspects of the original mother/nurturing adult relationship. They provide the images which the poet uses in his work either in central or peripheral function.[7]

Communication

Let us now return to the two-part structure of the novella and the change we observed in Nathanael from one part to the other. We have learned that he has a rich inner life, built up during his childhood, which came to the fore in two childhood episodes and which he dwells on in his letter and in his poetry. We have seen that the sandman is beneficial and essential to his development. Only after the sandman's third appearance something goes wrong. We must therefore look more closely at what happens in the communication between the lovers, and especially at how Nathanael's communications are received by Klara and Lothar. We might note that Nathanael's mother, though important as a provider, is always excluded from communications about the sandman and her son's distress. Her initial empathic failure dictates Nathanael's reticence (190;201).

In writing the story of his childhood, Nathanael has several objectives. By telling the story, he wants to face his fear and understand its cause. He dimly perceives that the act of writing can free him from the isolation into which fear has cast him. These feelings are reflected in the repeated attempts of his first paragraph to state what ails him and his several failures to do so. "I know you are all very uneasy ... But ... how could I write to you ... I must now tell you ... I must ... what shall I say ... I wish you were here ... But now you will ... take me for ..." (183). All his circumlocutions precede the sentence reporting the eyeglass dealer's visit. A further, important objective is to ask Lothar and Klara to help him overcome his fear, though he does not know how they can do so because he does not know what he fears. He is apprehensive that they will take him for a "superstitious ghost-seer" (183). He twice asks them to "laugh" at him, yet he obviously wants his fears to be taken seriously. The reader comes to wonder why he is so afraid they might laugh. Nathanael wants Klara and Lothar to confirm that his subjective world is important to them. He does not ask them to confirm the reality of Coppola's dangerousness, but the reality of his feelings about him. Through a reference he makes to Schiller's *Robbers* we learn what he fears. Asking them to laugh at him in the "frantic despair in which Franz Moor entreated Daniel to laugh" (184), Nathanael is comparing himself to Franz, who dreams of being condemned, at the Last Judgment, for his part in his father's death. The reference implies that Nathanael, feeling similar guilt, expects to be rejected because of this guilt. Yet he urgently, desperately needs Klara's and Lothar's acceptance.

Nathanael's instinct is healthy: acceptance by Klara and Lothar would break down his isolation and alleviate his fear and guilt. Klara's rationalistic explanation is sound enough: Nathanael's fear is inappropriate; Coppelius is a creature of his imagination. Failing to see that Nathanael already knows this, she underestimates his insight and thereby diminishes him. Instructing him to dismiss his dread, "Pluck up your spirits! Be cheerful!" she speaks as to a disobedient child. "I beg you, dear, strive to forget the ugly lawyer Coppelius as well as the peddler Guiseppe Coppola. Try and convince yourself that these foreign influences can have no power over you, that it is only belief in their hostile power which can ... make them dangerous to you....I'm not afraid ..." (193). Nathanael is angry at being thus deflated. His sarcastic answer to Klara's letter shows that he understands her meaning: "Coppelius and Coppola...are phantoms of my own self, which will at once be dissipated, as soon as I look upon them in that light" (193). He knows "in no way can I get rid of the impression which Coppelius's cursed face made upon me" (194). Nathanael's sensitivity and Klara's rejection lead to the first alienation of the lovers.

Nathanael is affected by Klara's rejection in an even more crucial sense. Explaining his fear by the account of his childhood, Nathanael tries to objectify his feelings, to bring his immediate emotional response into accord with verifiable past events, to make sense of his life and gain control of his feelings. Communicating the story of his childhood and his fears, he is attempting ego mastery over his inner and outer worlds. Klara fails to understand his need to have this mastery confirmed. Her reply gives him no credit for trying to help himself by writing out and objectifying his fears. Yet Nathanael still trusts her and Lothar enough to visit them, although their letter has undermined his trust in himself. He links his artistic and intellectual self-doubts to his unresolved encounter with Coppelius: "He went so far as to maintain that it was foolish to believe that a man could do anything ... of his own accord, for the inspiration in which alone any true artistic work could be done...was the result of the operation directed inwards of some Higher Principle existing without and beyond ourselves" (197-198). Note that his concern centers on his artistic work.

During the visit, Nathanael makes another bid to understand his continuing fears, overcome his increasing alienation from Klara, and gain her recognition of his ego mastery by writing a poem. The attention to form has a calming, sobering effect. He gains sufficient distance to see the poem aesthetically as "very successful" (199). He regains his gay, vivacious manner (200). Klara unwittingly persuades him to read the poem to her and, understandably, rejects it. "She drew him softly to her heart and said in a low but very grave and impressive tone, 'Nathanael, my darling Nathanael, throw that foolish, senseless, stupid thing into the fire'" (200). Nathanael sees this as rejection of himself and his bid for mastery, all the more so because her words are accompanied by a maternal gesture. Klara may mean the gesture as reassurance, but Nathanael responds as if it were meant to suppress him. "Nathanael leaped indignantly to his feet" (200). In this sentence and a half, Hoffmann's consummate skill manages to suggest the contradiction between Klara's words and gestures and the complex interaction between the lovers. As the quarrel leading to the duel shows, Nathanael has read Klara's words correctly — unwilling to see that his poem is an attempt at mastering his fears, she wants to suppress the entire matter. Thereby, she once again forces Nathanael into the submissive role of a willfully disobedient child.

To understand what Nathanael craves from Klara, what he believes could free him from fear and conflict, we might contrast Klara's reception of the poem with the reception of his poems by Olimpia, the automaton. Almost all his activity with her concerns his writing. He reads for hours everything that "he had ever written — poems, ... visions, romances, tales, and the heap was increased daily..." (209). The wording indicates that at this point Nathanael's writing has become mechanical and worthless. Olimpia says nothing, but merely gazes at him ardently. Seeming to accept him totally, she "expressed in respect to his works and his poetic genius the identical sentiments which he himself cherished deep down in his own heart,... as if it was his own heart's voice speaking to him" (209). This feeling is, of course, literally true. A Klara who could accept Nathanael and let him be himself might save him, but this requires an empathy Klara does not possess.

After the reading of the poem, neither Klara nor Nathanael distinguishes between inner and outer worlds. What Nathanael began as an attempt to gain control over his feelings by creation and communication becomes, because of Klara's reaction, a power-struggle for ascendency. As the duel shows, the conflict cannot be resolved in the present. However, by remembering how much he felt for Klara "in the happiest days of...golden youth" (201), Nathanael is able to submit: "he threw himself at Klara's feet" (201). He pays a heavy price. By asking brother and sister for pardon, he assumes responsibility for the quarrel. Through submission he forfeits his attempt to understand himself and also the right to his own feelings. We should remember that these feelings include guilt as well as fear. It is hardly a surprise that casting off his feelings gives him a temporary sense of relief: "Nathanael felt as if a heavy burden that had been weighing him down to the earth was now rolled off him" (201). Submission, denial, regression and repression leave him fatally weakened.[8] The rejected poem is fulfilled by the conclusion of the story. Nathanael no longer responds to real situations but to repressed, incomprehensible urges. In their power struggle, Klara has won a child, but lost Nathanael as a man and a poet. The form used, the three introductory letters, show how crucial the communication issue is to Hoffmann.

Alienation, Regression, Insanity

In the second half of the story, in three further episodes, Nathanael loses what he gained in the first part. He again encounters Coppola when he returns, fatally weakened, to the university. By a pair of binoculars obtained from Coppola, Nathanael increases his alienation and enters a fantastic world. He believes the glasses look out on the world although they, in fact, look in on his own psyche. Damaged by rejection, he loses the capacity to distinguish between his fears and the world around him. The automaton Olimpia is an actualization of his wishes concerning Klara. Whereas Klara has a will of her own, Olimpia is moved, literally and figuratively, by him alone. He gives her warmth and life: her "ice-cold lips met his burning ones...the kiss appeared to warm her lips" (207). Her lifelessness is his own. When he tries to become engaged to Olimpia, that is, to close himself off in his imagined world, Professor Spalanzani and Coppola/Coppelius tear Olimpia to pieces. This is to say that his self-love, like his earlier love for Klara, arouses fear of self-annihilation and castration, once again demanding that he give up love. On this occasion Nathanael cannot retreat, because giving up love means giving up his self. This is why he tries to strangle the sandman figure in the shape of Spalanzani.

After he recovers from this violent episode, Nathanael finds himself at home with his mother, Klara and Lothar. He makes no further attempt to rally his strength. His artistic ambition forgotten, he remains with the family "more childlike than he had ever been" (213). He and Klara plan a life together in the country, in isolation, never mentioning the past, in a timeless, infantile utopia in which Klara is "an angel...supremely pure and noble" (213). He has resolved the incongruence between feeling (fear of castration for loving) and reality (being an adult with biological and psychic readiness for love and responsibility) in favor of withdrawal to an almost uterine existence in the family womb. This, in a sense, is self-castration. Therefore it is not surprising that any self-assertion required of him brings another appearance of the sandman. Just before their marriage, Nathanael and Klara climb a tower. The ascent, symbol of phallic mastery, brings violence. Nathanael attacks Klara and when she is rescued, propels himself off the tower at Coppelius.[9]

In Nathanael's case, Hoffmann differentiates between adaptive and regressive ways of handling breaks in ego-boundaries. In the first half of the tale Nathanael's ego is repeatedly overwhelmed by unresolved emotions and conflicts welling up from the id. As Weissmann remarks in his essay "Ego Functions in Creativity" the "same id material in varying inspirational contents appears and reappears at different times in the life of a creative mind."[10] Such id materials emerge in the first, second, and third appearances of the sandman. In the second appearance, Nathanael simply represses the disturbing id elements. In the first and third appearances, they provide driving energy toward creativity. His creative impulse is the drive to assimilate his inner emotions and conflicts into his present circumstances. Put in another way, it is the impulse to grow by bringing inner and outer worlds into correlation by communication and by artistic/scientific work. As long as Nathanael receives some confirmation and mirroring, his ego is capable of integration.[11]

In the second half of the story, Hoffmann attributes devastating effect to the inundation of the ego by id materials. In the concluding episodes, Nathanael faints, denies, retreats from reality, and regresses to ever-earlier stages of psychosexual development. Klara and Lothar, with their rationalist stance, take Nathanael's childlikeness for childishness. Assuming the parental role, they imprison him in submission and regression. After the abortive duel, Nathanael's ego does not rally. His regression shows in his unsociability, his total devotion to fantasy, a devotion comparable to his dedication to fantasy during latency. Following his violence at the sandman's fifth appearance, Nathanael regresses to infancy. Increasingly he loses capacity to deal with slight demands on him, which he experiences as threats. Hoffmann, whose skill in describing psychotic states and dynamics of behavior is remarkable,[12] claims that the artist needs to be childlike, and to experience breaks in his ego boundaries. This necessary inundation becomes fatefully debilitating for Nathanael.

Freud's emphasis in interpreting this story was on its oedipal level and on the question of love, human closeness, and the hero's inability to deal with the oedipal conflict. He overlooked Nathanael's decided attempts in the first part of the story to use these conflicts as a spur toward creative achievement. Paying no attention to the structure of the story, and seeing the hero as inactive, Freud missed Nathanael's forward development through the first sandman appearances. In the third, pivotal appearance of the sandman, the hero is at first shown to increase his mastery over the conflict, but finally, because his feelings are not appropriately mirrored, he loses his mastery. In three further sandman appearances, the narrator explores the hero's regression which leads back over the same steps through which he had progressed — adulthood, adolescence, childhood, death. Hoffmann presents us with a theory of creation and shows success and failure in a circular evolution: the two halves of the story cancel each other. Nothing remains of Nathanael. We never know whether anyone remembers him or grieves for him. Coppelius disappears. Klara finds happiness with another. His name Nathanael means "gift of God," and by the story's structure this gift is taken back. Because Hoffmann's own name, Theodor, is Greek for the Hebrew name Nathanael, we may suspect that he saw a parallel with himself. Like his fictional alter ego, and through him and his opposite, the narrator, Hoffmann bares the origins of creativity.[13] Where Nathanael fails, Hoffmann succeeds, as author of the structured, concluded work.

Hoffmann achieves this feat by the introduction of the narrator into the story. It is the narrator who takes over just before Nathanael's last bid for mastery by creation is rejected. Right at the beginning of this section, the narrator insists on his "gracious" reader's (194) identification with him rather than with Nathanael. Through four long paragraphs, he cajoles "you", the reader, to experience, perceive, feel, imagine what the narrator does. Unlike Nathanael who has difficulties beginning his story, he expects "everybody...and also the whole world to boot" (195) to listen and hence does not hesitate to reveal what moves him. The narrator's very insistence on communication proclaims: art, to be life-giving, must be shared with listeners. The narrator then, from auctorial perspective, adds information on Nathanael's family, gives the preceding letters their context, and establishes himself as the narrative's authoritative source. Describing and ironizing his creature's failures in turn, the narrator finally destroys him. In fact, the greater his hero's failure and annihilation, the greater the narrator's triumph. From Nathanael's point of view, this is the story of the utter defeat of an artist. From Hoffmann's, it tells of the artist's victory over fear of experimentation with unusual states of mind, with regression, with return of the repressed, alienation, guilt and violence, failure of ego mastery, and rejection and punishment by the world. Through his insight into the artist who failed Hoffmann achieves victory. Yet this triumph somehow has a hollow ring. It is achieved by an almost mechanical formal regularity, and by an irony that is too heavy. If we attend to formal literary technique, the novella seems too contrived. The six episodes, with the two central ones mirroring each other, are too repetitive, the *leitmotifs* and ironies too obvious, the recurrence of key words and sentences too trite.

Still, Hoffmann reveals remarkable insight into what makes an artist. As the first psychologist of creativity, he offers a concise, penetrating psychology of art and artist in the brief compass of this novella. His insights came to constitute the romantic portrait of the artist, and the romantic theory of creation. It is a view which recurs with different accents in Nietzsche, Thomas and Heinrich Mann, and Freud. Perhaps Freud's "hands-off policy" toward creativity made him overlook the poet in Nathanael. Or maybe his fear of having been anticipated by another writer made him overlook Hoffmann's artist portrait.[14] Perhaps Freud paid too much attention to the story's latent content, to what author and protagonist are not aware of, the oedipal level, the sexual overtones and undercurrents. He therefore failed to attend to those levels which Hoffmann points to: the importance of childhood learning, reinforcement, play, the need for confirmation of self, for control of emotion and conflict by form, the significance of an approach/avoidance dilemma as an impulse toward creativity. In fact, latent and manifest content of this novella supplement each other. The latent levels lend a depth and richness to the theory of the artist which Hoffmann could not have hoped to reach in theoretical writing.

Hoffmann's Poetic Theory and its Relation to his Biography

The Hoffmann hero often experiences himself, other persons, and the world as fragmented, unintegrated, lifeless. When Nathanael gazes into Klara's eyes, death looks at him (220); when he loses Olimpia, she is torn to pieces limb by limb; Nathanael calls Klara an automaton (220). Since he sees Klara and Olimpia as extensions of himself, the two female figures reflect his experience of himself. As is revealed by works which express his theoretical position such as *The Golden Flower Pot* (1814), *The Serapion's Brothers* (1819), and *My Cousin's Corner Window* (1822), Hoffmann himself shared this experience of a fragmented world and generalized it into a philosophy. In what has been called "Serapion's Principle"[15] he formulates a dualistic world view. Art and the artist are to overcome this fragmentation.[16]

To return to Nathanael, we have seen that he too experiences the world dualistically. His inner vision of how he wants to be understood by Klara is remote from their actual relationship. Ideal and reality are at painful odds. The ordinary person manages this conflict between inner vision and outer world by denying the inner vision, but the madman denies reality (e.g., Nathanael sees Klara as death). To Hoffmann, the writer's most important gift is precisely his sensitivity to the discrepancy between inner and outer worlds and aliveness to the outer world in the inner world (that is the reality core in the madman's visions and the artist's paradisiac yearnings). The Serapion principle is that the artist, penetrating external reality, seeing a person's wellsprings of action, gives external reality to the inner worlds of his characters in his work.

The artist's task is therefore dual. He must observe and understand a person's inner world from details of dress and behavior. He must be able to use details to evoke his character's inner life. Put differently: Hoffmann's is the dualism of the factual world versus the world of feeling about fact. Through his creations, the artist integrates feeling into the world of fact and thereby helps readers to integrate and externalize their feelings into the world he has created. For instance, when Nathanael discovering that Olimpia is a doll, feels his beliefs shattered, his world fragments. Hoffmann portrays the emotional experience factually: Olimpia *is* torn apart. Or Nathanael, who fears his good father's anger sees two father figures: one kindly, the other malicious. His feeling intrudes into the world of fact, distorting it and giving it a nightmare quality (cf. Illustration I: Nathanael seeing the Sandman in his father's study). But, for the person who experiences himself as alienated, fragmented and dead (as Hoffmann did, and most of us do on occasion) the world of fact is indeed a nightmare world. To perform his arduous task as integrator, the Hoffmann artist needs the sustaining interpersonal relations and ego mastery we saw Nathanael muster at his best. We might add that for the Hoffmann artist the task is so difficult because his emotional states are mostly uncomfortable ones: emptiness, anxiety, fear, frustration and disorientation. Comfort, for the Hoffmann hero, is either illusory or short-lived, usually both (e.g., Nathanael's before the last attack).

As his diaries indicate, Hoffmann felt lifeless and fragmented. His self-portrait at age forty ironizes his disjointed self-image (cf. frontispiece). He was a heavy drinker and had been since his middle twenties. His first biographer and friend Hitzig remarked that drinking had become "a habit and compulsion."[17] His correspondence, reports by friends and contemporaries, but above all his diaries (1803-1804; 1809-1815) written at Plock, Bamberg, Dresden, Berlin comment regularly on the wines consumed, on hangovers, on "nerves excited by spiced wine,"(65) or give the sign of a glass. An indiscretion at a festivity in Posen (he allowed caricatures he had drawn of Prussian officers to be distributed), led to his being exiled from his government position. At Bamberg and Berlin, leaving his wife to her own resources, he spent his evenings at the wine cellars *Rose* and *Lutter und Wegner's* respectively. The bill he left at the latter at his death at 46 amounted to one and a half times his considerable annual salary as a judge. When he was a poor musician of thirty-four, married, he fell in love with his then fourteen year old voice

E. T. A. Hoffmann: Nathanael eavesdrops on his father and Coppelius
in the study, 1815.

pupil, Julia Mark, and this brought acute fear of self-disintegration and madness. Several of his diary entries, written in the shaky hand of the inebriate, refer to that fear: "Observations about the self which is threatened by disintegration — it is something unusual and never experienced before" (139).[18] The words used to express his feeling for Julia link his love to both a desire for merging with her and a fear of disintegration: "exalted mood" (112), "exalted to madness" (112), "exotic mood" (125) where exotic describes his being in love as an "uncomfortable,...terrifying, most fatal mood." For several years (1810-12), he attempted to control himself by fantasies about Julia, by frenzied composition, musical and literary, and by increasingly heavy drinking.

The pattern of wanting and fearing merger, and attempting to control wish and fear by ingestion, can best be understood through Kohut's self psychology of the addicted person:

> The narcissistically disturbed individual yearns for praise and approval or for merger with an idealized supportive other because he cannot sufficiently supply himself with self-approval or with a sense of strength through his own inner resources... the addict craves the drug [or the alcoholic alcohol] because the drug seems to him to be capable of curing the central defect in his self. It becomes for him the substitute for a selfobject [a nurturing parent] that failed him, with traumatizing intensity and suddenness, at a time when he should still have had the feeling of omnipotently controlling its responses in accordance with his needs as if it were a part of himself. By ingesting the drug, he symbolically compels the mirroring selfobject [usually mother] to soothe him, to accept him. Or he symbolically compels the idealized selfobject [usually father] to submit to his merging into it and thus to his partaking in its magical power.[19]

Hoffmann experienced love for Julia as merging with her. This shows in naming her his Kätchen (after Kleist's somnambulist heroine), in calling her his muse, and in the imagined relationship between them in his novella *Don Juan* (1812). In this work, the singer of the role of Donna Anna (Julia) mediates to him as narrator, a total understanding of Mozart's work, so much so that she merges into him and ceases to exist (she dies during the performance).

Simultaneously he, with the creation of his own *Don Juan,* loses his identity and becomes another Mozart.[20] This assumption of another identity parallels Hoffmann's life. He so much identified himself with Mozart that he discarded one of his own names and as signature to his works added Mozart's middle name, Amadeus. Significantly, the name abandoned, Wilhelm, belonged to his hated and disrespected father-substitute, his uncle Otto Wilhelm Doerfer, who raised him from the age of two. Amadeus — meaning beloved of god, reveals Hoffmann's need and desire for merger with an approving, strong, archaic, divine father. The desire to merge with the muse Julia leads to merger with an archaic father. Behind the seeming oedipal problem (fear of merging with Julia — muse — Klara because of punishment/castration — Coppelius) appears the older fear of self-disintegration. Merging with the archaic father, would be fearful because he possessed an angry, destructive side that we identified earlier as the image of the bad father/sandman/Coppelius.

Fear of self-disintegration is due to unempathic, weak, contradictory mirroring selfobjects (mother) as well as idealized selfobjects (father or any idealized adult). We have seen that Nathanael's mother's lack of empathy is complemented by the father's failure to control Coppelius, for instance.[21] Both fail and desert Nathanael the child. Hoffmann's parents similarly failed and deserted him. When he was two, his parents divorced. His melancholy mother returned to her family, and spent the rest of her days an invalid cloistered in her room. His dissolute, artistic father left him to be brought up in the maternal grandmother's household by a bachelor uncle and a maiden aunt. A childish, hypochondriac lawyer who retired at forty-two, the uncle saw that the boy received proper schooling. But his eccentricities made it impossible for the boy to respect him. By 18th century standards, Hoffmann was sent to school early (at six or seven), fortunately to a good school which gave him friends, models, and a classical education. A life-long friendship with Theodor von Hippel began there when Hoffmann was eleven. Teachers and peers, and the development of ego skills and intellectual tools, appear to have compensated for the shortcomings of his home (like Nathanael, Hoffmann sketched, wrote, composed and played music from childhood). We do not know whether the early selfobject who permitted Hoffmann the later Mozart identification was a teacher or his own father. The yearning for a powerful, idealized father, for a spiritual-intellectual identification, in any case led to Hoffmann's Mozart cult and an identification that gave promise of self-integration through imitation of Mozart's creativeness. This strength is Hoffmann's difference from Nathanael.

In real life, the maiden aunt gave the boy love and approval, but could not compensate for the mother deprivation he must have suffered.[22] Nevertheless, he received enough comfort, warmth and understanding to be capable of using women as love objects, even if only as distant, split-off love objects. Julia was too young: sexual and emotional closeness with her was impossible — she was a safe, distant love object. An earlier love of his late teens was much older and safe; he escaped from his fiancée just before marriage and the woman he finally married was not his intellectual equal, nor did he love her. Hoffmann's artistic inspiration therefore appears in pseudo-oedipal form, but the Mozart identification points to an earlier wish to merge into the father for self-cohesion.

The biographic information makes it obvious that Hoffmann's disrupted family was the root of his fragmented self and world. This information also explains why being an artist was one way for him to achieve self-integration. Art allowed controlled fusion (form, irony) into idealized selfobjects. We can now understand also another reason for Nathanael's failure. To him, the powerful selfobject, the idealized parent imago, is negative only; the benevolent father is weak. Another Hoffmann hero who is happy in his work, Anselmus of the *Golden Flower Pot,* has a father surrogate who is both powerful and benevolent. But the ending of this novella clearly states that such a father is a myth, a wish rather than actuality. Hoffmann's own situation reflects that of both Nathanael and Anselmus.

What was Hoffmann's situation when he wrote *The Sandman* and what was his purpose? Together with other stories of the time, it was a work of personal crisis which began with Hoffmann's dismissal as conductor from the Leipzig theater. Like all the men of his family, Hoffmann had become a lawyer, but he lost his position in the Prussian bureaucracy on Prussia's defeat by the armies of Napoleon in 1807. For a number of years he worked, never successfully, as a free-lance artist and music teacher in Bamberg, Leipzig, and Dresden. He added to his income by publishing criticism and fiction about music, with fiction gradually assuming more importance. The struggle for subsistence as an artist led him to a safe though disliked bureaucratic career in the judicial system after the 1815 Restoration. Despair over the failed artistic career initiated a personal crisis. The need to face the daily responsibilities of his new life prolonged the crisis. He needed to work through his negativeness and fears of what has been called the *Nachtseite des Lebens* (the side of life hidden from consciousness).[23] The poetic works of the *Nachtstücke* resulted. His art helped him to integrate himself into the realities of his age and time. He resolved the crisis well enough, by *Nachtstücke,* to play an important role in Prussian judicial history after 1815. He drove himself hard as an official and author. His writing turned decisively to social, political criticism and satire. But neither art nor social responsibility offered sufficient possibilities for self-cohesion to fight the urge to destroy himself by alcohol, which claimed him before the police did for his political engagement.[24]

Unlike Freud, we have interpreted *Sandman* as the story of an artist. Hoffmann's many-faceted portrayal, organized around the sandman symbol, makes the preoedipal and oedipal situations crucial factors in artistic development through childhood, adolescence and young manhood. Following Nathanael's childhood memories, we witness his acquisition of a treasury of primary process images. Through his brief life, the Sandman complex is the irritant which impels him toward ego mastery and self-integration by creation. In childhood, Nathanael achieves this through play, in adult life through poetry. Hoffmann's artist differs from the people around him by reason of his vulnerability to eruptions from the unconscious. This openness constitutes the childlikeness of the romantic artist.

Creation is possible and pleasurable only in community, through communication with others. The other striking facet of Hoffmann's theory of creativity is emphasis on interpersonal processes and communication. Nathanael's relations with others cause his psyche to be flooded by primary process imagery. Shaping this imagery to communicate it, the artist gains control over it. For this purpose, secondary process operations (ability to understand motivation and mediate understanding in rational, artistic form) become important. By mediating his inner world to others, the artist integrates himself into their social world and gives pleasure by doing so. From this activity he derives a sense of control, pleasure, and worth, that is, ego-mastery. The artist's struggle for ego-mastery via creation, bound as it is to interpersonal relations, is subject to many vicissitudes. Hoffmann concentrates on the power-struggle aspects. The artist can misuse his work to dominate others. Others can misuse or misunderstand the artist's childlikeness in their struggle with him for ascendancy, and hurt him by refusing confirmation of his efforts. When this confirmation is refused, the artist's inner world becomes destructive and his childlikeness becomes pathological. In *The Sandman,* Hoffmann portrays both the successful and unsuccessful creative process. Using a poet's life, Hoffmann shows how thin is the line dividing creativity from pathology. His own life situation paralleled his hero's, and he used Nathanael to overcome, in limited fashion, his own similar liabilities, which he nevertheless regarded as the *sine qua non* of the artist.

III
GEORG BÜCHNER'S *LENZ*:
SCHIZOPHRENIC DISINTEGRATION

In his novella *Lenz*[1] the twenty-two year old Georg Büchner (1813-1837) gives an account of the emotional death of a poet. The fifteen year long, futile struggle for sanity of the German poet Jakob Michael Reinhold Lenz (1751-1792) is telescoped into a tightly structured tale covering about three weeks of Lenz's life.[2] Büchner is not a Romantic. Nevertheless, his account shares much with Hoffmann's and helps us attain a deepened and more differentiated view of the creative process.

A few facts about Lenz may be helpful to the non-German reader. A parson's son and graduate theologian, young Lenz abandoned his career and his native Livonia against his father's wish and went to Strasbourg to join the Storm and Stress circle (Goethe, Herder, Lavater, Schlosser) congregated there. He found rapid success as a writer and became the group's most prominent critic of the repressive social order. After Goethe departed for Weimar and gradually turned to classicism, and to acceptance of the social order, many of the Strasbourg friends followed suit. Lenz, too, joined Goethe at the Weimar Court in 1776, but was expelled after a few months for offenses against protocol. Unsettled by this, Lenz spent the next year wandering through Alsace and Switzerland, soliciting help from several old friends, until he finally suffered several illnesses and psychotic breaks.[3] Büchner took as departure for his story a break-down which occurred in 1778 at the home of a parson at Waldbach, in the Alsace.

Büchner sees Lenz as a social critic who holds to the rebellious Storm and Stress movement ideals deserted by the Strasbourg friends, and gradually finds himself rejected by them. Alone in a hostile environment represented by the parsonage, unable to uphold himself as a writer, ignored by his family, uncertain of his faith, unwilling to compromise and undertake a bourgeois career, Lenz suffers mental disintegration. Büchner shows its steps and follows it into irredeemable alienation. Büchner knew that Lenz never wrote anything of worth after this period of his life; once removed from the Waldbach parsonage he struggled against madness for fifteen years until he died destitute in the streets of Moscow.

Büchner based the story on Parson Oberlin's diary.[4] After Oberlin had the crazed poet taken from his house, he found himself criticized by many. To defend himself, he published his account of the period. Using Oberlin's report extensively, Büchner made Lenz's relationship to Oberlin the crucial factor in the poet's silencing and death. What must have struck Büchner in this story was the stifling of the writer, Lenz's relinquishment of craft and social criticism at this crossroads of his life. Moreover, Lenz's death as a writer had a historical meaning, for the Storm and Stress protest died with it. Accounting for Lenz's schizophrenic episode,[5] Büchner exposes 18th and 19th century German political, social, and religious repression, to which he himself was also subjected. But the story as Büchner develops it is not only a case history or exposé.[6] It lays bare the psychological roots of Lenz's and his own artistic sensitivity, and at its center stands a consistent theory of artistic creation and human response to art.

In analyzing the story our concern is with the psychology of the artist Lenz, his creative process, his theory of art and his development. By partial identification with Lenz through his narrative method, Büchner discloses much about his own creative process. He thereby helps us to understand important similarities and to compare differences between the creative process, experience, and life history of an artist and a schizophrenic.

For guidance to the reader in a complex subject, I will briefly summarize a few results of my analysis. By his use of *erlebte Rede* with its hovering perspective, Büchner established close identification with

Lenz. The narrator and Lenz share an extraordinary sensitivity to stimuli from the world around them, and to stimuli from inner worlds (memories, conscious and unconscious impulses, wishes, fantasies, needs, feelings). This sensitivity results from a tendency to experience diffusion of the boundaries of the self, or breaks in the boundaries of the ego. The narrator's sensitivity has a center which helps to organize the stimuli and firm the boundaries. Lenz's has not. In the story, Lenz finds such a center in Oberlin. As long as he is in harmony with Oberlin, Lenz can create. In the course of Lenz's stay at the parsonage, Oberlin blends with the figure of his father and with God. In his relationship to Oberlin, Lenz therefore lives and relives preoedipal, infantile patterns. When he is rejected by this omnipotent figure, Lenz loses the center of his existence. His sensitivity intensifies. He defends himself against the onslaught of chaotic stimuli by maladaptive mental strategies and irrational actions, until he collapses in apathy. This is his death as a poet. In his struggle, he creates symptoms instead of works of art. The relationship to the father, or a paternal principle, is central to understand Lenz's and Büchner's psychology. The theory and practice of art which Büchner attributes to Lenz, and shares, exactly complements the psychology of the artist he portrays.

An author like Grillparzer, in *The Poor Fiddler,* deals with a chronic schizophrenic whose psychotic break lies in the distant past.[7] Büchner shows the painful process of the break before defenses have closed off further anguish. Hoffmann or Mörike (see chapter 4) show artists whose alienation is not as extensive as Lenz's. The pathology of Büchner's Lenz is more radical, its roots more archaic. For our study, Büchner's significance lies in establishing a link between the schizophrenic and creative process, and therewith between the most deeply regressed, pathological processes and the highest mental activity. Before we can begin to distinguish between the psychology of the two processes, we must study narrative method, *leitmotifs,* and other techniques to differentiate between narrator and character.

Narrative Structure, Technique and Leitmotifs

Büchner's account covers about twenty days in the life of the twenty-seven-year-old Lenz, from January 20 to February 10, 1778. The four distinctive sections of the narrative center on the hero's inner life and his relationship to a father figure. In the first section, Büchner shows Lenz in isolation as he is crossing the mountains. Lenz and the reader know neither the time of day, where they are, where they are going, where they came from. Büchner reflects Lenz's agitation, and rapid shifts in mood in evocations of the winter landscape. After describing his initial apathy and his peculiar thoughts ("he felt displeased that he could not walk on his head," 79), the story tells how the vigor of the stormy scene communicates itself to Lenz and makes him feel alive (the storm "tore his chest, he stood gasping, he thought he'd have to swallow the storm"). The excitement becomes too intense; Lenz escapes into fantasy and finally reverts to apathy. Several such mood cycles establish Lenz's extreme sensitivity subject to any pressure.[8] He can only escape into fantasy, alienation, apathy. As evening comes on, the slight orientation provided by the landscape lost, we witness Lenz's growing fear of isolation, experienced as emptiness, as being in nothingness, and being pursued by "something frightful" (80). As night falls, he arrives at Waldbach parsonage. The aimless wandering has found a goal, the hero has found light, comfort, and hospitality. The first section has established Lenz's inner state without a father figure to cling to.

The second section deals with Lenz's integration into the parsonage and his growing trust in Oberlin, the parson, a trust which gives Lenz confidence to work as an artist. The simple, homely parsonage contrasts sharply with the earlier stormy setting. On the first evening, the friendliness of the household brings out Lenz's sociability and points up his childlike openness to human contact. But, when he is left alone Lenz's earlier fears return; he attempts to free himself by infliction of pain, and awakens the household. During the following days he becomes calmer under the parson's influence. He visits parishioners with him, gives a sermon, he paints, and talks with Oberlin. After a few days Lenz's friend Kaufmann pays a visit, the three men join in lively conversation. Now at the height of emotional well-being, Lenz elaborates his aesthetic theories. He is in opposition to Kaufmann, but clearly master of himself and his subject. Kaufmann's subsequent conversation with Lenz disrupts this stability. Kaufmann brings a letter from Lenz's father, and argues that Lenz should return to Livonia to support his family. Lenz experiences this as an attack, and begs to be left in the peace of the parsonage. When Oberlin decides to depart with Kaufmann for a visit to Switzerland, Lenz is deprived of support.

The third section describes Lenz's reaction to Oberlin's departure and his attempts to find comfort without the presence of a benevolent father figure. The lightness of the second section gives way to the bleakness of the first. As Lenz resumes his wanderings, the environment takes on a hostile air, in his encounter with a religious community in the mountains, and in the Oberlin parsonage, where he tries to attach himself to Madame Oberlin without finding the comfort Oberlin had given him. Lenz's yearning for Oberlin and anger at his absence are shown through his growing religious torment and his vacillation between religious enthusiasm and atheism. His attempt to prove he is God's son by resurrecting a dead girl forms the climax of this section.

In the final section, Büchner describes the changed relationship after Oberlin's return from Switzerland. Oberlin joins Kaufmann in urging Lenz to obey his father. When Lenz loses Oberlin's support, his scruples about disobeying his father increase, his agitation grows, and his behavior increasingly disrupts the entire household. Lenz tries to quiet his mental pain by harming himself or by seeking refuge with Oberlin, now hypocritically supportive. After casting himself from the parsonage window, Lenz is brought to Strasbourg. Once there, he is overtaken by an apathy which Büchner describes as never again lifting, so that he lives on in a living death: "His existence was an inevitable burden to him. — Thus he lived on" (101).

The perspective of *Lenz* hovers between the narrator's dispassionate description and Lenz's interior monologue. This establishes a close link between character and narrator — the narrator sees all events from Lenz's viewpoint and never reports the feelings or thoughts of another character.[9] At the beginning of the story, there is often no definite demarcation between the voices of Lenz and the narrator — often the reader must judge from context whether an observation is Lenz's or Büchner's. This hovering perspective is produced by verbless sentences and phrases which leave open the speaker and the time frame. The phrases often give feeling reactions to landscape or situation ("but everything so close," 79 or "the homey room, and the still faces," 81) and the reader shares the feeling. The hovering perspective therefore engages the reader and simultaneously blurs the distinction between narrator and character. Let us look at the first sentences in detail.

The story begins from the narrator's perspective and promises dispassionate observation. "On January 20, Lenz went through the mountains" (79). The three following phrases move out of the past tense into a hovering perspective of what Lenz or the author sees: "Mountain peaks and high plateaus in the snow; down in the valleys: grey stone, green surfaces, rocks, and fir trees." The next sentences from the narrator's point of view add detail to the landscape: "It was wet and cold; the water rushed down the rocks and cascaded over the road. The branches of the firs hung down heavily in the damp air. In the sky, grey clouds moved, but everything so close,..." The last verbless phrase with its emotional reaction resumes the hovering perspective, but in continuing the sentence moves back to the narrator's point of view ("and then the fog steamed up and swept heavily and damply through the bushes,") only to revert to hovering perspective and emotional response ("so ponderously, so lazily"). By this time the perspective is established and the reader has begun to identify with narrator and character while evaluating their responses. When Büchner, in the following sentences, reports what Lenz does, thinks, feels, sees, the reader readily enters Lenz's inner world, but the narrator's perspective gives this inner world an impartial voice: "Initially there was pressure in his chest when the stones fell away, when the grey forest below him shook... there was an urge in him, he looked for something, such as lost dreams, but he found nothing. Everything was so small to him, so near, so wet."

In the first two sections of the story, Büchner repeatedly brings the reader back to hovering perspective by verbless constructions. As we near the end, we move toward the impartial observer's point of view from which internal and external events are reported, thus giving them an effect of inevitability. After the first two sections, the reader's responses are well established and he continues to share and evaluate Lenz's experience. The means by which Büchner establishes this intersubjective response is simple. The effect is powerful indeed. Through this perspective and response the reader comes to understand an artist's particular sensitivity.

Even though the narrator identifies closely with Lenz, he differentiates himself clearly and subordinates all events and thoughts to the central underlying idea and psychodynamics of the father/son relationship. In this structuring he demonstrates insight into the characters' motivations and subtly controls our response. A brief comparison with the historical Oberlin's account, Büchner's main source, makes it obvious how this differentiation is achieved. The historical Oberlin protected himself from involvement with Lenz's tragedy by moral judgments. From his rational stance, most of Lenz's words and actions are incomprehensible, unpredictable, mad. Oberlin never understood that, to Lenz, he represented Lenz's father. The poignancy of the real Oberlin's account is his tragic lack of awareness of Lenz's transference. Büchner, reading his source, understood by empathy the psychodynamics of Lenz's relationship to his father as revived in the relationship to Oberlin. He omitted Oberlin's judgments and subordinated all details, of thought, perception, feeling, all images and *leitmotifs,* to delineation of the perimeters, fluctuations, and motivating forces in that father/son relationship. Suicide attempts play a large role in both accounts, but Büchner details only defenestration, although Oberlin mentions it among several methods. Defenestration shows graphically that Büchner understood how Lenz, in his suicide attempts, was symbolically acting out his being cast out by Oberlin, the household, society. Büchner omits details which distract from this pattern of the poet-son's rejection by the father-clergyman.[10]

The *leitmotifs,* which provide a continuous pattern of parallelism and contrast, demonstrate the narrator's design and controlling hand. Simultaneously they establish wider, deeper meanings of the father-son relationship. Take for instance the recurring mountain metaphor. The wintry mountainscape forms a solid, constantly mentioned backdrop to the first three sections. In the first, the mountains are bleak, primeval space. In the second, when Lenz is calmed by Oberlin, they are sunny; the valley rests in them. In the third section, after Oberlin's departure, their light disappears and they grow wild. In all three parts, they are the permanent background to Lenz's existence. When Lenz tells Kaufmann he needs the mountains to calm him ("if I could not go up a mountain...I would go mad," 88) he speaks of a presence like Oberlin's, which gives him elementary stability and orientation. Since the mountains are closely associated with Oberlin in Lenz's mind, they take on the symbolic significance of paternal reality.

During the fourth section, when Lenz has lost Oberlin's support, references to the mountains disappear. Their absence suggests that Lenz has lost the firm ground under his feet. Lenz's chaotic world knows no stability. Mountain references recur in the last paragraph, when Lenz is sunk in apathy and permanent alienation. But their image is given a hallucinatory quality; they are not close and tangible but "like a deep blue crystal wave towering into the evening glow" (101). In the following sentences ("at the foot of the mountains lay a shimmering bluish haze") they lose their connection to earth and become a mirage. Through the turmoil of Lenz's life the mountains represent elemental support and reality. Their disappearance at the end indicates Lenz's total loss of reality.[11]

In contrast to the mountain image, we find volatile images of the flow of light, rush of water, press of clouds, movement of wind, mist, fog, storms. They reflect Lenz's state of mind and influence it. Büchner uses them to illustrate Lenz's susceptibility to sensory stimulation, his openness to every breath of nature, his lack of defense against sensuousness and hence against an important aspect of the primary process. This imagery, and the states of mind it suggests, dominates the first part of the narrative, which is independent of the real Oberlin's account. This sensitivity is prominent also in the second part, but less so in the third. In the first two sections, Lenz seeks sensory stimulation though he fears it, and lays himself open to states of fusion and self-loss. Gentle motion and soft colors mediate pleasant, calming experiences, while harsh, confused and violent motion, sound and color cause painful inner turmoil. Early on, this openness to stimulation by nature is Lenz's artistic ideal and renders forcefully his Werther-like yearning to be part of the flow of natural energies.

The sensitivity to stimuli and the volatile images disappear in the fourth part, but recur twice in altered, psychotic form. Toward the end of his stay at the parsonage, Lenz feels the household's rejection so terribly that he transforms it into "immense heaviness of the air" (100) because of which, he tells Oberlin, he must stay in bed. Feeling has changed to concretization and acting-out. The same evening, Lenz projects an inaudible cry for help into the valley and tells Oberlin about "the terrible voice which screams from the horizon and which we usually call the stillness" (100). When he says these terrible words, Lenz is emotionless. He has made his pain concrete and no longer feels it. The freezing of volatile imagery into the rigidity of stone and metal at the story's end ("the crystal wave of the mountains, the gold wave of the moon," 101), suggests death by petrification in which paternal nature is still contained in the dead self.

Openness to Sense Perception, Over— and Understimulation, Defensive Strategies

The use of imagery in the examples given above tells us that Lenz loses his sense of being a living self. What reasons does Büchner give for this loss and what measures of self-protection does he attribute to Lenz? It strikes us at the story's beginning that Lenz's journey has no goal. He is portrayed, and he experiences himself, as drifting in the world. Neither he nor we know his destination or his origins. Hence he is at the mercy of every impulse. In the following passage, the fusing of inner and outer perceptions, and the absence of a permanent sense of self, clearly appear:

> In the beginning, there was pressure in his chest when the rocks fell away, when the gray forest below him shook and when the fog swallowed the tree shapes and then revealed their giant limbs; he felt pressure in himself, he looked for something, such as lost dreams but he found nothing. Everything was so small to him, so near, so wet; he would have liked to put the earth behind a stove. He could not understand that he should need so much time to climb down a slope to reach a distant point; he thought that he should be able to span everything with a few steps. (79)

The impression of violent nature (precipitous slopes, shaking trees, giant limbs) creates pressures in Lenz which remain nameless, as if they were reawakened infantile reactions to a primal scene. He seeks something to relieve the onslaught. At first he looks for an external point of reference: "he looked for something." But, his mind can find nothing either external or internal to help him; the "something" is like "lost dreams," hence "nothing"; without external direction or inner stability, he cannot organize his impressions. Therefore, we find in the next sentence, without transition ("Everything so small") that he has distorted the world into a miniature world. We assume he has done this to make it manageable and thereby reduce the threat of overstimulation. Büchner continues Lenz's fantasy of a small world which, like a wet toy, can be put behind a stove to dry. In the next sentence the defensive maneuver results in discrepancy between the small world and the actual distances Lenz has to cope with. Lenz refuses to understand his fantasy as wish, and cannot grasp why the distances are so great.

In this first paragraph Büchner introduces us to the defensive strategies of Lenz's psyche and gives an example of his disordered thoughts. Lenz's mind leaps from perception of the threat of overstimulation to diminution of it by an omnipotence fantasy which reverses the perception (not giant limbs, but a small world, therefore tiny limbs). Lenz then relates to the wished-for world as if it were the real; therefore he cannot understand it. His defensive maneuver has the benefit of reducing the threat, but the disadvantage of depriving him of new perceptions. He is no longer open to the world. All through the first section, Lenz defends himself against sensory overload by such strategies. To make sense of the story, the reader must fill in the protagonist's leaps between threat and defense. By repeating the pattern several times, Büchner gets the reader to make connections between overload and consequent distortion to avoid it. The reader therefore experiences a pattern of meaningful cause-and-effect relationships. The hero has no such reassurance. His fantasies cause increasing anxiety ("a nameless fear took hold of him," 80) because he has cut off the reassurance of the real world. To counteract the anxiety, he seeks contact with the natural world. But sensory stimulation becomes overstimulation, and the cycle begins again.

The same pattern holds for the human world. Lenz's hold on reality is so tenuous that he has great difficulty in letting go to sleep. He tries to counteract night's terrifying emptiness by sharp sensations, ice-cold baths, hurling himself against walls — to assure himself he is not in a nightmare, he even wakes up the whole household. But objects become fantastic even as he clings to them ("forms quickly moved past him, he pressed against them, they were shadows, life receded from him," 82). In the course of his stay at the parsonage, self-stimulation must be stronger and stronger to give him the sense of being alive. During the period of Lenz's trust in Oberlin, his presence, a word from him, prayers he recommends, help Lenz. But after this trust is lost, only physical pain helps. His self-mutilations are not suicide attempts, but attempts "to bring him to himself" (100). Lenz is equally tormented by over- and understimulation. By showing Lenz's shifts to fantasy when sensory pressure gets too strong, and to self-stimulation when emptiness becomes too frightening, Büchner indicates that the schizophrenic process is a defense of the psyche against fears of total regression and disintegration. The defensive strategies are the exercise of an infantile omnipotence of thought.

It is Büchner's achievement to propel us through the hovering perspective at the beginning of the story into an identification with Lenz's and his own sensitivity. One's first reaction to the beginning pages is painful awareness of the chaotic sensory impressions. At the same time, Büchner gets the reader to differentiate between his narrator's and his protagonist's use of their sensitivity. By identification with Lenz, Büchner locates his own creative process in a similar sensitivity to stimulation. Lenz is controlled by the press of stimuli, and reacts with startling immediacy. In describing their pattern and demonstrating his understanding of its meaning, the narrator takes an ego controlling stance toward his sensitivity to Lenz and identification with him. The narrator's response is not a defensive closing off, but a controlled openness. He shows this control by using *leitmotifs* to reveal the state of Lenz's psyche, and by symbolic use of grammatical forms. Most importantly, he structures the narrative firmly around the father symbol. The narrator's creative process has the social function of mediating empathy with and understanding for another human being. Narrator and reader share a conscious, ego-directed, ego-strengthening goal.[12] Lenz has no such goal. The metaphors of the aimless journey, wandering in fog and darkness, help Büchner to describe a self without center, focus or orientation. Lenz does not know that he attempts to escape stimulation by fantasy, nor that he seeks someone or something to cling to. Büchner shows that Lenz needs Oberlin to give boundaries to his disintegrating sense of self. He has no capacity to limit himself.

The nature imagery of the beginning section points up the importance to Lenz of stimulation. He is just as oversensitive to nature as to the human world. Human beings, unlike nature, can actively affect another human. Hence we might assign them exclusive responsibility for Lenz's spiritual death, and make Büchner's psychosocial treatment of the artist theme a purely social issue, which it is not. Büchner is concerned with what it is in Lenz's psychology and early development, and his own, that makes them vulnerable to the natural and social world. Lenz's relationships fall into a pattern which reflects his early childhood and allows us to reconstruct his early development and the origins of sensitivity and defenses.

The Social World

Out of the dark storm comes Lenz, deeply troubled, to a friendly village with "children at table, old women, girls" (80) and a brightly lit parsonage. By heavy emphasis on children, Lenz's childlikeness, his childhood memories and fears, Büchner indicates the degree of regression in Lenz's social relations and shapes our expectations. Oberlin greets Lenz with the welcoming, unconditional acceptance which a good father would give a child just born. "Welcome, even though I do not know you" (80), he tells Lenz, and thereby elicits Lenz's trust. Through these words he allows Lenz a child's entrance to the parsonage, without a name or social identity or responsibilities. How much Lenz needs to be accepted in just this way appears from his disavowal of his identity as writer. When he is asked if he is the writer whose plays Oberlin has read, Lenz repudiates them by, "Do not judge me by them." We must keep in mind that although Lenz had a literary reputation next to Goethe's, he was already an outcast, and the literary identity was the only positive one he had.

Being a clergyman's son, Lenz finds the parsonage a familiar environment and quickly feels at home. As he tells stories of his childhood home, the present and past parsonages merge: "it seemed to him as if old figures, forgotten faces emerged from the darkness" (81). His wish for a home seems to be realized. Yet the very comfort seems to be too much for Lenz and his recollections become fantasies which lead him "far, far away" (81).

How deceptive the homeyness is, and how little he has really been accepted, becomes obvious at bedtime when he is quartered across the street in the empty schoolhouse attic.[13] When he is left alone in the dark, his fear of emptiness immediately overwhelms him, and he seeks to fill it with whatever stimulation he can muster. Oberlin's power over him appears even on the first evening, for his appearance calms Lenz at once. The rest of that night, when Lenz repeats the Lord's Prayer, he is expressing his desperate need for help from a father, heavenly or on earth. Lenz cannot tell Oberlin what he fears, nor does Oberlin question his strange behavior. Indirectly, Lenz expresses his need and fear by the uproar he causes, like a child who dare not admit he is afraid. Oberlin, through his silence, indirectly expresses unwillingness or incapacity to help.

This non-communication remains typical of their relations and contributes to Lenz's increasing but always oblique efforts to obtain an unequivocal response from Oberlin. The immediacy and strength of Lenz's attachment betrays that it is a transference in which we can see Lenz's actual father reflected. Büchner's genius knows how to evoke the past relationship in the present. The first evening establishes the pattern and the participants' reactions to it. As in the natural world, Lenz swings from desire for stimulation through human contact to recoil from it, from craving contact to dread of it. Since Oberlin refuses an unequivocal response, Lenz's problems develop and accelerate. We are concerned with a regressed, infantile pattern, so let us look first at Lenz's relationship to mother figures in the story, since after all mothers shape these early patterns.

The Relationship with the Mother

On his first evening in the Oberlin household, Lenz observes the mother in the shadows, sitting "quietly and like an angel" (81). She is curiously insubstantial and neither greets him nor speaks to him. During a later walk in the valley, when Lenz no longer feels threatened and is at one with the world ("he felt so much at home...a feeling of Christmas came over him," 83) he is reminded of his mother. He feels that she "should step forth from behind a tree, tall, and tell him she had given all this to him as a present" (83). The vision is a child's (the mother is tall and gives presents) and insubstantial, a quickly fading image. Nevertheless, Lenz feels its blessing: "When he went down, he saw a rainbow of colors surround his shadow, he felt that something had touched his forehead, the being spoke to him" (83). Lenz takes the rainbow as a revelation of his divine sonship (Revelation 4:3) and it encourages him to ask Oberlin to allow him to preach next Sunday. We should note that Lenz does not attribute the blessing to the maternal vision, but to a nonsexual "something," a "being." His experience of the mother precedes sexual differentiation. The regression seems to be to such an early stage that the mother is experienced preverbally, for the words spoken are not given. The relationship to maternal beings makes it clear that Lenz relates to others like an infant, and rarely as the adult he is.

Considering the importance of maternal figures, their insubstantiality is striking. Lenz's description to Madame Oberlin of a girl he loved has the lightness and grace of a young mother observed by a child: "When she went through the room and sang quietly half to herself and every step was a kind of music, such happiness was in her and that flowed over into me, I was almost calm when I looked at her" (92). Note that she neither turns to him nor addresses him, but is a self-contained presence from whom happiness "flowed." Lenz's relationship to the woman is on the preverbal level, like his earlier relationship to the mother image. It is receiving, rather than give-and-take. And the woman herself is not strong. The description evokes a pathetic, childlike creature, an anxious girl for whom "the world is too big" (92). She reacts by withdrawal "into herself." To protect herself, she seeks "the narrowest corner in the entire house, and there she sat as if all her happiness were only in that one spot." The woman's name matters little, or who she was in Lenz's life, Friederike Brion, with whose forsakenness he identified, or Goethe's sister, Cornelia Schlosser, with whom he sought shelter.[14] Büchner gives her different forms in the story, she is the girl whom Lenz tries to resurrect, the sick girl in the healer's cabin, the woman he calls to at night, the woman he describes to Madame Oberlin. The girl-woman is a prototype of Lenz's experience of women, mother and lover alike.[15] He craves support that they are incapable of giving.

Lenz's dream about his mother confirms our analysis of his wish and need for a sustaining mother. He falls asleep at a time when he wants to be alone and yet feels deserted. He has cried himself to sleep, like a child, and the author emphasizes the depth of his abandonment: "He lay there alone, and everything was quiet and calm and cold, and the moon shone all night long and stood over the mountains" (85). Thus abandoned, he dreams of his mother's funeral. She is pictured as a white figure against a dark graveyard wall, a young erotic woman with "a white and red rose pinned to her breast." The erotic picture is quickly erased as "she sank into a corner and the roses slowly grew over her" (85). The mother as nurturer is experienced as sexual and seductive (the roses on her breast); she is also weak and insubstantial, for the wish to eliminate her seductiveness eliminates her when she sinks into the earth and roses grow over her.

On waking, Lenz immediately goes to Oberlin to tell him he believes his mother has died. The dream and its immediate communication to Oberlin express Lenz's wish to eliminate the ineffective, seductive mother and replace her with a father as nurturer and provider.

Because the dream realizes an unconscious angry wish, Lenz feels neither loss nor sadness; he accepts the father in the mother's stead. Later, however, he acknowledges guilt when he says that he has murdered his mother, and sacrificed the woman he loved (92). In terms of psychosocial development, Lenz's dream expresses sacrifice of the oedipal drive in favor of nurture. Because he experiences the mother as weak and the father as strong, he assigns the mother's role to the father. The experience of woman as unsatisfactory mother gives overwhelming importance to Lenz's relationship with the father and father figures, for this is the only sustaining relationship he has. He needs the father to define himself against him and to mirror himself in him. He needs his acceptance so that he can accept himself.[16] Lenz's relationship to mother figures clarifies that his regression reaches back to preverbal infancy. Furthermore, in terms of early development, the support he got from a mother was so tenuous that it left him with a fatal weakness of his self. In Büchner's portrayal of Lenz's perception of mother figures, the schizophrenogenic child-mother comes alive.[17] The mother figure we found to be the artist/son's muse in Nathanael's history appears only in faint outline in Lenz's Christmas vision. Lenz's psyche is too incoherent and too regressed to experience a genuine oedipal encounter and dilemma.

The Changing Relationship to the Father

All through the story, Oberlin is the only person to whom Lenz turns. By his profession as understanding and practical country pastor, Oberlin promises fatherly guidance and ministration ("everywhere trusting glances...people told him dreams, misgivings, a quick turn to practical things" 82.) His eyes mediate greater calm to Lenz than nature at rest (82). As Lenz quiets down under their influence, the country seems bathed in sunlight. Oberlin's liking reassures Lenz and comforts him ("Oberlin liked his conversation and took great pleasure in his gracious, childlike face" 82.) Oberlin's existence gives Lenz a gentler image of the divine than he had before. During the first days, Oberlin's calm eyes, closeness, unconditional acceptance, approving glance soothe Lenz like an infant.

Feeling at one with his host, Lenz is able to help Oberlin with the parish (83), go for walks, read, even imagine a future for himself. At the beginning, he is still afraid at night when he is not with Oberlin, and needs Oberlin's physical presence to soothe him. But when he has established a symbolic identification with Oberlin by getting his permission to preach, he works steadily on his sermon, his night terrors disappear, he can sleep (83). The sermon and the conversation about art show Lenz at the peak of well-being. Strengthened by identification with the good father in his role as preacher, Lenz ceases to respond in a chaotic way and becomes capable of developing a consistent artistic theory and using the full range of a finely differentiated sensitivity and intellect. He commands a rich cultural heritage, about which he has deep feeling and insight, and withstands opposition such as Kaufmann's with liveliness and grace. Though still childlike in his spontaneity and openness, he is neither simple nor regressed.

Lenz does not find an intellectual equal in Oberlin, but experiences him as elemental because he is endowed with a sense for the elemental in nature (85). It is this elemental quality that gives support. By merging with Oberlin, Lenz "saves himself" (89). But the support has shaky, deceptive foundations. There are many indications, even at the beginning that Oberlin cannot understand Lenz's thoughts and enthusiasms or empathize. He makes no effort to question his troubled guest and gives no thought to Lenz when he suddenly decides to accompany Kaufmann on a visit to Switzerland. His departure is a disaster for Lenz, who does not know how to make Oberlin understand his need for him to stay.[18]

The third section covers Oberlin's absence, describes aspects of a distant, unsympathetic father, and delimits new aspects of the father/son relationship. One of these aspects is the healer in whose cabin Lenz spends a night; the other is God in Lenz's religious quest. Like Oberlin, the healer speaks of visions in the mountains; unlike Oberlin, he does not address Lenz but speaks to the room (90). Oberlin lives in communication with his parishioners, the healer prays in isolation, in a room busy with people coming and going. The cabin scene forms a clear contrast to the first evening at the parsonage. The hut is dark and unfriendly, its inhabitants alienated from each another and unconcerned with Lenz, their religious life is confused and centered on suffering. The entire scene is uncanny, compared to the homelike parsonage. Yet Lenz feels the experience as positive ("the world had been light," 91). He who has trouble sleeping, falls asleep in the cabin without the fears which plague him at the parsonage. This seems to indicate that an alienated, unfriendly environment and father figure do not disturb him as much as the elusive emotional support from Oberlin.

During Oberlin's absence, Lenz repeatedly works himself into frenzy searching for a divine father but when he receives no response the frenzy collapses. The cycles continue until he hears a child has died, after he begged God for a sign. The pitch of his expectations heightens until imagining a sign changes to acting out, demanding a sign. He supports his delusion by dressing as a penitent, and fasting. At the child's body, he "concentrates his will in one point" (93) and then speaks Christ's words, "Arise" (Mark 5:41). He wants proof that he is God's son,[19] a confirmed share in His omnipotence. At the same time, coming in penitent's garb, he secures forgiveness in advance. When his hope collapses, he angrily concludes that God is impotent, and he himself is omnipotent ("he felt that he could...seize God and drag Him through His clouds,...could squash the world with his teeth and spit it into the creator's face," 93-94). He takes the light of the "simpleminded" moon (94) as an answer to his rebellion, an answer which confirms his conviction of the impotent father. Atheism gives him temporary strength and he finds sleep. Next day, however, he is overtaken by horror at his empty existence and returns to a tormented, uneasy faith. Without faith or father, Lenz does not have the inner resources to give coherence to his feelings and thoughts.

The issue of rejection by the father takes center stage on Oberlin's return. Despite a friendly manner, Oberlin busies himself while he talks to Lenz, and urges him to submit to his father's wishes. Realizing that Oberlin does not understand him at all, Lenz tells Oberlin explicitly that he lacks faith and therefore cannot obey his father and become a pastor. He asks Oberlin directly: "Are you rejecting me?" (94) and is told that he should turn to Christ to help him with his faith. Lenz responds to Oberlin's evasion by one of his own, a sudden, irrational question "what the woman is doing," designed to test Oberlin's forbearance.[20] At the same time, Lenz puts the question in such a way as to let Oberlin know that he is no longer capable of rational discourse, is helpless, and should not be rejected.

Later that day Lenz again tests Oberlin. To fully understand the significance of this test we need to remind ourselves that Lenz's first name, by which his family called him, was Jacob and that like the Biblical Jacob, he was a second son. That morning Oberlin had brought a letter from Lenz's friends and "a bundle of rods" (94).[21] Oberlin had no hesitation in delivering this cruel gift. Now Lenz asks Oberlin to beat him with the rods and thus execute the punishment implied. Oberlin refuses, takes no responsibility for his own cruelty, disguises it with hypocritical kisses, and passes further responsibility to God, with whom Lenz "should settle his account" (95). In addition to the request for clarification ("do you want me beaten," Lenz seems to say) Lenz implies another request. He wears a piece of fur on his left shoulder, indicating that he is enacting the role of Jacob come to receive his father's blessing (Genesis 27:16). Since his communication is to another theologian, Lenz could expect Oberlin to understand the symbolism and to realize that the request for a beating is actually a plea for a paternal blessing. Oberlin refuses to understand the plea. The Jacob and rod symbolism together form a suggestive fabric, like that of the resurrection scene, concerning Lenz's wish to be acknowledged the beloved child of an all-powerful father who shares His omnipotence. Lenz's abject terror at Oberlin's rejection is shown by his "whining with a hollow, terrible, despairing voice" (95) all through the night following the Jacob episode. And no one even thinks of going to comfort him.

The incident shows Oberlin's insensitivity and unwillingness to take responsibility for his rejection. His kisses are kisses of betrayal. Oberlin prizes his image of good Christian, shepherd of his flock. But when asked to help, he evades responsibility, passing it to God. In this way, he contributes to Lenz's isolation and gradual disintegration. Lenz wants to believe in the promises and assistance of the good shepherd. But every time he needs help he is disappointed and confused by surface friendliness and underlying rejection. Oberlin keeps him in this double bind until he finally sends him away.[22]

Because of preoccupations with children and household, Mme. Oberlin remains outside the double binding relationship, but Oberlin is as firmly tied into it as Lenz. After Oberlin's return,[23] Lenz feels increasingly abandoned and displays amazing ingenuity in new strategies to command an honest response — staying in bed, blaspheming, referring to women he supposedly harmed, running away, pleading, mystifying, casting himself from a window — again and again trying to move by his enormous suffering this man of God who remains a tantalizing undecipherable hieroglyph to his creative son. Lenz cannot tell what is real and what is dream. When he says to Oberlin, "if only I could distinguish if I am awake or dreaming...let's investigate that" (96), he is begging for straightforward communication. It is dreadful irony that the double binding brings forth the inventive strategies of the artist. Instead of works of art, Lenz creates ever new symptoms of illness. The ambiguous father, to whom the son can only relate with confusion and ambivalence, generates the artist.

Despite his regression, Lenz displays considerable cunning in trying to trap Oberlin into helping him. At the same time he gradually loses the capacity to organize his perceptions, thoughts, feelings, and impulses. As his sense of self fragments, the still predictable cycles of over- and understimulation also fragment. He could formerly rally defenses against the intense pain of rejection, but he can no longer do so because he loses the capacity to tell what might help or harm him, what is imaginary, what is real. A harmless cat can take on the aspect of a terrifying enemy, when Lenz's anger and hostility is projected on it. Worst of all, his sense of time disappears. Alone in nature in the first section, Lenz experienced a similar incapacity to separate fantasy from the real world, but this was only a foretaste of the hell he experiences once time has turned into eternity: "It seemed to him...as if the world were only his idea...and he was eternally damned, Satan, alone with his tormenting fantasy" (99). "For him there was no peace and no hope in death" (100). The more he tries to control thoughts, words, and actions the less he can. Attempting to hold to a thought in conversation, for instance, he is afraid of losing the end of his sentence and must repeat its last word over and over. The meaning and context no longer matter. His struggle to control such impulses is the more desperate the more he loses confidence in Oberlin. His isolation seems more terrible because it occurs in the midst of a lively household.

We have seen that Lenz needs a father as a steadying presence and support. He also required him to provide a focus for his emotional and intellectual life, and, most advanced in terms of psychosocial development, he needs a father to support his artistic mission. On the other hand, what does his father want from Lenz, and what reasons does the narrator give for Lenz's disobedience? The father/Oberlin wants him to return to Livonia, assume a clergyman's position, and support him and his social order. This means to Lenz that he must renounce his own needs, and achieve only what his father wishes. Since Lenz's needs have never been met by his parents, he cannot renounce them: such renunciation would be an intolerable strain. "Everyone needs something," he tells Kaufmann. "If he can rest," (as he does at Oberlin's) "what more could he have?" He rejects the achievement ethic of his father's Protestantism: He feels he cannot "always climb, struggle and ever throw away what the moment gives and to deprive oneself" (89). The plain terms in which Lenz describes his needs at the height of his happiness at the parsonage show that for him the artist's needs are simple: "to go out into the mountains and to look out from them," (we should recall that mountains represented paternal, safe space), to have a house to come to, "a garden to go through and a window to look in on" (89). Lenz need not own the house, or even be in the room — he only wants to look in at the window. A safe space, psychically and physically containing, distant but not too distant from fellow men, the support of a paternal, undemanding being[24] — these are the needs Büchner claims for the artist. A century later, Virginia Woolf was demanding a similar space for work and self-development for the woman writer, and spelled it out as "a room of one's own."

In view of these needs, the end of the story is the more horrifying. Lenz is in no condition to care for himself, has repeatedly hurt himself, is incapacitated physically. Nevertheless, he is put into a carriage and put down somewhere in Strasbourg. No thought is given by anyone, least of all Oberlin, to where he will go. Nor do we know who accompanies him. "They" bring him. Humans have deserted Lenz, and once again the landscape is made to express and reflect his abandonment and isolation. Büchner's description conveys more effectively than Oberlin's defensive account that Lenz, like other schizophrenics of his day, was palmed off by one person onto the next without concern for his need or pain. Since no one cares, he loses the capacity to care for himself. Describing the journey from Waldbach to Strasbourg, Büchner evokes the gradual deadening and the walled-off apathetic state reached by the chronic schizophrenic after years of suffering.

Unlike Oberlin and his own contemporaries, Büchner empathizes with Lenz's pain and terror. As *Woyzeck* correlates madness and aggression with a social environment, Lenz's madness is related to his treatment by the father figure representing social and religious institutions.[25] He demonstrates his understanding by the actions, interrelationships, feelings and thoughts he attributes to Lenz, by the symbols and images he uses. Every one of the seemingly irrational words and actions of the sick man makes good sense considering his background and his situation in the parsonage and in society. By making Lenz's defensive strategies increasingly extreme and his sensitivity increasingly lacerated, Büchner builds up a convincing and deeply moving record of an accelerating, more and more frightening self-disintegration.

From the narrative, we cannot tell if Büchner meant Oberlin's attitudes, reactions and values to be similar to those of Lenz's real father. Judging by the impact they have on Lenz, we assume that Büchner saw them as familiar patterns experienced from early childhood. Initially, Oberlin's presence gives Lenz enough self-cohesion so he can use his artistic gift. When support is withdrawn, Lenz cannot find other support, or muster inner resources to sustain himself. In terms of his psychosocial development this inability means he has never had sufficiently strong, unequivocal parental support to internalize it as psychic structure, that is, to become emotionally self-supporting.[26] At the same time, the double bind relationship with the parent has generated a heightened sensitivity to stimuli and a strong, inventive capacity to master them. Because Lenz experienced a too traumatic self-development, because he continues to hold himself open to regression and vulnerability, he needs external support from a generous father figure or from the social environment to fulfill himself as an artist. The casting out by the father spells spiritual death and the end of the ability to create. In his account, Büchner establishes a close connection between chaos and creation, pathology and creativity. Unlike Woyzeck, Lenz is more than a victim of society or pathology. He has a task as an artist and writer, and must keep open to memories, fantasies, feelings — his primary process. He must let himself regress. That is his tragedy.

The Artist

Once we accept that Büchner is concerned with a poet's psychic death, we can no longer consider Lenz's writing as irrelevant, or the conversation on art as an unrelated addition which explains only Büchner's own aesthetic theory.[27] Unlike Hoffmann, Büchner does not assign primary process qualities to one part of a split self (Nathanael), and the secondary process to another (the narrator). Lenz

himself covers the whole range from regressed psychotic to incisive
theorist and poet, indicating that Büchner links the processes more
closely and has a unified concept of the artist's self. The most important function of this conversation is to emphasize the fact that Lenz
is an artist and his interests when he is at ease are those of an artist.
Lenz's sermon realizes his poetic mission. Portraying him as he
preaches, Büchner establishes a relationship between art and religion
that illuminates their common ground. This again appears in the
choice of the paintings Lenz discusses, whose religious subject
emphasizes the communion between aesthetic and religious feeling.

Büchner shows several stages of a creative process in the sermon
incident. Inspiration comes during Lenz's Christmas vision and
causes him to ask Oberlin's permission to preach. Permission gained,
he chooses a text and begins to compose in his head. Since the sermon is treated as oral poetry, Büchner carefully sets the surrealistic
scene: a sunny winter valley, resonant with bells, fragrant with
flowers, the church overlooking the village. Thus Büchner prepares us
for an experience of oceanic bliss and mystical union: "as if everything were dissolving into one harmonious wave" (84). The hymn sung
by women and girls blends into this wave of harmony. During the
hymn Lenz feels taken up into the community, and loses his shyness.
As he relaxes, painful feelings awaken, but by putting them in simple
words and sharing them with everyone, he believes he has become the
voice of the community. Speaking of his own suffering, he thinks he
consoles theirs and helps them express it within the human commun-
ity(84). In speaking to them, he gains strength. The feeling comes to
an end with the sermon, for the community responds by a Pietist
hymn affirming suffering as "service to God." Because the response is
negative, Lenz feels "deep, unnameable pain." He feels he has failed
to move their hearts and "the universe itself was for him in
wounds."[28]

Lenz's conflict with society continues in the conversation about art
with Kaufmann and Oberlin. Kaufmann's is the idealist position,
which Lenz rejects. He does not isolate aesthetics from other aspects
of life, but finds the possibility of art in every living form, from the
most sublime to the humblest. He demands respect for human life in
all its manifestations, and that is why he uses illustrations from
peasant life. His concept is dynamic, opposed to Kaufmann's static
idealism. Since he finds his own position and that of the peasants

barely tolerable, he must advocate change. Like Hoffmann's, Lenz's (Büchner's) artistic theory derives from personal sources. Unlike Hoffmann's, theirs is impelled by a strong interpersonal impulse and has a social-political aim. Lenz prefers the simple, prosaic life of the people as the subject of art, because it directly reveals the "vein of feeling... alike in almost all men" (87). He asks that the artist feel, and convey his feeling, that the artist "love humankind in order to penetrate into the individual" (87). To communicate understanding, the artist can freely create humans "out of himself," out of his feeling for human nature, "without copying anything of external reality into them" (87). Dynamic, truthful, humanitarian, Lenz's conception of art sees the artist as mediator of the inner workings of the psychic, social, and natural worlds. The individuals and phenomena of the external world are part of "an infinite beauty which assumes now this form and now that, eternally unfolding, changing" (87). To bring them to the attention of his fellows, the artist fixes in permanent form the changing, fleeting manifestations of life. He is a re-creator of God's world — and we are once again face to face with the theme of the artist son of a divine father. Lenz's view of art, his experience of existence, his sensitivity, are opposed to the normative approach of Oberlin and Kaufmann: "reality contains no types for an Apollo of Belvedere" (87), bounded by prescription and insensitivity.

Lenz's examples illustrating his theories express his idea of a satisfactory life. The works he chooses are counterworlds to his present existence, but not escapes into different worlds. Savoy's *Christ and the Disciples at Emaus* and Nicolaes Maes' *Woman at the Window*[29] are so rooted in the German/Dutch rural world that they could be scenes from the Steintal or the parsonage. The "picture" Lenz observed that day, the two peasant girls on a rock, also shows ordinary human beings in community. The two girls help each other; the disciples encounter the divine in their everyday world; the woman at the window, though alone, follows the community's church service. Humans are at peace with one another and their environment. They actively relate to each other. There is a quality of solemn yet homey celebration of life. Their world is no idyll without disappointment and grief. The girls are serious, the disciples are grieving on "a dull quiet evening," frightened by the unknown. The woman sitting in a Sunday-clean room cannot go to church. The experiences shown are tolerable and enriching because the people feel they are part of a supporting world which offers comfort and fellowship. The contrast to Lenz's isolation, deprivation, exposure to overwhelming feeling, is striking. We might also note that in these pictures Lenz's idea of women is different from the real-life view we observed earlier. The girls symbolize simple human cooperation, the solitary woman is an image of self-acceptance and work well done. The pictures radiate strength.

In sum: for Büchner, the artist must expose himself to a dynamic experience of life. He cannot shield himself by preconceived ideals, rules or traditions. In psychoanalytic language, we might say that he must be entirely open to reality and the primary process. He needs this openness (which appears as Lenz's childlikeness and his sensitivity to stimulation) to participate with feeling in the created world. He puts his view of the dynamic world in communicable form, to increase his own well-being and contribute to his fellow man's. He needs support from a father (and social order) who accepts him and his efforts. If he is rejected, if the father stifles him by demanding conformity, or if he is ambiguous and indifferent to his son, then the son exhausts himself in emotional turmoil. He dies an emotional and spiritual death, though outwardly he lives on and does "everything as the others did" (101).

By embedding the artist theme in the psychological situation of Lenz, Büchner establishes similarities in the psychic processes of schizophrenic and artist. The schizophrenic is subject to constant change in his emotional world and impulses. The artist must keep himself open to the same kind of constant change. Potentially, his artistic strategies in the uses of this openness integrate him into the community. Lenz's artistic theory has developed from painful attempts to help his fellow men through his art and to resolve his psychic situation through creation. Büchner, as writer, was heard by his contemporaries. Lenz, during his sermon, is at one with the community. But the schizophrenic's defenses isolate him. The Lenz of the last section, no longer creating symbols, but living them, alienates the entire household by behavior dictated by his past, and his uncontrollable impulses. Büchner shows how Lenz, "prophet of modern, homeless, pathological man,"[30] himself becomes a homeless, pathological outcast.

Büchner's motives in writing *Lenz* were political. The Young German writer Gutzkow wrote him in 1835, in his Strasbourg exile,

"Conduct your smuggling of freedom as I do; wine hidden under the straw of novellas." (As rifles were sometimes hidden under the straw of peasant carts.) "I believe in this way we can be more useful than when we run into their rifles blindly, all the more as these rifles are aimed at us and loaded" (II, 476-477). Büchner seems to have taken the suggestion up immediately, for Gutzkow's next letter asks "your novella is to have the shipwrecked poet as a subject?" (II, 479).

In addition to social criticism, Büchner was trying to understand and portray the danger to the artist, the forces which undermine the creative capacity, the assistance a writer needs, and the effect which rejection has on him. Büchner differs from his *Lenz* because he understands the difference between the psychic and social processes of the schizophrenic and the artist, and is able to convey his understanding in a symbolic form. Büchner drew from Oberlin's account, Lenz's biography by Stöber, the study of Lenz's works, oral reports, and letters acquired during the Strasbourg exile.[31] From these sources he developed a portrait of such psychodynamic accuracy that the contemporary reader, although he has the benefit of more detailed information on Lenz, can add little. To better understand Büchner, who succeeded in integrating the dangers, and Lenz who was overcome, let us look at their lives.

Life Histories[32]

Lenz's father and Büchner's worked their way up into the educated bourgeoisie, but their mothers belonged there by birth. Both fathers had strong opinions. Having done well under the existing power structure, both supported the status quo, in Lenz's case Imperial Russian hegemony in Livonia, in Büchner's the Metternich-style Restoration in Hesse. Both fathers' world view contained an essential contradiction. Despite his Pietist (individualist) enthusiasm, father Lenz subscribed to submission to the state, the social order, and a rigid Protestant morality. Despite enthusiasm for the French Revolution and Enlightenment, father Büchner was a reactionary. Both profoundly influenced their sons' early development — Büchner's father inspiring him with enthusiasm for the Revolution, and father Lenz supporting his son's mystical bent. Both sons were interested in writing from their early adolescence, and Lenz's father at least delighted in his early publication. Both invested much in their sons and expected much.[33] Each took up his father's profession. Büchner transformed his father's medical profession into a teaching career in physiology. Lenz reluctantly became a clergyman. Both rebelled, Lenz went to Strasbourg to be a writer and Büchner became involved in political activity which led to his exile. Both fathers withdrew support, emotional and financial.

Of significant difference were the degree of stress the sons were subjected to, and the degree of distress in their families. Once Büchner had qualified himself for a position as university lecturer in science (despite revolutionary activities he did not lose much time finishing his studies), his father ungrudgingly rewarded his achievement. Moreover, at the beginning of the 1830s, the study of science was challenging and offered a wide variety of options. Lenz's future in theology, and the prospect of struggling for a living in rural Livonia, offered none. Once Lenz lost his father's support, he never regained it.

A vital difference appears in the role of the two mothers. The one extant letter of Büchner's mother shows an active, lively, concerned woman, involved in the lives of children and friends, enjoying their company (II, 497-499). Lenz's mother seems a mere shadow of the father. She is described as being ill, and in fact she died in 1778, the summer after the Waldbach episode.[34] She seems to have rejected Lenz when he left Livonia. Büchner as the first child of a healthy, energetic woman, must have received great support from his mother, whereas Lenz, a sick woman's fourth or fifth child in a family of eight, would have received little if any.

Their political and intellectual situation was also vitally different, as well as the availability of friends and companions. Lenz began writing on religion when still a high school student. Leaving Königsberg University, he turned his back on his religious convictions as well as his father. Initially he was much admired by the Strasbourg circle. His was the most decided political bent of the group. He linked economic-political exploitation and repression with sexual repression. His rebellion was couched in concrete, everyday terms, not the mytho-religious vein of most of his contemporaries. More exposed by his desertion of family and bourgeois prospects, and his stronger stand, Lenz had more to lose than his friends. When they abandoned him he must have dreaded that he would totally submit to paternal authority and lose his identity if he returned to Livonia. It was small wonder that he was increasingly incapacitated by illness both physical and mental. By 1777 his literary career was finished, and when he went home his worst fears were realized.

Even in high school, young Büchner's friends shared his dislike of conditions in Hesse. Unlike Lenz, his intellectual development was continuous. In the freer atmosphere of Strasbourg his liberalism was strengthened and he joined the radical, but legitimate Société des Droits de l'Homme et du Citoyen. He also got engaged in Strasbourg. He had to complete his studies at a Hessian university to qualify for a position in Hesse, and therefore enrolled at the University of Giessen. The repressive atmosphere, his outrage at the slavish bourgeoisie and the treatment of the urban and rural poor led him to engage in political agitation though he had promised his parents not to do so. At Giessen he was alienated from fellow students and environment, and suffered severe depression and states of alienation like those he attributes to Lenz. When some pamphlets were discovered, his friends were proved loyal, and though his revolutionary hopes were ended, he found shelter and emotional support at home. He had sufficient peace of mind to write his play, *Danton's Death,* hoping to use the proceeds to leave Germany. When he finally fled to Strasbourg, he was returning to a town he loved, where his fiancée awaited him, where he could complete his studies. Meanwhile he had won admiration and encouragement from the German writer Gutzkow, and a ready outlet in Gutzkow's journal for further work.

The bare facts of their lives tell eloquently of the strengths and weaknesses of the two writers, and give us some understanding why one disintegrated under stress and the other did not. Because of his experience of early conflict with his father, persecution, anxiety, states of alienation, Büchner was qualified to write about inner turmoil in a hostile world. We do not understand how Büchner, young as he was, could know that Lenz's treatment by Oberlin repeated old, familiar childhood patterns. The life histories show the importance to the writer of his father. An insignificant role is given the oedipal relationship. Büchner connects the sensitivity to nature and his human environment of the writer Lenz to his past and present vulnerability. He probably wrote the novella in an attempt to integrate his own experience of alienation and vulnerability into his recent role of acclaimed writer. Physical and emotional support from parents and friends allowed Büchner this achievement. Considering his understanding of human interactions, his keen grasp of developmental patterns, and the fineness of his empathy at twenty-two, there is no telling what he might have accomplished as a writer had he not died two years later.

IV
EDUARD MÖRIKE'S
MOZART ON THE WAY TO PRAGUE:
ACHIEVEMENT OF INTEGRATION THROUGH MASTERY OF AN
OEDIPAL CRISIS

To Romantics like E.T.A. Hoffmann and post-Romantics like Mörike (1804-1875), Mozart was the paradigm of the exuberant, effortless creator. Mörike's novella[1] telescopes Mozart's entire life into a seventy-page story describing a single autumn day two years before the French Revolution and four years before Mozart's early death. The thirty-one year old composer, still working on *Don Giovanni,* is traveling by coach through Moravia to Prague. Because of the telescoping technique, each detail of the day represents a fundamental aspect of the composer's life.

From youth, Mörike was intimately familiar with Mozart's life and music[2] and he used no biography while writing the novella.[3] Hoffmann's *Don Juan* had also made a lasting impression on him.[4] Although Mörike invented the other characters, and the events of the day, the observations on the creative process are his own.[5] His portrayal of Mozart is based on identification with the composer, to whom he attributed the rich imagination, numerous moments of inspiration, and ease of composition which he himself conspicuously lacked, except during two brief periods in his seventy-odd years.

Even then he took eight years to finish the tale. The Mozart portrayal is a projection and wish fulfillment. After completing this story, Mörike, except for a few poems, ceased to write.

Among the day's distinct but interlinked episodes, three stand out as moments during which the composer is creating. We shall look closely at the symbolism in these episodes to shed light on Mörike's insights into the different motivations, stages, and results of creativity. In each incident, he is describing a different originating impulse, at a different developmental level (oral, phallic, oedipal), resulting in a different mode of expression (lyrical-idyllic-intimate; festive-social-humorous; tragic-elegiac-sublime). The modes of expression which Mörike attributes to Mozart correspond to his own three favorite moods.[6] The story interests the student of creativity because we find not merely one wellspring of creation, but clearly differentiated sources, occasions, and products of creativity. A brief account of the plot will furnish the background for further analysis.

Plot and Structure

The plot is made up of six episodes in the sequence of their occurrence on this autumn day.[7] Several episodes flash back to past occurrences to elucidate present action. Each event is on a realistic and allegorical level. The symbolic orchestration of these levels will concern us later in our analysis of creativity. The novella has two complementary symbolical-allegorical object symbols or integrative devices;[8] one from nature, the orange tree and the orange; the other a human artifact, the opera *Don Giovanni*. All episodes directly or indirectly concern the composition of the opera and the despoilment of the tree. In the first episode, Mozart and his wife are traveling to Prague, where he is to conduct the first performance of *Don Giovanni*. The reader discovers their worries and wishes from their conversation and the author's comments. Arrived at a village inn by noon, Mozart leaves his wife to rest and goes for a walk. He enters the park of a manor house and discovers a pavilion by a fountain. A little orange tree inspires memory of a boyhood stay in Italy. Involuntarily, Mozart picks an orange. A gardener surprises him and threatens him as a thief. The embarrassed composer sends the gardener with a letter of apology to the owner of the manor, a count.

At the manor house, preparations are in progress for betrothal of the count's niece. The orange tree, its nine oranges representing the nine muses, has been designated as a gift to the bride. Hence Mozart's violation of the tree causes anger. The count's wife, who knows of the composer, calms the count, explaining that Mozart's presence will be a substitute for the gift, since Eugenia, the bride, is a singer and ardent admirer of Mozart. The count requests Mozart and his wife to join the celebration.

During the festive meal, the bride is given presents. In restitution for the missing orange, Mozart presents her with the wedding duet from *Don Giovanni,* inspired by the orange tree, and confides his feelings about its inspiration. Eugenia is also given the tree, and a poem explaining its significance. It is both an allegory of the cultural European tradition and a mythological tree of life from the garden of Eden. The tree is an heirloom, brought by the bride's great-great aunt to Austria from the court of Louis XIV, the Sun King of France. Mozart's song fittingly substitutes for the ninth-broken-off orange. Thus, on the allegorical level, the composer integrates himself into educated, aristocratic society. Initially his appearance seemed to disrupt cultural, mythological and family traditions. Through his gift he adds to the value of all three. Small wonder that the assembled guests idolize him and create, during the festivities, a canon of praise for him in spontaneous song and dance.

In late afternoon the men and women separate, and Mozart's wife Constance entertains the ladies with incidents from his life. She relates how Mozart once assisted another bride, a peasant girl, by buying garden tools and household goods from her. Constance gives Eugenia a saltbox, one of the household objects whose story she told.

After this interlude, the tale's fifth episode returns to a more serious tone. After nightfall, Mozart is asked to play from his *Don Giovanni.* Playing it for the first time, he adds the recently finished finale, which describes the death and punishment of Don Juan. As he did earlier for the wedding song, the composer tells his audience the occasion for its inspiration, discovery of the completed libretto. He confides at this time his own fears of death.

Next morning, the Mozarts leave in a coach which the count has presented to them. The tale ends when Eugenia, with a premonition of Mozart's early death, locks the piano he played. She believes her premonitions confirmed by the words of a folk song she comes on by chance.

The Symbolism of Quest and Paradise

On the symbolical level, Mozart's journey to Prague is a quest whose expressed aim is the composition and performance of *Don Giovanni*. It is a quest in several stages, three of which result in artistic creation. In our analysis we are using the term symbolical in Rank's meaning, that is to say, one member of the symbolic equation is unconscious to author, protagonist and reader.[9] By explicating the symbolic structure of the tale, we gain insight into Mörike's conscious and unconscious knowledge of the creative process and his intuitive awareness of primary and secondary processes. In the structure of the tale, realistic details, narrator's comment, symbol and allegory supplement each other. Though we will be dealing primarily with the symbolic level, we cannot exclude other levels.

Mozart travels to Prague to work on *Don Giovanni* and to see it performed. Describing the effect of the opera, Mörike compares it to two other tragedies of similar stature, *Oedipus* and *Macbeth* (371). By doing this, he draws attention to the theme they share, the killing of a father authority figure by a protagonist son. All three deal with variations on the oedipal problem. By choosing Mozart's journey made when composing this opera, Mörike portrays the artist's quest as an attempt to resolve his conflict with various forms of paternal authority.[10]

The quest takes place in a world which Mörike sees as maternal. The paradise which Mozart encounters on his journey rests in maternal surroundings. The women who populate the paradise are mother and sister figures in various disguises. The males who own and guard the paradise represent paternal and fraternal authority. The artist's life journey involves both mother and father; his creative process in turn involves the self-forgetting in the maternal ground and identification with paternal authority, discipline and form. In following the quest which Mörike attributes to Mozart, we move between the maternal and paternal worlds in various patterns of interchange.

The First Creative Episode

The symbolism of the first creative episode and first stage of the journey is the oral stage of development. The garden where Mozart discovers the orange tree with its "golden apples" contains a circle of orange trees, laurels, and oleanders surrounding a fountain's large, oval basin, with an arbor opening on it. Mozart jokingly refers to the garden as "Paradise"...where, "like Adam," I have "eaten the apple" (338). The ironic reference only thinly disguises the truth, for the place where his inspiration occurs is, on the symbolical level, a maternal paradise, protected and protecting, round and sensual.[11] The fountain's gentle murmur invokes a boyhood recollection which shares with the present scene the emphasis on roundness, gentleness, and the sound of water. He recalls sitting by the "shimmering curve of the lovely coast" (346) of the gulf of Naples. All his senses participate as he touches the orange's "glorious roundness and juicy fullness" (336). He smells "delicious perfume" (337) and when he picks it and cuts it in half he moves the halves back and forth, closing and opening them while gazing at the "soft yellow mass" (337).

On the unconscious level the scene unites elements of infantile enjoyment at the mother's breast with elements of an erotic union. The composer regresses to a polymorphous perverse state. The oceanic bliss of this stage finds joyous outpouring in song. The memory of Neopolitan youths and maidens singing as they play a game with orange balls is a screen memory for the earlier experience. The recollection provides the melody, the reminiscences of Sicilian dances and ballads furnish the lyrics of the duet which he hears in his mind. The earlier, primal memory of union with the mother provides the first driving impulse of musical inspiration. Mozart himself says it is "a tune which seemed to flow into the words" (350).

Mozart as the intruding male, is totally unconscious of his actions and motives. He wanders aimlessly into the garden, finds the orangery by chance, caresses the orange absent-mindedly and breaks it off inadvertently. Lost in revery, he cuts open the orange. He hears the music which will become the wedding song, and his inner eye gazes at a scene twenty years in the past. He is open to all sensory impressions (all six are mentioned specifically) and he is awake to internal mental and emotional processes.[12] Boundaries between inner and outer experience, present and past, cease to exist. How distant he is from ordinary reality appears from the comment of the gardener who considers him "not quite right in the head" (339).

The description of the unity of inner and outer event supports Freud's later notions of a primary ego-feeling, a limitless narcissism enjoyed by the infant at his mother's breast and recalled in artistic or mystic trance.[13] This reactivation of narcissistic libido, to use Marcuse's formulation, occurs at the beginning of the creative process and provides its energy. Mörike is describing in this incident a creator whose "productivity...is sensuousness, play and song," who experiences existence as "gratification, which unites man and nature," who is dominated by the pleasure principle.[14] Creativity, here, has an erotic component and is not the result of sublimation of sexual interests.[15]

Mörike's novella, with its description of paradisiac happiness, runs against the mainstream of German post-Romantic letters which is inclined to praise the performance principle. Mörike differs from the Romantics who extolled narcissism because his paradise, an actual garden, has an unromantic concreteness, sensuousness, and realism. He achieves richness of sensual gratification for the reader by telling incidents twice, each time from different perspectives. In the above analysis I have blended outer with inner events as they are experienced by Mozart. The first-time reader of the story, however, first observes Mozart in an environment where nothing distracts from the reality of the senses. A few pages later the reader re-lives the events in the garden in the composer's narrative, from his inner perspective and memories. Memory and garden scene share so many sensuous features that all sensations seem doubled.

Given over to pleasure as he is, Mozart when awakened by the gardener from his revery reacts as if caught in a shameful act. "... visibly blushing" he wants to hide the orange but puts it down in full sight "with a...defiant flourish" (337). The gardener appears to him a "monster" (338) whom he calls Nemesis, cruel as the Emperor Tiberius. The terror caused by the gardener's appearance seems to Mozart out of keeping, "I cannot remember, in all my life, anyone terrifying me out of my wits by simply being there" (351). He comically imagines further terrors at being caught: "If the man looks like that...what will the master look like?" (351) The count, by this description, is established as an authority, a father figure, and the gardener who invoked such fright is never again mentioned. The oedipal core of the scene, that paradise means union with the mother, is confirmed by the gardener's appearance and the protagonist's reaction. Sensuous pleasure and the rape of the tree are transgressions against the father's authority and property. The fear aroused is fear of castration, hence the reference to the sword of Nemesis.

In the story we find confirmation of Marcuse's arguments concerning interdependence of the pleasure and reality principles, of an all-inclusive narcissism and scarcity, of repression and sublimation in Western European civilization. Mozart in this scene transforms erotic, sensuous libido into the language of symbolism, into music. He does so playfully; his sensuousness flows into the melody. The origin of his art is in a non-repressed state. But when in that state, he does violence to reality, the orange tree, because he lives in a world of scarcity. In this world, the 18th-century Austrian household, the orange tree was exotic, its fruit an expensive delicacy. The world of scarcity is patriarchal. The tree belongs to the count, as does the manor house, garden, and family. The allegorical-spiritual level also stresses the scarcity theme: the tree's nine oranges represent the nine muses; each is irreplaceable. Mozart's taking one ruins the bride's present and destroys the allegorical meaning, hence the count's angry outburst. Because the offense exists on the spiritual level of meaning, a fitting restitution, Mozart's gift of Zerlina's song, is possible.

While inspiration for the song comes during the narcissistic experience, writing down the music, the use of the inspiration, is an act of symbolic substitution and restitution. The work of art owes its existence outside the composer's mind to his wish for pardon for transgressing against the father's world. It expresses his need for acceptance in the father's world. "Per dio," Mozart reflects, that is the "way out of my plight! I shall sit down, write the song as best I can, give a truthful account of the idiotic mishap, and it will all be a splendid frolic. I had plenty of time and managed to discover a clean sheet of green-lined paper! And here is the result" (351). Although the song is given to the bride, the composer clearly feels she is an intercessor to the father's world: "I was actually counting on the help of the ladies" (351).

Restitution follows a different law than inspiration, which occurs under the sway of primary process. Putting inspiration on paper involves "all the rules of his art," that is, secondary process. Inspiration binds the composer to the sensuous forms of the maternal

sphere: he integrates himself into the paternal sphere by using a mental process which his culture holds to be paternal. Mörike gives considerable space in this novella to the paternal processes, presenting
Mozart as a disciplined, knowledgeable craftsman, who composes and
performs to make a living. His attitude to composition is methodical.
He follows a regular work schedule: "Part of his night was always
devoted to composition. In the morning, often in bed, some hours
were spent finishing the work of the night" (328-329). Writing a
larger work, he composes individual pieces in chronological order.
"...it is not a habit of mine to compose out of order, no matter how
enticing it may be; that is a bad habit that can lead to very unhappy
results" (373).

This particular work of art owes its existence to the continuum of
experience which begins with the oceanic feeling, regression to the
oral stage of development, and ends with an act of restitution. The
work of art which originates in the oral stage bears the marks of its
origin: folk song-like simplicity, repetitiveness, and the infantile "tra
la la" of the refrain. It is an idyllic country air, joyous and sensuous.
As the composer says, "the smiling beauty of the Bay of Naples"
joined in the song (350).

The Second Stage: The Social Function of Art

The success of restitution depends on the culprit's finding a recep-
tive audience. The charm of the Mörike tale is that all participants
in the festivities accept and enjoy the gift. All understand its allegorical significance, and the bride intuits its symbolical meaning. Mozart
not only makes good his offense, but improves on nature by substitut-
ing song for the orange. The count and Eugenia's foster brother Max
at once incorporate the song into their own gifts. Max re-shapes his
poem (354) to the ceremonial presentation of the tree, which is
greeted by the assembly with increased delight. Because the male
audience use and enjoy Mozart's gift, they share in his creativeness.
Beginning with the count, Max and Mozart, and joined by only one
woman, an elderly aunt with a "cracked soprano" (358), they spontaneously compose a humorous canon in praise of the artist and his
work. During this scene, rich in sensuous-erotic stimulation, the
father figure is no threat to the frolic, but a participant. Because
there is no need for restitution, the spontaneous impromptu remains

unrecorded. Mörike notes: "Afterward Mozart promised that when he had time he would write down the whole impromptu according to all the rules of his art" (358). He later sent it to them from Vienna. During the celebration, Mozart comes to appear an Apollo, an immortal, to his co-revellers, and becomes ever more expansive and exuberant.

On the allegorical level, the manor house group represents the best European aristocratic culture. It is an elite which derives its ideas, forms and conventions via Renaissance and French classicism, from Greco-Roman sources. The daily life and the festivals of this society are carefully planned and ordered. The betrothal being celebrated assures the future of the society. The entire tradition is represented by the orange tree. Mozart is not a member of this society but a non-noble, non-propertied interloper who breaks up the order. His rape of the orange tree destroys part of the tradition. Mörike sees the French Revolution similarly, as destructive of the splendor of court life. Yet, through his talent, Mozart, the bourgeois artist, restores meaning to tradition and renews it by new creation. The Austrian nobles Mörike portrays also have basically bourgeois virtues with "sound principles and beliefs" (353) and do not share the French court's lack of "moral seriousness" (352). Mörike sees them as preserving the best of the courtly cultural tradition. Mozart integrates himself into this society by his effort to make restitution through his art.

On the symbolic level, Mozart creates a social paradise in the manor. To quote Marcuse again: "Libido can take the road of self-sublimation only as a social phenomenon: as an unrepressed force, it can promote the formation of a culture only under conditions which relate associated individuals to each other in the cultivation of the environment for the developing needs and faculties."[16] During the festivities we seem to see a non-repressive society emerge, the composer playing the role of catalyst. His ability to transform libidinal and social energy into symbol, is contagious. Breaking into song, he brings the men to participate in his creativeness. The count, father figure and symbol of order, discovers to his own surprise that he can rhyme and sing "inspired only by himself" (357). In this episode, father (count) and son (artist) identify with each other, work and play together, strengthen their bonds with each other and thus advance culture. Their earlier animosity is transcended in their new society.

The exuberance, expansiveness, emphasis on masculinity and male identification of the second episode place it in the phallic stage of development. The work of art originating in this stage is the spontaneous, occasional piece, a *divertimento*. For effect, it depends on "time and place,...general gaiety,...brilliance" (357). It belongs to the art of living, rather than to the realm of art, "But such things can hardly be reported in a story" (357).

The Third Stage: Reemergence and Resolution of the Don Juan Theme

Narrating the third creative experience, Mozart's playing the opera's piano score, Mörike directly confronts the father-son theme, earlier touched in a playful, even comic manner.[17] The first creative episode concerned the oral stage; the second moved forward to the phallic stage; the third, with expressed parallelism to *Oedipus Rex,* deals in all earnestness with the oedipal phase. How serious this is to narrator and composer alike appears from their delaying tactics in order not to arrive at Don Juan's rebellion. Between the second and third creative episodes, Mörike inserts the interlude of Mozart's patriarchal fantasies, reported by his wife. Mozart delays by playing those excerpts unconcerned with the Don's rebellion. He ends the first part of his performance with the "ravishing beauty of the sextette" (372), the sinner's death and the triumph of the survivors. A comment that "parts of the [supposedly incomplete] finale would involve immense labor" (372) brings Mozart to drop his evasive, protective attitude.

In the second part of the entertainment, Mozart/Mörike evoke, in equally strong poetry and music, the don's graveyard encounter with the murdered father. (We note in passing that Don Juan murdered the commander in his garden, and that father figure and garden hence appear in association.) When the ghost demands atonement, the rebel refuses, "defying eternal laws in his monstrous self-will" (374). At this point in the narrative, when rebellion comes into the open, author and composer break through the literary and social conventions. Mörike's digressions and play in the preceding scenes have ill-prepared the reader for the violence and passion which now erupt. Similarly, the composer, by the symbolic gesture of extinguishing the candles, casts his drawing room audience into darkness and confusion.

Unprepared, their defenses weakened, audience and reader are forced into identification with the rebel. Mörike expends some of his most moving sentences on the greatness of this rebellion. The force offended by the don has a voice whose "notes fall down through the blue night from silver trumpets, icy cold, piercing heart and soul." The dialogue between ghost and rebel carries "the soberest mind to the very frontiers of the human imagination...where we...feel...helplessly...tossed from one extreme to the other" (374). At the don's rebellion, audience and reader experience "mingled delight and terror" *(Lust und Angst)* "as...when watching the glorious spectacle of an ungovernable force of nature.... Against our will we range ourselves on the side of this blind greatness, and, with clenched teeth, share its agony in the headlong course of its self-destruction" (375). For the Aristotelian "pity and fear" *(Mitleid und Furcht)* expected in a discussion of tragedy, Mörike substitutes unexpected, and hence startling "delight and terror." He thus emphasizes that this is no intellectual, sublimated, pitying sympathy with the rebel but rather passionate, lustful identification. It is not chance that Mörike substitutes *Angst* for *Furcht*. *Furcht* refers to fear of something definite and known. *Angst* is a generalized, all pervasive fear whose source remains unconscious.

Identified with the protagonist, composer, narrator, and audience share his death struggle. As he is killed, each experiences the rebel's death as the death of his own rebellious self, as a symbolic self-sacrifice and restitution offered to the father.[18] Completion of the death scene means that the composer has attained maturity: now he can contemplate his own future death and be at peace (375).

By the symbolic sacrifice, a new relationship to the father and his order becomes possible. Mörike portrays this new relationship in two ways: 1) Thinking back to the first creative episode, the reader understands in retrospect why the composer could so easily resolve his conflict with the gardener authority-figure, which at first caused such inordinate fear. We now realize that Mozart had, three weeks earlier, exorcized his rebellious self in composing Don Juan's death. Consequently he afterward can find socially acceptable ways in his life and art to resolve the authority conflicts he or any man is heir to, ways which benefit himself and improve his society. The finale of the music points back to and deepens the meaning of the creativity theme at the beginning of the tale. 2) Mörike strengthens the reconciliation between father and son in a further symbolic episode. Don Juan's rebellion is unproductive; the artist's is productive in a double sense. His portrayal of rebellion heals himself and his audience. It also wins the respect and admiration of the father. Mörike expresses this paternal respect by the count/father's parting gift. A closer look at the symbolism of the coach will conclude discussion of the reconciliation.

At the beginning of the tale we are given a detailed description of Mozart's coach, which stands, in the language of the unconscious, for the mother's womb. Mozart's coach, lent him by a patroness, is ornate and contrasts sharply with the open country and Mozart's relaxed appearance. The coach given him on departure from the manor symbolizes his changed estate. The vehicle is simpler, emphasis is given to its comfort. In praise of it, Mozart repeatedly exclaims, "This carriage is to be mine!" (377) At the journey's beginning, Mozart is a dependent without means of his own, under the protection of a mother figure. At the end, the father figure gives him means to continue the journey. The artist is now free; he has earned independence by his unique skills. He has made his contribution to the society he now leaves behind to continue his own quest. Through this gift, the father gives his blessing, contributes to furtherance of the quest, and in fact wants to be included in it. Note the almost religious language the count uses in presenting the coach: "do me the pleasure of keeping it in memory of me" (377).

The composer's mature achievement, the work of art of the oedipal phase proper, is deeply serious, passionate, and tragic in its outcome. It is classical in the sense that it deals weightily with serious subject matter. In Mörike's view, Mozart acquired by this work the characteristic lightness and social grace which he demonstrated earlier in the story. Mörike seems to say that only by making this symbolic self-sacrifice can an artist, through his art, contribute to his culture.

From this vantage point, let us reconsider Marcuse's theory of the function of art in society. He maintains that "Reactivation of polymorphous and narcissistic sexuality ceases to be a threat to culture and it can itself lead to culture-building if the organism exists...as a subject of self-realization." Further: "The culture-building power of Eros *is* non-repressive sublimation; sexuality is neither deflected from nor blocked in its objective; rather, in attaining its objective, it transcends it to others, searching for fuller gratification."[19] Mörike would agree, with the following emendations: Reactivation of polymorphous and narcissistic sexuality, like reactivation of oedipal anger, is no threat to culture but is necessary to enrich culture, provided it is expressed by a creator who has learned to transform it into symbol and use its product for social purposes. Unlike Marcuse, Mörike the 19th-century *Bürger* stresses that libidinal energies must be transformed for use in culture-building. Mörike would agree with Marcuse that such transformation and sublimation must be freely chosen, cannot be enforced by fathers or authorities. Mörike is, in this respect, the anti-paternalistic heir of the French Revolution. Art has the function of making self-realization possible in a community.[20]

At the end of the story, Mozart's quest continues, for the opera is not complete. This seems to mean that self-realization of man and artist in society is a continuous process. On the formal level, Mörike indicates continuity by the relationship between the first and third creative episodes. Only after the reader has appreciated the third, can he fully understand the first. Since the artist's quest is a circular process, artistic paradise is neither a land in the past nor a goal in the future, but an ever-present possibility which everyone, but the artist most easily, can attain. As we have seen in the second episode, the artist can show others how to realize themselves, how to create in their own lives the heightened paradisiac estate. This is his gift and his mission.

Woman as Source and Destroyer of Life

All would be well if the story ended with reconciliation and the gift of the coach. But Mörike ends with Eugenia's premonition, her locking the piano and her discovery of the oracle folk song. This makes us ask: 1) what is the role of Eugenia in the story? 2) How are we to interpret her actions? 3) What is the artist's relationship to woman?

The tale takes place in a paternal society. Women form the background against which the men act. Eugenia, whose name means the well-born, on her betrothal day, represents the feminine continuation of aristocratic culture, incorporating in herself all women of the society: bride and mother, sister and wife. At the same time, she is the composer's muse. She inspires him and she understands his moods and his music better than anyone else, even his wife. Mozart looks to her for applause (346). It is she who receives a song from him, she who sings it with him. During the performance of Don Juan's love adventures, she is so absorbed that "she could hardly give a coherent reply when her betrothed spoke to her" (372). She seems more intimate with the composer than with her fiancé, and Mozart's interest in her surpasses the tribute due a bride on her day of honor. A strong erotic undercurrent enlivens and intensifies the allegory of the artist and his muse.

The bond between them draws the reader's attention to the fact that Eugenia, as his muse, personifies the ever-youthful feminine matrix, the maternal ground from which the composer's inspiration derives. Though she participates less than the other women, she is, as bride and muse, the center of the day and the center of life. Hence the importance of her premonition, and her act in locking the piano Mozart played.

Eugenia sees deeper than the other revellers, and divines the danger to Mozart's existence. "She was so sure, so utterly sure, that this man would burn himself up in his own flame...that he could be but a transient visitor on earth because it could not, in reality, support the riches he poured forth on it" (378). None of the others, to whom she tells her feeling, share her pessimism. Are her premonitions due to special sensitivity, and is her action merely pious preservation of Mozart's memory? Or do her thoughts and acts betray rejection of him, his art, and his quest? We have seen that the artist needs the feminine matrix, but must transcend it and leave it behind. The woman cannot hold him. Since she cannot, would she prefer him dead? Until the end of the story, Mörike has praised the social function of art. Does Eugenia negate it even if she intends her gesture to be pious? Her finding the folk song may be chance; what she makes of it is not: she sees it as confirming her premonition. Her tears for Mozart's early death are tears for her own present loss. Is Eugenia the "earth" which could not support him? (378).[21]

The creator, through his art, enriches his society. Beginning as narcissistic enjoyment in a maternal environment, his art leads him to rebellion and restitution. By giving pleasure to his fellows, he earns the father's blessing and acceptance. Together with the father, he builds a culture. In so doing, he collides with another life-threatening force, the jealous female who will not share with anyone the gifts he so freely bestows. Hence he must die.

The Role of "Mozart on the Way to Prague"
in Mörike's Life

Except for a few poems, Mörike stopped writing after finishing his
Mozart tale.[22] He planned but never began another tale on the darker
side of Mozart's genius. The pouring forth of the inspiration of even
the lighter side had brought him into too-close contact with a deadly
muse. Rather than expose himself to this danger, he ceased writing.
A brief look at his early relationships, which led to such unhappy,
unconscious convictions may clarify the discussion of the novella.

Mörike grew up in a family constellation closely resembling
Goethe's, typical of the 19th-century German middle class. His
father was a physician, stern, self-disciplined, dedicated to life's serious business, who had little time for his children. In an autobiographical account, Mörike mentions his father's neglect with resentment
and regret.[23] Nevertheless, the father provided a good example of
male strength and achievement. The mother was a happier person,
devoted to her children. It was she who instructed them in manners
and morals and introduced them to culture by telling stories and sharing her interest in art. The third living child of seven, six years
younger than his elder, and closely followed by five more siblings,
Mörike was lonely and sensitive. He liked to hide in the attic and
write poetry. When he was eleven his father had a stroke. During the
following three years, the boy watched his father die. Impatient with
paralysis, the father still wanted to help others. Increasingly he
failed to do so. The family attributed the stroke to overwork and
emotional stress on the death of his mother, which occurred just
before his illness.

After his father's death, Mörike had an undistinguished career at
schools designed for the protestant clergy, the cheapest education
available to an orphan. Though he was often ill, and found study
difficult, he, unlike his brothers, completed his education. After much
hesitation over his suitability as a clergyman, and unsuccessful bids
for love and marriage during his university studies and early vicar-
ships, he settled down with his mother, sister and ever visiting brothers to an indolent, semi-invalid bachelor existence in a country parsonage. Mörike's illnesses followed a definite pattern. Whenever
family pressures rose to an unbearable pitch, and his detested parish
chores   became   unbearable,   he   developed   either   abdominal

inflammations, rheumatism, nerve weakness, laryngitis, etc.[24] Occasionally, he had hallucinations. For instance, a few weeks after Mörike and his family moved into Cleversulzbach parsonage, a ghost appeared! A month later, Mörike developed an "abdominal inflammation" (bladder infection?), which persisted through November and December. In the early part of the following year, Mörike was trying, despite family disapproval, to help his brother Karl get a job, and barely managing to fulfill his pastoral duties. By July, he had taken to his bed with "general weakness of nerves" and on September 3 he suffered a "spinal hemorrhage." He could not do his parish work and had to ask for the help of a curate. Mörike's money problems and illness led his friend Hartlaub to suggest in January 1836 that his friends take up a collection for him. By March, Mörike was able to leave his bed, six weeks later he was spending time in his garden. During May to September, he took curative baths, and in September he requested time off to recover, which was granted for September/October. During this time, Mörike incurred new debts to help of his brother Adolf. In January, the ghost once more appeared to him, and by February his doctor was experimenting with galvanizing treatments. In April he was worse, and so the pattern repeated. He was the only one of five brothers with a steady income and lent himself to their exploitation. His years of hope (1822-1834) were rich in poetry, which ceased almost entirely during his parsonage imprisonment (1834-1843). After his mother died, he retired at thirty-seven, escaping on the excuse of ill health. Over the next ten years, he gradually made a new life, gaining a wife, a new profession, and a second lease on creation (1846-1854), of which the Mozart novella is the last product.

In Mörike's life we find a suspension between paternal and maternal poles similar to that observed in the Mozart novella. Estranged from the awe-inspiring father, over-attached to the loving mother, the adolescent must have felt the father's illness as a punishment for which he, the son, was to blame. It was unfortunate for young Mörike that his father fell ill just when his oedipal feelings for his mother and rebellion against his father were reawakened at puberty. The adolescent could not resolve the oedipal conflict with a male parent heart-rendingly ill and helpless; it had to be repressed. Moreover, he appears to have assumed responsibility for his siblings even then. After his father's death he suffered from ill health and even from occasional attacks of paralysis similar to his father's. His invalidism was atonement for oedipal guilt feelings and protection against the father's role he was thrown into. Moreover, because of the family explanation for the father's illness, Mörike must have come to associate hard work, achievement, and emotional exertion with death. His invalid state was therefore partly a protection against death.

But Mörike had a positive father identification as well as the negative one. As poet and artist, he could see himself as the spiritual heir of his father, hardworking healer of his fellows. Mörike's theory of art includes a therapeutic function as well as the socializing, harmonizing effect found in the novella. Art heals by establishing psychic equilibrium.[25] Assumption of this health-giving role, however, would have threatened Mörike with death from exhaustion.

His image of his mother seems to have been as split as that of the father. She was life giver and protectress, but her love (and the family burden it brought along) could stifle him. She might draw him into her death, as his grandmother did his father. While living with mother, sister, and those brothers presently in financial or legal difficulties in the parsonage, fulfilling the roles of provider for his family (father) and of child, he found his role increasingly difficult and withdrew more and more into illness. At this point, the invalidism must also have had the function of atonement, protecting him against his oedipal feelings, and keeping him in pre-oedipal dependency. His contemporaries repeatedly commented on Mörike's childlike appearance and behavior. But dependency and invalidism stifled creativity. When his mother died, his ill-health increased at first, probably in self-punishment. But her death freed him from the fear that, like his father, he might die at her death; it also freed him from bondage to his siblings and from his hated profession. (This hate was never expressed, except that he, the man of letters, found it impossible to compose sermons.) For a while, he must have felt sufficiently free to dare a new life, new involvement, new creation. With the completion of the Mozart novella, the old pattern must have reasserted itself. It is characteristic that the menage Mörike set up with his wife after a few years alone included his sister; within four years two daughters were born, so that one or possibly both women took over the mother's role. In any case, indolence and hypochondria returned; illness and women held creation and death at bay. He never outgrew the feeling that his art was a form of atonement. It was the happier, more spiritual, finally the all-too dangerous counterpart of his invalidism.

Summary

Mörike describes the artist's life as a symbolic journey and observes three distinct creative occasions, each reflecting a different developmental stage: oral, phallic, and oedipal. Each stage inspires a different form of art, with a distinct subject and style. For the artist, the creative process involves regression, openness to the primary process modes of experience of these stages. But oceanic bliss, transgression against paternal limits, exuberance over godlike powers, and indulgence in rebellion cause anxiety and a wish to atone. The actual production of a work of art is, therefore, a restitution for the broken law of the father. On one level (as Greenacre believes) the work of art is, for Mörike, the artist's love-gift to the world. On another level, the artist's gift is Melanie Klein's gesture of restitution.

The artist resolves his personal oedipal strivings through his production. By communicating these strivings, he brings his audience to share them, vicariously enjoy them, and then reject them. Through his achievement, he wins the love and respect of the paternal and fraternal world. Together with this audience, he builds a culture.

Mörike's artist succeeds in transcending the father figure, but fails to transcend the mother. His maternal muse claims him and his achievement for herself, thus defeating and killing him. Mörike, with Novalis and Hoffmann, believes in a deadly muse. Novalis's muse, however, opened a transcendent world in which the poet could experience rebirth. Mörike does not share the optimism which led Novalis to believe he could survive death and realize himself in a spiritual existence transcending the mother figure. The embrace of Mörike's muse meant annihilation. Had he had the conviction that the feminine could not harm him, his inspiration might not have failed, and he might have explored other themes. Unfortunately, he remained in the grip of the unconscious conviction that creation meant death. He did not manage to free himself through writing the Mozart tale, but lived on for another twenty years, indolent, silenced.

V

ADALBERT STIFTER'S *PROGENY*:
MANAGEMENT OF DISINTEGRATION FEAR

When suffering from the depression that led to his retirement and suicide three years later in 1868, Stifter wrote his publisher Heckenast a description of how he treated what the doctors called "lingering typhoid" and he himself: "anxiety, restlessness, a terrible aversion to noise, or to being told anything unpleasant, finally an oversensitivity of the intestine leading to revulsion from food" *(Letters,* XX, 180).[1] Writing was an important part of this self-prescribed cure, "the medicine which all medical men banned but whose refreshing effect I knew well." Though family, friends, and physicians claimed that the strain of writing caused his illness, Stifter insisted that writing cured: "I must write, else I would die" (XIX, 260). For Stifter, art's presence meant a healthy culture; its absence meant degeneration. "When a people degenerates, art leaves first" *(Gesammelte Werke,* XIV, 207). Stifter assigns to art "the highest, most important power in human life...it outranks everything as a human end in itself" (XIV, 26).[2] This crucially curative role of art, his novella *Progeny* (1864), contemporary with all this theory, seemingly contradicts. In it, two artists, a poet and a painter, end in renouncing art for practical, 19th-century bourgeois life.

A close look at the story brings out several contradictions. Some critics, like Joachim Müller, argue that Stifter is satirizing romantic, would-be artists, and that this novella demonstrates the humor of his maturity.[3] There is no doubt that the painter-narrator pokes fun at himself and other characters, and that the happy outcome, a marriage between an avowed bachelor and the daughter of his long-lost relative, is a subject for comedy. Other critics support this point of view by pointing out that Stifter in his mature work turns from artists and makes his characters seek integration in the bourgeois social world, preserving links to the art world only by restoration of medieval or Renaissance art.[4] Stifter was himself painter as well as writer, and Polheim has shown with convincing detail that the two artists are self-portraits, and their theories Stifter's own.[5] If one believes that in this work Stifter is rejecting the artistic existence, either seriously or in jest, one must accept that he is also rejecting himself and theories of art he held dear even as he wrote the story.

Would a writer so dependent on succoring values repudiate his remedy, art, for bourgeois ideals just at a time when he needed it most? Once the story had been sent to the publisher, did Stifter fall into severe depression because he had betrayed his own values?[6] Why was it so hard for him to release his work for publication? Why did he insist on constant revision?[7] Furthermore, in his case, we have an autobiographical fragment which sheds light on his early childhood development and on the psychological functions of his double talent, painter/writer.[8] We have, therefore, sufficient material, a problematic question concerning the role of art, and some intriguing psychological questions, to make *Progeny* the center of our inquiry into Stifter's creative process. A comparison between *Julius,* an earlier fragment,[9] and *Progeny* will be used to acquaint the reader with salient themes.

Since it is available only in German, let us first acquaint the English reader with the story told in *Progeny*. A young painter, Friedrich Roderer, gives an account of becoming a painter, and moving near a moor to paint it. As in other artist novellas, we are given the symbols of the explorer and the journey. Behind a surface of humorous, everyday events, there is danger and crisis. Friedrich lives in an inn run by a talkative landlady. An old man comes to the inn evenings, an estate owner and cultivator of the moorland. The young man at first makes fun of Peter's ideas of turning the moor to farmland, but afterwards he accepts the friendship of the older man and the two spend their evenings talking of Peter's work and Friedrich's painting. Friedrich, although he hides his identity as well as his paintings from everyone, allows Peter to see his sketches. Days afterward, the old man predicts that Friedrich will stop painting some day. Asked for a reason, he says that Friedrich reminds him of the men of his own family, the Roderers, who trace their history back to the Middle Ages. All have been initiators, all have been rootless, and all have achieved goals different than they intended. Peter himself when young wanted to become a poet, but after comparing his work with the great poets, renounced his ambition. When his father died shortly afterward, he began a commercial career, quickly acquiring property and family. He has only recently settled in this region, where he plans to found a permanently-settled Roderer clan.

Friedrich reacts to the prophecy by reaffirming his devotion to painting, and building his studio at the moor's edge. Once established, he makes excursions into the forest beyond, and daily encounters a young woman he knows to be Roderer's daughter, Susanna. One day when the summer is almost past, the young woman fails to appear, and Friedrich gives up his lonely rambling and joins the villagers of Lüpfing who hold a celebration on a meadow. Wishing to sketch the scene, he lies down behind a low wall. A group including Peter, his family, and some of Susanna's admirers approach, but only Susanna knows of his presence. When the young men joke about Friedrich, and when he is about to attack them in anger, Susanna secretly tells him by a calming gesture that she loves him. Friedrich returns home undiscovered and the next day when the two meet, they confess their love for each other. That evening, Friedrich asks Peter for an appointment at Castle Firnberg at which he reveals himself as a member of the Roderer clan and asks for Susanna's hand. The lovers are given permission to court and get to know each other.

During the rest of the summer Friedrich completes his painting and establishes bonds with Susanna and her family. That winter, Peter visits Friedrich's family in Vienna and confirms that the two families are related. The following spring, the two long-separated branches celebrate their reunion when Friedrich and Susanna are betrothed. After locking himself in with his painting for three days, Friedrich asks Susanna's permission to destroy it and renounce his career as a painter. She agrees, trusting that whatever profession he takes up, they will achieve something of importance together. The picture destroyed, the marriage takes place.

The Julius Fragment and Stifter's Development as an Author

Almost all *Progeny's* themes are prefigured in Stifter's first story, *Julius,* written in 1828-1832 when he was in his early twenties. He was a student in Vienna then and during summers at home in Bohemia was courting Fanni Greipl, daughter of a wealthy linen merchant. Like a first memory, a first literary work often reveals in thin disguise the author's unconscious wishes and fears.[10] Since the problems depicted in *Julius* reappear thirty-five years later in *Progeny*, we can assume that they still concerned Stifter. In both stories, the problem of the artist is intertwined with a love story. The narrator of *Julius* tells of the hero's encounter with a father and daughter twenty years after all participants have died.[11] This point of departure casts a tragic light on the story, the implication being that the encounter led to their early deaths. The Vienna university student Julius has thrown over his law studies (Stifter did the same thing in 1829), returned to the valley town where he spent his adolescence and become a painter of huge, melancholy alpine paintings. Abandoned at the age of ten, Julius has no family and is an outcast (Stifter's father died when he was twelve). Julius is a veritable Kaspar Hauser (Stifter knew his story and was familiar with the foundling theme in Jean Paul), and yearns for roots.[12] One day he rescues the daughter of the lord of the manor, a widowed, hot-tempered general, from a runaway carriage. The grateful father invites the mysterious hero to his castle. Julius feels unworthy and therefore refuses the invitation. By chance a piece of note paper reveals his identity, whereupon the father personally fetches him to the castle. The young people fall in love. Julius's courage and his graceful bearing on horseback prompt the general to prophesy that he will not remain a painter. He invites Julius to dueling practice next day. Here the narrative breaks off. From the framework we surmise that Julius' identity, his being closely related to father and daughter, and the encounter at arms were to lead to tragedy. Aggression and sexuality are irrevocably linked.

Julius reveals young Stifter's fears of love, which had been revived through his courting of Fanni Greipl. The father figure, though friendly, is potentially threatening, as was Fanni's father to Stifter. As a half-orphan of humble peasant origin, young Stifter felt himself a social outcast. He felt implicated in the death of his father, as Julius does. This sense of guilt appeared in the twelve year old Stifter's wish to starve himself as punishment for his father's death.[13] If we consider this story's themes of potential patricide and incest, and what they tell us about Stifter's oedipal fears, we are not surprised that he failed all tests on the way to winning Fanni in marriage. He omitted to take a qualifying legal examination (1829). A few years later he slept through a science examination which he needed to qualify for a teaching position. Several years afterward he partially overcame his unconscious fear of marriage and competition with a father (1837) when he married Amalia Mohrhaupt, whom he did not love and whose family did not insist on his winning a bourgeois social position. In *Julius,* notes on a painting lead to the characters' encounter and propel the action toward eventual catastrophe. Writing, therefore, rather than painting, is implicated in oedipal entanglements. The choice of writing to deal with the oedipal situation is common to all fiction dealing with artistic development. By this choice, authors imply that the creative impulse assumes narrative form in the oedipal situation.

Writing *Progeny* thirty-four years later, Stifter transmuted many of *Julius's* themes, subdued melodrama and self-pity, and toned down violence, mystery and passion.[14] The mysterious young painter Julius is still discernible in Friedrich's reluctance to reveal his identity. Father and daughter become relatives distant by several degrees and a mother is added: therefore the incest theme fades. The older man's prophecy forms the core of both stories. In both, Stifter sets a high castle to reflect the social and psychological exaltation of father and daughter (mother), and a low valley to suggest the son-painter's position. The most meaningful change is in perspective. In *Progeny,* the hero tells his own story; in *Julius,* the story is told after the hero is dead. In *Progeny,* Friedrich depicts his artistic development and love against the background of his daily life and these concerns, not passionate mystery or violent tragedy, occupy center stage. Moreover, the later work has a tone of comedy in contrast to the ominous melancholy of impending tragedy in *Julius.* A small, significant symbol from both stories may demonstrate how the oedipal dilemma has been transformed, if not resolved. In *Progeny*, the young painter no longer rescues the girl. The runaway horses (passion) from which Julius saves Maria are shown waiting patiently as Susanna goes to meet Friedrich. There is only a faint indication that the horses were once wild; early in the novella Friedrich remarks that he sees the horses abducting Susanna ("entführen," 281) with his rival. The passion is taken from the hero and projected faintly onto his rival. But it still lives in Susanna's "fiery eyes" (282) and in Friedrich's violent destruction of his painting.[15]

The rescue theme has not been jettisoned; it has been transferred from loved women to the moor. When Friedrich arrives at the Lüpfing moor, he feels an urgent need to "save" the moor by painting it before "the rich man finally destroys it" (237). At the beginning of the story he regards himself as Peter's rival. He suffers through rainy days, unhappy because he cannot go out and paint, while Peter's men "are not handicapped" (250). He is irritated because Peter bears the same name, "And who is he, even if he *is* Mr. Roderer?"(240)[16] For one man, oedipal energy has turned to the cultivation of the land, for the other, into recording a symbol. The riding and fencing of *Julius* develop into nightly discussions of land-use and aesthetic theory in *Progeny*. The struggle between the two men changes from a physical encounter to figurative wrestling over land. Friedrich wants to plumb the depths of the moor and Peter wants to fill it up. Both, as the name suggests, (Lüpfing = lift) want to "lift" the moor to their respective planes, one to agriculture, the other to an aesthetic object. As their name Roderer (*roden* = make arable) indicates, both want to make the moor useful to their differing purposes. As the concreteness of Peter's endeavor shows, the shift to the symbolic level is incomplete.

The change from physical conflict in *Julius* to a partially sublimated level in *Progeny* reflects Stifter's mature perspective. His interest has shifted from depiction of struggle and disintegration, to tracing the origin of conflict, and the development and re-integration of individuals and families. The young Stifter's direct attempt to deal with oedipal conflict in *Julius* led him to a fearful and tragic view of life. He was unable to work through it in real encounters with Father Greipl and Fanni, could not transform it into a valid symbol and hence abandoned it as a failure. Just as *Julius*, Stifter's many early literary efforts are astonishingly trite and imitative. Only following his marriage at thirty-two, and Fanni's death two years later, he began to produce tales of sufficient symbolic transformation to be acceptable to the public.[17] He stopped the venting of oedipal passion and began to explore its origins in more archaic layers of the psyche and its possible transformation. This subject matter represented a way out of tragedy into idyll. The father-daughter-young man theme remained dominant in much of his work, but by assuming a developmental, psychological attitude and toning down conflict, Stifter was able to re-shape the theme of intruder-in-the-house-of-the-father and find a way to deal with his situation in which all can survive.[18] As author, Stifter transformed himself from a potential dramatist into a psychologist.

As he advanced in age, Stifter's interest in process grew. While writing *Progeny,* he was working on a long historical novel, *Witiko* (1858-1867), which treated the development of a culture hero and a culture in the Bohemian Forest. In *Progeny* the Roderers are cultivators of new land and therefore also initiators and culture heroes, though in humbler scope. What does concern Stifter at greater depth in *Progeny* than in *Witiko* is the individual development of the hero, who is for him the artist. The shorter work, with its more autobiographical account, its contemporary framework and its symbol, the moor, has a psychological aspect absent from *Witiko.* To better understand this perspective, let us look at Friedrich's development as painter and writer and the moor as symbol.

The Meaning of the Moor and the Development of the Painter and Writer

Friedrich views painting the moor as a test. He equates the moor with a mountain, the Dachstein, he had earlier attempted to paint. On coming to the moor, he is a stranger and alone. At the Dachstein he had plenty of company. Stifter opposes psychic spaces of height against psychic spaces of depth (256). He contrasts the drama of the icy mountain reflected in the Gosau Lake with the simple, even primitive moor landscape joined by a unicolored fir forest and backed by a meadow and blue, distant mountains. In one sense, Friedrich's coming to the moor is progression, for he has gone past the alpine subjects on which Julius foundered. In another sense, coming to the moor is regression to a simpler subject lying in the depths of time. In a seemingly unmotivated aside, Friedrich says, "I have been here earlier." His sense of the antiquity of the moor is reflected in his remark that the landlady's family has lived there "since the Flood" (237).[19]

Friedrich's feeling of *déjà vu* and hostility toward Peter indicate that to him the moor represents the maternal element. It seems to be an early form of a specific mother. Monotonous, solitary, with few variations in form or color, the moor represents the psychic space of earliest childhood, of the dyad mother and infant. She is no joyous mother, but is melancholy and threatening, the source of a deadly fever (236). Peter Roderer protects his workmen by relieving them often, and by providing fresh well water (243). Initially, having escaped the fever earlier, Friedrich feels safe and does not protect himself (236). On his first actual excursion into the moor, on an exceptionally hot day (243) he cannot find water and has to ask Peter's men for some. Later he is more careful. Water and fever symbolism point to passion as the moor's danger. Peter sees the danger as social; that is why he wants to drain it. Thanks to his efforts, the fever has greatly decreased. Friedrich avoids another danger by staying on dry ground when on the moor. For entire days, the workmen throw load after load of earth and stones into "soft ground which swallowed them" (245), illustrating the moor's capacity for engulfment. To the down-to-earth landlady, the moor's danger is psychic. Intuitively she fears that Friedrich's autistic existence and the loneliness of his studio-camp will make him "sick to his soul" (277). The actions of the characters, and the descriptions of nature, bear a consistent symbolic message which gives Stifter's mature tales their typical evocativeness.

The reality of a threat may be measured by the number of people who come to the aid of the person endangered. Friedrich meets some of these helpers during his evenings at the Lüpfing inn, itself an Eden complete with apple tree. The landlady, as the good oral mother, provides meat and drink for father and son. Her cheerfulness, ignorant chatter, and concern with the well-being of the men is contrasted with the other face of the early mother — the devouring, gloomy moor. As provider of the inn's supplies, Peter is once again identified as the father figure, who has older claims on the landlady than Friedrich. In keeping with the symbolism, Peter's wife and the landlady's husband remain shadowy, but the relationship between Peter, Friedrich and the landlady dominates the beginning of the story. As lodger at the inn, Friedrich is dependent on the landlady. Their bond, though newer than the landlady's with Peter, is closer. She worries over Friedrich, is curious about him, wants to show him off to the villagers, hopes he will sell his sketches, and makes plans for his future. Being an image of the early, elemental mother, she cannot understand his aspirations or his spiritual quest. She sees only his dangers. Stifter uses her misunderstanding of Friedrich as a rich source of fun, but the comedy should not deceive us about her importance. She is the stable ground from which he forays onto the moor. To the safety of her inn he brings his sketches and transposes them on canvas. The base coat of his painting is done under the landlady's roof (250). Even when he builds a studio to have more space, he stays close to the inn, and retains the landlady's care instead of hiring a servant.

Peter Roderer complements the help of the landlady. In the beginning, he is the initiator of the relationship. He comes to the inn every day, even through rain and fog. At the first meeting, it is he who salutes Friedrich, absorbed in contemplation of "his" moor (238). Even at the first meeting Peter introduces reality to the young painter, talking about road building, coal mining, river regulation — subjects on which the young man is ignorant but willing to listen. From the first encounter, the older man serves as guide to the young one.

Following initial mistrust, Friedrich begins to trust Peter, who becomes the first and only person Friedrich will admit to his studio. The old man reciprocates with careful scrutiny of the paintings, and with his prophecy. In a scene like a verbal duel, Peter challenges Friedrich. "One day, you will probably stop painting, and never again touch a brush," (254) and thus confronts Friedrich with the choice he must make to achieve adulthood. Unlike the novella's reader, Peter knows the young man's talents and aspirations. After confronting Friedrich, he assures him of his respect for his ideals and achievement, thus ensuring that his challenge will be heard and will not harm Friedrich. Friedrich's reply indicates that the thrust went home ("If you take away this activity, my life has no value," 257). Yet one purpose of the challenge has been met. With his assertion, "I will never renounce landscape painting," (257) Friedrich acquires the firmness of purpose he needs to separate himself from the engulfing aspects of the early mother — the moor. At the same time, by relating the history of Friedrich's ancestors, Peter helps Friedrich to find an identity in a common past, an identity which allows a change of goal. The independent gesture with which Friedrich responds, building his studio on the moor, symbolizes the firm ground Friedrich has gained, and the paternal support he had (unknown to him, it was built with Peter's wood). Thus by empathically mirroring to Friedrich his lack of boundaries and by giving him support for his ideals, Peter serves the double function of mirroring-approving selfobject and idealized parent imago.[20]

Friedrich portrays his existence as a painter in playful, breathlessly excited tones: "I like painting better than anything in the whole world; nothing on earth could move me more. When morning dawns I wake up looking forward to handling my lovely colors" (233). Absorbed in his paints and his subject, he is unconcerned with past or future, has neither plans, goals, nor a permanent home. The protecting inn, idyllic inn yard, nurturing landlady, supportive grandfatherly mentor, guarantee his freedom from responsibility, a life of try-out and play in the pure present. Like Mörike, Stifter gives his young hero-artist a safe space to play in, an artistic existence reminiscent of early childhood. In fact, this existence has many of the characteristics Winnicott describes as the "intermediate playground" which the mother creates for the infant, where "the baby begins to enjoy experiences based on a 'marriage' of the omnipotence of intrapsychic processes with the baby's control of the actual."[21] Friedrich's omnipotence is reflected in his wealth, his freedom from having to work and from human ties, freedom to destroy work he does not like.[22] Yet the moor does contain actual dangers (thirst, fever, sunstroke, etc.) against which he must guard. Like any child-adventurer, Friedrich can pretend to withhold his name, to keep his activities secret, to be without family, knowledge of whom, he says revealingly, "would have depressed [my] spirit and mind" (293). Peter's challenge causes Friedrich apprehension and forces his attention on a shared past, a different present, and a projected future. It is no wonder that, immediately after this challenge, Friedrich builds a separate, secure play space, the studio with windows looking onto the moor. Friedrich is projected forward, and must define himself against Peter's reality. With this in mind, the name Peter (rock) takes on new significance.

Another helper who comes to Friedrich is Susanna. Her name (Susanna = lily) indicates purity. Not by chance she and Friedrich meet daily in the forest, beyond the moor, only after Friedrich has left the landlady's roof. Like her father, she takes the initiative. She tests Friedrich's constancy. Their silent greeting gives him another fixed point in his solitary existence. As Peter's daughter, Susanna represents an aspect of the mother; from the symbolism which surrounds her, she is the oedipal mother. In the symbolic family group Friedrich encounters on Lüpfing meadow, she is the queen reigning over the family. She is distinct from the moor as oral mother. This appears to be the reason why Friedrich experiences conscious love only when he sees her farther from the moor than the forest. His speaking of his love represents the step into the oedipal phase. The story makes it clear that this is a phase of socialization. From then on, Friedrich is dressed appropriately to his station when he sees the Roderers in a higher social setting, Castle Firnberg.

The change of level does not affect Friedrich's painting. He paints the greater part of the day "with a diligence and enthusiasm" (296) he never knew before. As connoisseurs Peter and Susanna testify, he paints better than ever. Why, after long deliberation, does he insist on the destruction of the painting? Why does he fear losing Susanna if he destroys the picture? Why must he seek her permission to destroy it? And why must he cut it into small pieces and then burn it, with all his painting materials?[23] This cool violence bespeaks either a great deal of anger, or demonstrates the force needed to break the power of the oral mother. Does forcible destruction indicate that sexual maturity, social stature, and separation from the early mother can be won only at the expense of art? If we consider that Peter Roderer once made a similar decision, after which his father died, and he gained position, place, and wife [24], this seems to be the obvious message. But why can painting, a symbolical representation of the oral mother, not be continued into married adulthood? To answer these questions we must explore at greater depth the emotional meaning of his art to Friedrich. What does he want from painting?

Friedrich's goal is to capture "the real reality" ("die wirkliche Wirklichkeit," 271) a goal that has caused a flurry of critical discussion.[25] The way he literally settles down before his subject until he has achieved this goal strikes us as ridiculous, but there is nevertheless an underlying seriousness in the situation, since because of this

single-minded devotion he wins Susanna. Friedrich's persistence tells
us that through painting he wants to experience an emotional state.
By the systematic study he makes of the moor, exploring it, living
with it, painting it through all times of the day and the seasons (243),
he shows that he prefers participation in a natural process to the
finished product. The very phrase "real reality" demonstrates that he
wants to produce an absolute likeness. In human experience, the
state of absolute identity is achieved only by the infant merged with
the mother. Everything Friedrich says shows that he seeks a merger
with the processes of nature. He is so immersed that he doesn't know
when to stop, and continues to work on a picture "until I ruin it"
(235). The activity itself is the meaning of his life. Because the process is so vital to him, he will not part with his paintings and spends
incredibly long hours at work.[26]

Another distinctive characteristic is his unwillingness to let others
even see his work. The secretiveness is not related to concern about
quality, or fear that the work may reveal more than he wants it to. In
his first refusal to let Susanna and her friends watch him sketch, he
seems to be rationalizing when he describes his pictures as "strokes
and hooks which make sense only to the person who develops them"
(248). But there is emotional truth to this statement. If he wants to
give through his picture the experience of fusion with subject matter
which he experiences in the painting process, then line and color are
indeed nothing but meaningless strokes and hooks. If his audience
participated in the process, he might communicate this experience.
Yet he is intolerant of onlookers, and finds it "repugnant" when the
landlady's invitation to the villagers brings so many people to the inn
that he must lock himself away. House companions and friends are
allowed to watch him paint (252). The reason behind this discrimination seems to be that familiars, being part of him, do not interrupt
the process, but strangers do. Only an intimate can participate in
Friedrich's painting, life process, and emotional experience.

Analysis of one final incident — the encounter on the meadow —
may summarize our discussion of the meaning and goal of painting to
him. When he is surprised by Peter and his group, Friedrich is lying
on his stomach behind a low wall, shaded by bushes. He lies supported by the rise of the earth and sheltered like an infant. His
embarrassment is shown by his dramatic shift to the present to
report his thoughts.[27] His first idea, as always when he is painting, is

to hide. Next he forcefully rejects the conventional act of rising to greet the company — "That I cannot do at all"(285). He projects the annoyance on the conversation of his rivals who ridicule and humiliate him. Susanna, the only one who knows he is there, stops him from attacking them with a protective gesture: "her hand groped down the wall, she held the hand on my head and gently pressed me down" (286). This wordless declaration of love and acceptance makes it possible for Friedrich to declare his love (287). The interrupted process of painting, supported on mother earth, is transformed into another process, that of living with the Roderer family.

This scene shows that Friedrich associates the early supporting mother earth with the later oedipal mother-figure Susanna. The need to differentiate between them leads him to involve Susanna in the decision about his painting. He is testing her identification with the oral mother/picture, which he wants to renounce. The oral mother in the painting retains her engulfing qualities; he has not transformed her into a symbol. The fear of ridicule portrayed in the meadow scene reveals that this union is experienced as shameful in a social setting. The thoroughness with which Friedrich destroys the painting indicates its danger for his growth, and the strength of his renunciation.

Susanna believes that the issue is growth: "our hearts will accomplish something and it will not be small, base, and insignificant"(301). She cannot say what the goal will be: she is after all not an engulfing mother-figure. The assumption of critics has been that Friedrich joins Peter in administration of the estate. But Peter has a son who is preparing himself for this. There is hardly a place for Friedrich. However, in describing how he ceased being a painter, Friedrich has become a writer. The playground of art has shifted, without our knowledge, from painting to literature.

We must pay attention to the form of the story. Friedrich writes an autobiography. As a storyteller, he has involved his readers in a time process within the narrative. The many time-designations are devices to help us participate. Almost all events and characters are introduced by such phrases as "during those five days" (250), "after a short time," "another time came," etc. Moreover, Friedrich hovers between diary and autobiography, forms in which outcomes are unknown and processes are stressed. Insistence on duration and process determines the very title *Progeny,* and is the base of the portrayal of generation after generation integrated into an everlasting process ("Roderer auf grenzenlose Zeit," 302). Because Friedrich, in all his endeavors, seeks a feeling of involvement in a process, his painting being only one manifestation of the search, his change of goal is natural. Painting frustrates him because the finished product is static, not dynamic. This may be why he destroys his picture so thoroughly. Writing stories is more satisfying because, as a process in time, it sweeps up narrator and audience alike.

Friedrich's secretiveness as painter extends to his role as story-teller. That critical literature has paid no attention to his being the writer attests the success of his denial strategy. Without our having become aware, he has defined himself as writer. In addition, he has triumphed over the father-figure Peter, who sacrificed his pursuit of Romantic poetry. Friedrich becomes a different kind of poet, whose subject is the growth of a modest, contemporary author who records the history of a bourgeois family. He is what Stifter became: a writer concerned not so much with small dimensions as with processes of change and growth. If we note Stifter's defense of his writing in the preface to *Bunte Steine* (1852), we appreciate the irony of *Progeny* and of Friedrich's triumph over Peter:

> Someone, [Hebbel, his contemporary] observed against me that I form only small things...I was never concerned in my writing whether I was forming great or small things, I was guided by quite different laws....I consider great the move-ment of the air, the flowing of the water, the growth of grain, the tides of the ocean, the greening of the earth... I consider great a life lived in justice, simplicity, self-discipline, reasonableness, effectiveness in one's own sphere and admiration of the beautiful... Let us seek to grasp the gentle law by which mankind is guided (V, 3-6).

In contrast to *Julius,* where oedipal fears lead to annihilation of all the actors, in *Progeny* the revelation of Friedrich's identity, his change of life goal, and the realization of the father-figure's prophecy lead to a happy ending. The destructive potential of the earlier story is spent on the painting, the artist survives. He has his cake and eats it too: he creates (stories), he marries (the mother figure), he is vic-torious over the father-figure (he becomes a writer which Peter did not) and wins his recognition. Once again, however, secrecy indicates that writing is problematic too. To understand what writing means to

Friedrich (and Stifter), we must look at Friedrich as a story-teller, the forms of his story and his narrative techniques. But before turning to this, let us briefly consider parallels between Stifter and Friedrich.

Friedrich unobtrusively, almost accidentally, slips into the writer's role. This matches Stifter's situation during the 1830's. He gradually slipped into marriage (he and Amalia lived together first) and he remained loyal to Fanni during early marriage.[28] When she died he is reported to have told Amalia, "Only now am I wholly yours." According to legend, he likewise fell into the role of writer. A friend discovered one of his stories, *The Condor* (1840), and interested a publisher in it. If this is true, it illustrates Stifter's characteristic passivity.[29] It seems remarkable that after writing inferior stories and poems for years, he suddenly came into his own at thirty-five. Events suggest that Stifter's identity was forced on him: first by the involvement with Amalia, then by Fanni's death, and finally by discovery as a writer. When his identity as writer became firmer, his painting decreased in importance; it became partly a compulsive ritual and partly a continuous experiment. His picture *Motion* (*Bewegung*) is typical. It was an unpainterly subject at the time, though the idea of rendering motion foreshadows Duchamp's *Nude Descending Staircase* in 1912. With the techniques available in the 1850's, it was an unfinishable painting. In fact, Stifter acted out its title literally and worked on it for about nine years, sketching, putting paint on the canvas and scratching it off, version after version. As a painter, Stifter repeatedly showed interest in the contrast between fluidity and firmness, masses of water and of rock. (Novotny, 8, 9, 21, 27, 28 etc.) The first version of *Die Bewegung* still has an alpine mountainscape backdrop, which was typical of Stifter's early painting. The second version (available only as a tracing) centers on the first version's foreground of rocky river bed, and the background is almost eliminated. The contrast of water and rock and the motif of river's edge dominate (Illustration II). The transitions from dry stones to wet stones to water occupy the fragment of the painting (Illustration III). Even in the tracing, the viewer cannot be certain if the rock forms are convex or concave. As in a trompe l'oeil picture, the eye sees these forms now raised, now lowered, so that the forms themselves seem to move. Also, these forms vaguely suggest faces or forms of animals. Yet, in the painting the foreground stones are of

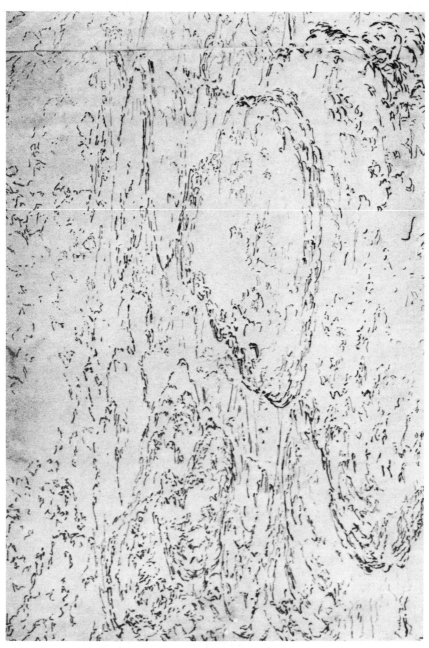

Adalbert Stifter: Fragment of the painting, *Motion (die Bewegung)*, 2. Version, 1858-1862.

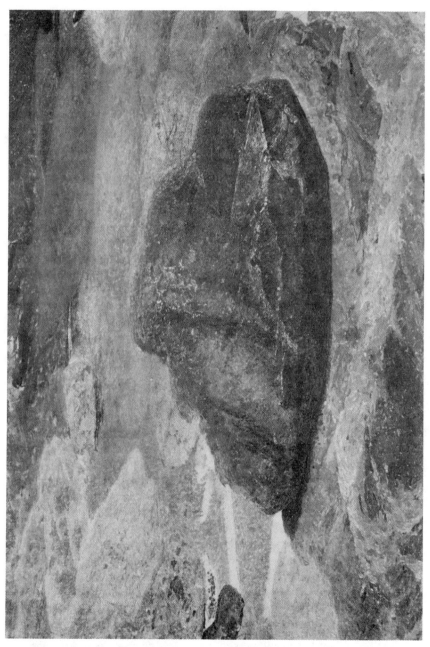

Adalbert Stifter: Paper tracing of the painting *Motion (die Bewegung),*
2. Version, 1858-1862, detail.

photographic detail. The center stone can be seen either as a sculpted head with beard and large nose, with its back buried in sand, or as a futurist sculpture. The nervous "hooks and strokes" of the drawing (reminiscent of Friedrich's "unfinished strokes and hooks," 248) resemble now firm, now hazy forms or mysterious inscriptions. The drawing vibrates with hidden energy and meaning. Despite the impression of energetic movement, the lines do not point beyond the picture plane. The movement seems to occur below the surface and to form concentric circles toward the center of the drawing. By employing the same kind of hooks and strokes for water and stone, the two elements are made alike, and firm forms become fluid. Stifter achieves similar effects in the painting by coloring, for the viewer can see rocks as colored stones or as water reflecting or covering stones. By repeatedly painting over stone forms, but leaving fragments of earlier forms exposed as at right front, Stifter achieves a highlighting of the last layer painted and suggest extraordinary, almost three dimensional depth. We might therefore see his pictures less as unfinished fragments and more as results of his intent to portray a continuous process of natural movements by a continuous play of forms and of layers of paint. Analysis of *Progeny* shows how effectively Stifter's writing used similar techniques of play with form: doing and undoing, saying and unsaying, hiding and revealing, shaping and reshaping ever finer gradations of meaning in a continuous process.

Strategies of Denial and Techniques of Revelation in Progeny[30]

If we agree with Noy that artistic form is "the means used to express, represent, or organize meanings"[31] we have a deeper definition, encompassing more than that of late classical rhetoric, which regards form as an external sugar-coating of the pill of unpleasant instruction. Noy's definition permits us to recognize the similar function attributed to form in analytic theory and in classical aesthetics, namely, that form and formality themselves mediate meaning. The story contrasts the form of the painting with the form of the narrative. The painting is huge, so huge that Friedrich will have to take down the wall of the house to move it. The landlady describes it, "a...huge sheet, stretched on wood... painted...and on which there are only clouds" (276). The painting's formlessness contrasts with the firm narrative sequence, which uses seventy pages to encompass some sixteen months of time as well as two flashbacks, one to Friedrich's childhood and the other to Peter's formative years and family history. We have noted the lack of firm, differentiated forms in the moor which is the painting subject, and have interpreted this fluidity as a characteristic representation of the perception of the early mother. The greater form capacity of writing would therefore better control the formless subject. The contrast of form and shapelessness also dominates the characters' actions. At the first meeting, Friedrich commits a breach of good manners by failing to greet the older man first. At the story's end, our attention is once more drawn to politeness: replying to Peter's toast, Friedrich and Susanna "thank... most courteously" (302). The superlative, as well as setting this sentence off by a paragraph of its own, gives the matter of formality a striking emphasis.

This opposition between beginning and end of the story extends to many other stylistic aspects and expresses Friedrich's transformation. Initially, his report is playfully exuberant, using humorous exaggerations to illustrate his existence as a painter. His bantering creates a safe narrative space. In fact, with his lengthy digressions on painting, Friedrich reproduces the formlessness of the painting itself, taking much space to tell little. His playful wordiness contrasts sharply with Peter's restrained wit. In six pages (as many as Friedrich takes to suggest his paintings are superfluous) Peter gives the history of his family from the Middle Ages to the separation of its two branches three generations ago. He makes his account vivid by well-chosen examples demonstrating the thesis which the history is designed to illustrate. The thesis (that Roderers achieve goals different from those intended) precedes the examples, so that the instructive intent is clearly discernible throughout. In the story's middle section, concerned with his life at Lüpfing Inn, Friedrich curbs his exuberance. With greater restraint, he compresses several months in this section. In the last part, his integration into the Roderer family, Friedrich covers a year. Decisive events rapidly follow each other. Destruction of the painting and the marriage take one page each. From this stylistic change, the reader receives the impression that Friedrich has become another man and that his purpose and skill as narrator has increased. While writing his story, he has become a serious and accomplished craftsman.

Most of the story's techniques are designed simultaneously to tell and conceal who the hero is, to reveal and conceal his goals. They let us know that he changes, but hide what he changes to. In Stifter's denial of personal involvement, the most important strategy is the fiction of the autobiography. In a fictional work presented as autobiography, the author's identity merges completely into that of the hero.[32] A story using this convention has two effects. It is an immediate, subjective account, and claims to have no distance from or choice about events or characters. The reader has a front-row view of the hero's inescapable necessities and the choices he makes, of his total life. In fictional autobiography the author seems to have no voice in, control over, or responsibility for events. The convention of autobiography is that the writer is telling the truth as he sees it. Although the choice of this form gives the material the inevitability of life itself, the author in fact has total freedom. What Stifter chooses to put into the narrative is for Friedrich one of life's necessities. Since we read the story from Friedrich's point of view, we are caught up in his necessities and overlook Stifter's license to decide happenings, characters, and outcome. We have no way to gauge the author's degree of subjectivity or objectivity and we cannot tell which techniques of narration are Stifter's and which are Friedrich's. Since the techniques used here appear in other Stifter works, we will attribute them to Stifter. It is important to note, however, that Friedrich's intent was to hide in the story itself. He tries to achieve a merger with the writing process, as he did earlier with painting. Being hidden, the author has a great deal of control. With painting, or Friedrich as a painter, the issue of control did not arise. But it is basic to his writing. The greater the secrecy, the less our awareness, the greater Friedrich/Stifter's control. Painting had the exclusive function of holding Friedrich in a process, but writing keeps him in control of the process. Seemingly realistic details in the story, Stifter's famous nature descriptions only shield by their concreteness the omnipotent thought which controls. The painter's need is to be; the writer's, to control.

As a young man, Stifter was unabashed about the writer's freedom to manipulate characters and events, and clearly stated his enjoyment of this aspect: "I enjoy the activity itself, I can create people as I want them, I can let them love each other to death, sacrifice themselves, enjoy themselves,...and I live with them and forget that others are around me."[33] For the Stifter of *Progeny,* this control was still the incentive toward fiction, but by this time designing in thought became increasingly more satisfactory than actual writing (cf. *Letters,* XIX, 215). From the multitude of techniques for hiding and manipulating the reader's response, let us choose a few for discussion.

By splitting basic figures and meanings into a multitude, a writer can form an entire social universe. We have seen this process at work in Stifter's splitting of the mother- figure into the landlady as care-taking oral mother, the moor as devouring oral mother, and Susanna as oedipal mother. With the aspects safely separated, the hero can vanquish some and integrate others into his life. Splitting is thus one aspect of ego mastery. A similar splitting occurs with the father figure. Friedrich expresses difference between father figures by the color of their beards, the symbol of their vitality. "The beards of the Roderers were brown," he says, "only that of my father was mixed with white... That of the elder Peter was white" (300). His own father, whom he experiences as an oedipal threat, plays no role in the story. Peter, the father who provides stability in Friedrich's fluid existence, becomes a grandfather figure of lessened physical strength.[34]

Removal in time or geography, like splitting, are unconscious devices of mastery. The treatment of the family theme is in part conscious, designed to make acceptable the idea of incest. Participation in a family, to Stifter, was synonymous with complete acceptance and integration into a historical process. Passion drove the Roderers apart, three generations ago. The separate development of the families of Peter and Friedrich make their reunion possible. At the same time, by his history of the destinies of a bourgeois family, Stifter gives a European dimension. The Peter Roderers, with their Dutch and English associations, represent the industrial and commercial north. The Friedrich Roderers, with their Russian, Silesian and Balkan connections, stand for the agrarian south-east of Stifter's Austria. Moreover, the northern Roderers and Peter, the self-made man, embody one bourgeois pattern, and the Friedrich Roderers with their inherited wealth represent another.

Another conscious technique Stifter uses to achieve Friedrich's integration into a process is his control over the perspective and time frame.[35] Friedrich begins his story as a journal. As he gives the background of his life and passion for painting, the form changes to autobiography, and he moves back and forth between journal and autobiography. This indefiniteness renders his painter's existence in the present. Peter's prophecy, though reported by Friedrich in autobiographical manner, breaks through into the future. The time frame lengthens with Peter's narration of the family history, expanding back into the Middle Ages. Peter's assumption of the autobiographical form brings us back to the present, and his plans for the future of the family extend the time frame into "forever" (269). For the remaining half of his own story, Friedrich moves into this wide time frame. More and more the story seems to describe a historical process in which Friedrich comes to participate actively, but over which he seemingly has little control. Right after Peter's narrative, Friedrich emphatically places himself outside Peter's plans. He decides not to follow the family pattern. Note the use of the future tense in contrast to Peter's vision: "I shall paint my moor in my log cabin" (273). The next sentence shows that in fact Friedrich is moving according to the law of his family and will attain a goal different from the one he sought, his will notwithstanding. This sentence says: "The day after talking to Roderer I did not paint" (272). Instead, he builds his house — with Peter's wood.[36] Stifter's handling of the time frame draws our attention to the importance of merger, allowing us to distinguish two different kinds. Friedrich, the painter, wants to blend into an undefined present; Friedrich, the writer, finds his existential safety integrated into the flow of definite historical time, a succession of generations, each different from the one preceding.

Humor can give an objective cast to language and provide distance for reader and narrator from the story. In the early part of his tale, Friedrich uses self-ridicule to distance himself from his obsession with painting. The first sentence begins the game of playing with surprise, giving a promise and fulfilling it in a way the reader does not anticipate. The title *Progeny* suggests sequence, inheritance, succession, orderly change. The first sentence, "And so I unintentionally became a landscape painter" (299), juxtaposes lacking intent, foresight, or surprise. Startled to attention, the reader asks "Why *And so* as the first words?" *And so* and *unintentionally* presuppose preceding events and promise explanation, but the surface impression is that of a narrator whose lack of skill forces him to throw us into the midst of events with a big splash. The next sentence continues the game, "It is terrible." Now, what is so terrible about becoming a landscape painter? The question leads us to an explanation which teases us by nonsense piled on nonsense — he became a painter because there were already so many bad painters and his paintings are bad too. Once again the reader witnesses a provisional, ever changing playspace erected and destroyed in turns.

The central prophecy containing the all-important problem of identity likewise appears in humorous form. Friedrich's initial fears about the prophecy (a reminiscence of its tragic oedipal potential)[37] are soon calmed by Peter's family's story. The first Roderer, in romantic fashion associated with the mighty Emperor Friedrich Barbarossa,[38] wants "to build a castle on a high mountain, marry a noble lady, and found a family whose fame would spread...over the globe"(257). Realization is different, but by no means bad: "He gained riches, married a noble lady and, in his old age, administered a large estate and rode about counting his cattle, sheep, and horses" (258). Compared to Barbarossa's fate, Roderer's is neither annihilating nor demeaning to those who prefer cattle to soldiers and counting wealth to drowning on crusades. The prophecy acknowledges that something was gained in life. The humorous Oedipus did not gain what he said, and thus far his destiny resembles that of the tragic Oedipus. Similarly, the humor at the expense of the landlady and her ignorance of Friedrich's aspirations reconcile us to the lighter aspect of the oral mother and differentiate her from the devouring mother.

Control of the reader's response, and involvement in a process, are the heart of another narrative technique: doubling.[39] Almost all events, characters, statements, and descriptions appear twice. This duplication applies not only to major events (reunions of the Roderers for betrothal and marriage), major characters (Peter and Friedrich wear similar clothes and beards), topics (painting and poetry), and settings (Lüpfing moor and Firnberg castle); it extends into minor details. For instance, Susanna and Friedrich are married on Peter and Paul's day; their families mirror each other (father, mother, brother, sister).

Doubling emphasizes contrasts and parallels between pairs. Its dominance compels the reader to compare, all the more so as Stifter/Friedrich withhold value judgments but by doubling imply them. The reader is therefore involved in a continuous process of value judgments. Friedrich and Peter both have ambition as artists, like the same kind of women, and share character traits as well as appearance. But there are major and minor contrasts in age, appearance, chosen art, and style — differences which diminish or alter in the course of the tale. Differentiation and transformation of characters and actions remain implied and give extraordinary denseness to the story. Each character's actions reverberate with implications, but little is said, not much emotion is expressed, and anticipated communications are omitted.

Take for instance the daily silent meeting of the future lovers. When Susanna comes late, but Friedrich nevertheless meets her, she blushes. When she comes early, and he meets her just the same, she blushes once more. From then on "her eyes became ever more beautiful and radiant" (282). Emotion is indicated by the most ordinary means (note the common adjectives), by trivial acts (a walk in the woods) and by seemingly realistic details (time designation, location). If we add the implied symbolism of the moor and the characters' names, we see that a rich narrative texture is achieved by simple means. Moreover, the author need not once state his case; he gets us to make judgments and comparisons within the flow of the narrative.

Negation, together with doubling, makes possible a process of doing and undoing: every action is undone, every assertion denied.[40] Friedrich paints many pictures, but burns them all. His family was large, is now small; it was fertile, but he will not contribute to its growth. He has come to the moor to paint it, but there is not much to paint. The history of the Roderers is a continuous process of saying and unsaying. All Roderers strive for something, none gets what he wanted. Individual, unattained goals are given space varying from a few sentences to many paragraphs. Individual Roderers' achievements receive scant notice, at best a laconic sentence or two.[41] This compilation of negations together with the story's main action — Friedrich *not* becoming a painter — gives us a thin positive line indeed, the ironic implication that Friedrich as a writer achieves "something not small and insignificant."

Devices of humor, negation, doubling, displacement and omission all work together to almost eradicate content and dissolve it into form. The strong emphasis on negation indicates that almost all materials of the primary process are unacceptable to Stifter, from the orality of the devouring moor to the merger into painting and writing, the oedipal family romance and rivalries, and the violent self-rejection in the destruction of the painting. He manages them as writer by raising them to consciousness in a safely negated, playfully distanced, displaced secondary process form, and gives us a veritable compendium of defensive techniques. Stifter's and Friedrich's art of narration is not that of resolving conflict tragically or comically, of showing a winner or a loser. At the time he wrote *Julius* this was still possible for him. Increasingly, his became the art of keeping even imaginary conflicts at a safe distance, holding them unresolved in the medium of words, their tension still reverberating in vital images and symbolic actions. As readers, we remain unaware of the many implications we respond to in his doublings, his contrasts, parallels, names, symbolic actions, and locales. It takes effort to penetrate the disguise of irony and humor and elucidate the effect of the many forms of negation. The narrative seems straight, natural, even simple. Stifter's narrative process might be compared to superimposition of two almost matching photographic negatives. The story's actual events are the slight differences between the negatives. The matching parts are the weight to which we unknowingly respond. This weight became heavier in Stifter's last stories. Some critics have called this tendency in his latest stories an inclination to de-realize reality and to impersonalize subjectivity.[42]

The psychic gains realized by these techniques are slightly different from those found in painting. The writer, like the painter, remains in a process of existential safety because it is removed from reality, both the external reality of personal and historical situation, and the emotional reality of the threatening oral mother and oral/oedipal father. Hence it allows him symbolic mastery. Being in this process as its continuous creator, Stifter could control it completely. The only problem was that his professional and family obligations painfully interfered with his wish to keep on writing. Hence his frequent illnesses helped creation.[43] But the longest story must end, and the best materials cannot be indefinitely converted into smaller and smaller segments of forms of denial. As a counter-measure, Stifter revised and revised version after version of the same story. Even one already published was not safe from revision.[44] His were not revisions to sharpen intent and meaning as he became clearer about the story. Different versions show drastic changes of incident and meaning. The later in Stifter's writing career the work or version appears, the more proliferating are the denial techniques. Increasingly, the author lost himself in the process of composing. Control of feeling became more important than completion. Like Balzac and Dostoevski (but for different reasons) Stifter remained in debt, no doubt in an unconscious attempt to save at least some works from being revised to death, the usual fate of his paintings.[45] Even so: the melancholy, devouring mother symbolized in *Progeny* as the moor could never be entirely appeased. The denial which managed her became a compulsion which generalized to every aspect of life. More and more aspects too charged with emotion must be denied; less and less could be told. It seems to me that, in *Progeny* , Stifter attempted to deal with the oral mother but did not succeed in exorcizing her. He only managed to freeze her into the story for the time being.[46] To better understand the psychological questions involved in Stifter's art, let us turn to a childhood memory for clarification of the sources and functions of his double talent.

The Sources of the Compulsion to Paint and to Write

He was born in 1805, the first of six children of a rural Austrian-Bohemian peasant weaver. His young parents lived with the father's family, and Adalbert as first-born child received much attention. He was nearly illegitimate, born only two months after his parents' marriage, a fact which all his life caused him enough embarrassment to make him secretive about his age.[47] His father was enterprising, fond of reading, and on his way up in the world. During the boy's childhood, he built up a trade in linen to supplement the family weaving and small farming operations. When the baby was two, he suffered a major trauma — a sister was born and he lost the exclusive attention of his mother. He never seems to have regained the mother's love for even after his sister died a year later and he became the center of the household again, he remembers his mother as preoccupied (depressed?) and ever angry. The paternal grandmother largely took her place, especially after he was five when, in rapid succession, four more siblings were born. When he was twelve his father died, and he might have stayed a farmhand helping his grandfather raise the family, if his maternal grandfather had not arranged for the gifted boy to be placed in a monastery boarding school.

Though Stifter later denied that his father had much influence on his life, he shared the father's upward mobility. The greater attention he received as first- born undoubtedly contributed to a greater capacity for achievement. All his siblings remained in the peasant class. The mother's withdrawal of attention appears to have happened at a time when he could not master it in an active way. He must have felt his separation from her as a misfortune to be outwaited, and clung to the memory of complete possession in the dogged way a child shows in its first years. The basic fault (Balint), the weakness of the core of his self which necessitated later compulsions and denials as devices to protect weak cohesion of the self, must have originated then.[48] Moreover, his image of the mother seems to have split into good and bad, later into oral and oedipal mother. These splits never surfaced and never healed, but caused ambivalence and denial. His later compulsion to double and repeat appears to be rooted in early loss.

The rapid births of his siblings during the oedipal and latency periods and the severe parental punishment earned by his anger and jealousy seem to have made impossible a working through of oedipal and sibling rivalries. His father's premature death during his early adolescence halted their resolution. Births and deaths, out of his control as they were, must have strained the weak core of the self, and occasioned the conviction that feelings, his own and those of others, were dangerous. Hence, strong feelings — violence, anger, jealousy, desire could only be tamed by passive withdrawal, or be made tolerable by various forms of denial. At best, and this was the case with his writing, a partial transformation of feeling into symbol could occur.

To support these observations, let us now turn to two remarkable memories of his infancy, memories so early that they are unique in our record of writers' lives and creative processes. Though stylized, they are sufficiently free of later superimpositions to provide insight not only into Stifter's development, but into the development of creativity in general. They associate, for Stifter, visual and auditory sensitivity with embeddedness in the maternal, undifferentiated environment preceding socialization. Writing emerges out of it at the entry into the social world, a world of interaction with several others, and of guilt for action.

> Far back in empty nothingness there is something like delight and ecstasy which embraces me powerfully, almost annihilates me, penetrates my being and resembles nothing

else in my later life. Its remembered characteristics are: there was radiance, there was a bustling about, it was down below. ...a high, extended wall of dark nothingness surrounds it.

There also was something else which went through me softly and calming. Its characteristics were: it was sounds.

Then I swam in something like a breeze. I swam back and forth in it and became softer and softer; then I became as if intoxicated; then there was nothing. ...

The following peaks become more definite: the resounding of bells, a wide band of light, a red darkness.

Something...always repeated itself: a voice that spoke to me, eyes that looked at me and arms that comforted everything. I cried for these things.

Then there was something lamentable, insufferable, then something sweet and soothing. I remember urges that got nowhere and the cessation of something terrible and ruinous. I remember splendor and colors which were in my eyes, sounds which were in my ears and sweetnesses which were in my being.

More and more I feel the eyes which looked at me, the voice that spoke to me and the arms which comforted everything, I remember that I called this "Ma".

Once I felt these arms carry me. There were dark spots in me. Memory tells me later that these must have been the woods outside of me. Then there was a sensation like the first one of my life, radiance and bustling about, and then nothing. ...

Later the external world arose before me since up to then only sensations had been noticed. Even Ma, eyes, voice and arms had only been in me as sensations, even the woods, as I just said. It is strange that the first sensation of my life was of something external, something spatial, a down below, something that enters our consciousness only late. That shows how powerful an effect that sensation must have had.[49]

These memories well render the infant's experience of partial merging with the mother and reflect his global sense perceptions. He perceives the mother's presence as part of himself; he is not yet a clearly differentiated *I*. Most remarkably, memory itself (and hence the child) emerges from "empty nothingness" and always returns to it, a melancholy perception indeed of the source of life. Against this perception of the source of life is contrasted another, comforting stable experience of the mother (no doubt later in developmental sequence than the impersonal nothingness), a mother still experienced as voice, arms, and eyes, that is to say as part objects. Global sensations of comfort and discomfort play on this maternal background. Experiences of ecstasy are predominantly associated with visual, spatial, and kinaesthetic sensations *(radiance, bustling, down below, dark, breeze, softly, intoxicated)*. Experiences of extreme discomfort are not associated with a particular sense but generalized to "something terrible and ruinous," so overwhelming that only their cessation is remembered. The experience of engulfment and the terror of it no doubt have their source here; but so does a preference for spatial representation and vision. Moreover, the maternal presence recurs, whether as nothingness or as arms, voice, and eyes, and, like a steadying canvas, outlasts the sense perceptions that play against it.

The second memory given below shows that the child and the mother are distinct, separate identities and that the universe is now a social world populated by an entire family.

Ma whom I now called mother presently stood before me as a figure and I could tell her movements, then father, grandfather, grandmother, aunt. I called them by these names, felt sweetness from them but I don't remember a difference between them. I must have been able to distinguish other things as well without being able to remember an individual figure or difference. One event which occurred at that time proves that. Once again I found myself in the terrible and ruinous condition of which I spoke above. Then there was a ringing, confusion , pain in my hands and blood on them, mother put on bandages and then there was a picture which stands clearly before me even now as if painted in pure colors on porcelain. I stood in the garden which has been fixed in my imagination from that time on, mother was there and then my other grandmother, whose figure too entered my memory at that moment, I felt that ease which always followed the recession of the terrible and ruinous something, and I said, "Mother, there grows a blade of rye."

Grandmother answered to that, "One does not speak to a boy who has broken a window." I did not understand the connection but the extraordinary something which had just receded from me returned instantly; mother didn't say a word and I remember that something monstrous lay on my soul. This event even now is alive in me. I can see the high, slender blade of rye as clearly as if it were standing next to my desk; I see the figures of mother and grandmother working in the garden, I see the plants only as an indefinite green gloss; but the sunshine which flowed around us is now clearly there.[50]

In this episode we can observe that the earlier feeling of inexplicable, generalized discomfort ("something ruinous and terrible") is assigned a series of causes, and that the child does not wait it out but attempts to master it. The sequence of events can be rendered as follows: there is an offense (terrible condition, a ringing which translates into anger and breaking a window); there is punishment (pain and blood) and there is forgiveness (the mother bandaging the hand). In this first chain of events the child does not see himself as the initiator of actions, he only notes their results. The occurrences contain feeling and meaning but the child does not transform them into verbal expression. His anger externalizes into a destructive gesture and his punishment into hurting his hands. In the first chain of events, we observe the acting-out stage.

The second chain of events follows the same sequence but has different results. His offense is speaking, his punishment the grandmother's reproof and the adults' silence; the forgiveness is partial. Nature ("sunshine which flowed around us") consoles and unites, but the feeling of "the terrible and ruinous" remains, is aggravated to "something monstrous," and stays with him "even now," some fifty years later. In this second chain of events the child is the initiator as he attempts, by verbal, symbolic expression, to reestablish the bond to the mother. They are both bandaging the relationship broken by his anger. Transformation of the feeling of this scene into language and symbol was so important to Stifter's later writing that the symbolic blade of rye still seemed to be standing next to his desk. The offending sentence with its additional phallic connotations indicates that the original offense may have had an oedipal basis, anger of the five-year-old at his parents' union and their presenting him with a sibling.[51] Note that the adults act in concert and that the rejection comes from a relative stranger (the maternal grandmother did not live with the young family), who may serve as a screen memory for the too-threatening father.

The bond with the mother was too weak, the mother image too split, and the relationship too ambivalent to sustain the child through a conflict with adults. Mother and child unquestioningly obey the grandmother. The close association of acting out (window breaking) and speaking out (the offending sentence) indicates that the child closely links the two in this experience of punishment. He did not establish a clear difference between acting out an emotion and expressing it symbolically. This insufficient differentiation later led to Stifter's need to restrain even the creatures of his imagination, and to curtail especially their speaking out. Note that Friedrich does not say his name or put into words his love until he is accepted by a physical gesture. The danger of speaking out and punishment for it became a major theme of Stifter's.[52]

The child retreats in silence to a partial and isolated reconciliation with nature, the green of the garden and the shining sun. No doubt this precurses the evocations of abiding, silent, succoring nature which take over when the expression of love fails in Stifter's later writings.[53] Therewith the memory returns from the symbolical (language) and agent (relationship with persons) level of the social and literate stage to the nonagent level of the first chain of events.

The two childhood memories reveal typical facets of Stifter the painter and Stifter the writer, and help us understand why his writing was more successful even though it probably was more of a psychic risk than painting. Both arts were coping techniques. Painting seems to have helped him maintain his most rewarding sensuous fulfillment in the world and helped him to cling to the maternal matrix represented as canvas or as natural process. At the same time, when immersed in the activity of painting he was insufficiently differentiated from the mother of the earliest stage of psychosocial development. This meant that Stifter, the painter, could not communicate his vision to the social world. He did not produce enough or win buyers or patrons — and this not for lack of talent or effort. If he had attempted to use painting to master the oral mother, he would have had to seek formal instruction in the art. Except for the lessons he received at Kremsmünster monastery school, he did not. And since the earliest mother contained empty black nothingness as we saw from his first memory, we need not be surprised that he feared her. *Progeny* was but one attempt to save himself from her fearful aspects. There he sought to deal with her threat by juxtaposing it to a safe, permanently settled family, by soliciting the assistance of grandparent-helpers, and by using a more effective technique than painting to conquer her, namely writing. We saw that writing, though more clearly associated with active mastery was insufficiently differentiated from acting out, and therefore also contained dangers. The child of the second memory achieved some mastery over the "ruinous condition" by acting out his anger in a way that included self-punishment and a wound bad enough to arouse the mother's solicitude. The inevitable stresses of Stifter's mature life, as husband, father to a foster child, and school inspector, must have occasioned similar frustrations and angers to those which the child experienced, but Stifter never expressed anger or any violent emotion as an adult. Instead, he turned some of the anger against himself, punishment reflected in his many gastric ailments through these years. They in turn could be relieved by the quiet solicitude of his motherly wife. Internalized anger also expressed itself as continuous depression.[54] And he could channel anger and passion into his writing. The ever-increasing, stringent censorship which his superego vented on his fictional characters must have consumed emotional energy, as did the proliferating techniques of denial. Both let him hide himself in the process of composing, extend and control it, express emotion although denying it. In many respects, writing acted like a protective compulsion.[55] In addition, of course, his ego was strengthened by completed tales, and the monetary rewards and social acclaim received. During the years of his maturity, he achieved a precarious balance.

The secondary process elaborations of his narrative art, contaminated by incompletely symbolized emotion and primary process, could lead him into producing so much that it threatened to engulf him, awakening all the fears discussed earlier. This seems to be the meaning of the two worst depressions of his life. The first occurred during 1854-1855 when Stifter was working on three inordinately long, complex novels *(Nachsommer, Witiko,* and *Zawesch)*. In January 1854 he reported that he had been at work on 10-15 books simultaneously. The process of narration had got out of hand. A minor upset stopped all work. A depression followed and incapacitated him until he decided to abandon the two historical novels and finish *Nachsommer*. Freed from engulfment by material, the depression eased enough to allow him to wrest the novel from himself by slow installments.

The depression of 1863-1865 came at a similar stage during the completion of *Witiko*. Through 1858-1863 Stifter reported work in progress on *Witiko, Zawesch,* and a new work *Wok*. All through this time, he was plagued by quarrels, depressions and losses, but none was incapacitating.[56] The writing of *Progeny* appears to have been an attempt to free himself from engulfment by producing a finished work unrelated to the historical novels. Their threat of engulfment is represented by the moor in the novella. The several doublings which dominate the moor's destruction (Friedrich's double destruction of the painting, Peter draining the moor and filling it with stones), allow us to gauge the power of the threat and the counter-force needed. Presentation of the threat in the simple and effective image of the moor allowed Stifter a relatively direct working out of the problem, so much so that during the novella's composition he felt at ease and even mastered difficult negotiations as a school inspector. We saw that the threat of engulfment was by no means entirely resolved by the novella. Its completion strengthened him sufficiently to resume the longer works, but the strength was insufficient to head off the severe depression of the early winter of 1863. This incapacitated him and interrupted all work until January 1865 when he decided on the cure with whose description we began and settled on finishing *Witiko*. The depression then lifted enough that he could send parcels of work to his publisher, but in very slow installments.[57] His retirement occurred during his work on *Witiko* but brought little change. In these later years, Stifter alternated between language proliferation and silent psychosomatic acting out. At best, he managed a balance between fearing engulfment by too much narrative material, on the one hand, and panicking at loss of these materials, that is, losing the supportive narrative process with its safety devices, on the other. Hence the painful slowness of *Witiko;* hence, also, the deepening depression and return of panic once *Witiko* was published.

Stifter was about to make himself master of the balancing process by resuming work on a new version of an earlier, longer work, the *Journal of my Greatgrandfather,* when his entire household fell ill with influenza. The illness made him unable to either paint or write, and depression returned in full force. Bereft of his usual coping devices, and weakened by illness, panic and fear overwhelmed him. He ended his life, in a last, final denial of his expressive gift, by a painful gesture of self-punishment, the cutting of his throat.

VI
FRANZ KAFKA'S
JOSEPHINE THE SINGER, OR THE MOUSE FOLK:
SELF-COHESION BY STRUGGLE

Kafka's last story about Josephine, the mouse singer[1] was written in late March, 1924, in Prague, just after his return to his father's house from Berlin, a forty-one year old Napoleon whose "Russian mission"[2] had failed. His situation that month must have activated all the conflicts which had made him turn to writing. He had known for two years that he was dying.[3] Despite his fatal illness, he had found a companion, Dora Diamant, he was hoping to marry. He was again under his father's roof, his hate/love feelings for him unchanged. Shortly after producing this story in the characteristic creative frenzy,[4] Kafka left for Vienna, where he died of tuberculosis two months afterward. As in other artist stories written in these last two years, Kafka attempts in *Josephine* to deal with his death, and record and sum up his life and career. The story is specially valuable for a psychological study of Kafka's creative process, because it traces the split in his psyche that caused the specific nature of his art.

The artist-theme occupied Kafka from the beginning of his career as a writer. His writing was a way of living via self-observation and self-creation. An artist's experience, gained by living through the creation of an artistic work, seemed to him the best escape from the dilemma of existence as son in a world populated by authoritarian father-figures. The artist figure in his earlier stories and novels appears off center stage in various disguises: a letter-writing friend in *The Judgment,* a hack painter in *The Trial.* The performing ape of *A Report to an Academy* (1917) sets the artist, still disguised, center-stage. During Kafka's last two years, the figure of the artist dropped the disguise and became the main theme. Through a succession of fragments and complete stories, Kafka worked out an accounting of his creative process and the role of art in his life.

On the surface, *Josephine* is a story dealing with the role an artist plays as member of an oppressed minority, such as the Central European Jews of Kafka's lifetime. *Josephine* was at least partly inspired by Kafka's 1911 encounter with the Yiddish Theater Group in Prague, which awakened his interest in the Jewish national movement, drew his attention to the role of a minority artist in the life of his people, and made him reconsider his own identity as a Western Jew.[5] In the year preceding his death this interest was revived by his encounter in Germany with Eastern European Jews preparing for emigration to Palestine. Ill as he was, he briefly considered joining the immigrants. *Josephine* reflects people he met, issues he considered important, and hopes he held up to that time.[6] As usual with Kafka's writing the specific biographical point of departure is a more personal issue than the surface suggests, because all characters are aspects of his inner life, and more universal, because Kafka succeeds in making universal the problem of a dying artist of a deprived people.[7] It is important to the story that he combines references to German, Jewish and Hebrew traditions of art, folk traditions, and reflections about art; that he was again hoping to get married, was ill of tuberculosis, and had recently experienced discrimination, pogrom, police protection, and hunger.[8] Nevertheless, I am primarily concerned with internal psychological questions: What does the story tell us about the meaning, to the dying author, of literary and artistic creation? What personal and social function did he assign to art in his last years? What function did the creative process play in his life and early death?

Style and the Structure of Spielraum (play space)

The story's action between a people, their singer, and the narrator occurs in the animal kingdom. This alienated point of view allows the reader freedom from normal human perspective. While author and reader explore the mouse world, they discover familiar facts in new surroundings. A good deal of the novella's humor and poignance lies in the cultural and linguistic play allowed by the mouse perspective on art and society. For instance, the narrator-mouse uses stately rhetoric to speak of his people's culture, art, and heroes. The mouse folk have a bureaucratic language with ponderous multisyllabic words like "Gesuchsbegründung" that is: a justification for an application for redress (181). The mice have their own vocabulary, appropriate to mice. *Erdarbeiter,* for instance, is mouse for the human *Landarbeiter.* Because *pfeifen* describes their singing, their expression for *Volkslied* is *Volkspfeifen.* The German reader, finding the expression "Sie pfeift auf dem letzten Loch," (she is dying), recalls the rat song of Mephistopheles in Goethe's *Faust,* and its association with poison, pregnancy and diabolic laughter at human tragedy. The play with language contrasts with, but often leads up to and accentuates the fatal struggle between the singer, the narrator and her people. Many points which the narrator debates about the artist, his creative process, and his role in society, are found in the tradition of the artist novella since the Romantics. Any point can be supported from the story; but so can its opposite. For instance, art has an important social function. As symbol for the community Josephine can give the people strength and comfort. But art can also disrupt: the artist can lead people astray and bring about their annihilation. The artist is narcissistic and egotistical; devotion to art promotes irresponsibility, isolates, and debilitates. Yet Josephine can think of her art as an exalted and inspired calling, demanding a high degree of skill, rigorous discipline and devotion. A detractor might call it a self-indulgent temper tantrum requiring neither skill nor effort. The reader's guide for this exploration, the mouse-narrator, generally reports from the *we* perspective of the mouse folk, but identifies himself as *I,* has opinions of his own, and is an active, important character. As usual with a novella, the action can be summed up in one sentence. Josephine, her people's songstress, conducts a lifelong quarrel with the mouse folk for recognition of her art, and finally disappears from among them to achieve this. The narrator reports a series of ten progressive appearances before the people. The tale's key symbol is Josephine's singing/piping, which represents her art. Her performances, the mouse folk reaction, and the narrator's descriptions and reflections, define and refine the nature and effect of this art.

The novella is tightly structured. After an initial five-paragraph reflection by the narrator on the lack of musical tradition among the mice, and art and technique in general, he turns to examples of interaction between performer and audience. The introduction, presenting the key symbol, raises aesthetic questions which a discourse on poetics or music might deal with: the tradition the artist stands in, the nature of his medium, and the role of technique.[9] Unable to account for the effect of Josephine's singing, "this piping of hers is no piping" (362), the narrator considers actual performances to see what general truths about Josephine's art can be derived. He groups two or three examples and reflections together, and draws conclusions from each group in a general discourse, each discourse revealing need for more examples to carry on the argument. With the third group, and with two-thirds of the story told, Josephine's struggle for recognition comes to a climax. The narrator reports that, as a sign of recognition, she demands freedom from having to work. Three further examples of her performances, with comment, illustrate her increasingly dramatic recitals. Her vocal art changes to dramatic acting. The concluding three paragraphs report her disappearance and the narrator's reflections and summary.

This tightly organized work is a striking mixture of essay and narrative technique.[10] If we follow the plot line as it proceeds for Josephine, we find that her actions become more and more desperate. Within each series of episodes there is a heightening of drama, a widening of the radius of her actions, and an increase in the intensity of her emotions. For instance, in the first three episodes, Josephine asserts herself first against a small disturbance; in the second, she combats the hardships of thousands of mice, and in the third she battles the general mousehood condition of life in crisis. In each episode she spends greater effort. Against the disturbance "Josephine struck up her most triumphal notes" (363), against the thousand burdens "she...concentrated all her strength," against the life in crisis, "she actually bites" (364). The drama of her existence culminates in her final disappearance.

The tension generated by Josephine's struggle conflicts with the narrator's language, attitude, and tone. He presents successive arguments regarding Josephine's art and people, examines each, rejects some, finds others lacking, and proceeds to further documentation and argumentation. It is a logical, rather than a narrative progression. His tone is dry and he displays studied neutrality, assuming the pose of a chronicler reporting "a small episode in the eternal history of our people" (376). Yet, using the present tense throughout, he narrates from an eternally present perspective and thus cancels the historical one. Moreover, as Josephine's actions grow more dramatic, his arguments and reflections become denser and more complex. In the course of the story he often eliminates the historical drama and presents us instead with a dissertation on aesthetic principles. The narrator's perspective can be described as distant, and differs markedly and increasingly from the drama of Josephine's struggle. The narrator and Josephine have different ways of separating themselves from the mouse folk.

By the mousehood fable, by the linguistic fun and games, and by the setting up of two perspectives (Josephine's and the narrator's) on their common reality (the mouse folk and mousehood), Kafka achieves an emotional/intellectual *Spielraum* within the story, a space for the reader's imagination to play in. Within this play space, the reader's knowledge of the cultural tradition of the artist story and its conventions reverberates against the reported actions of Josephine and against the argumentations of the narrator. The geographical space for play and art we have found in other artist stories (e.g. Mozart's arbor) in Kafka's tale has become an invisible stage for the inner drama between author/characters/readers and their respective contexts.

The narrator appears to be uninvolved with his topic and to have complete control over it. On close scrutiny, we realize that he is unreliable and pretends omniscience. For instance, he begins: "Our singer is called Josephine. Anyone who has not heard her does not know the power of song" (360). This suggests that Josephine is an active member of the tribe. At the end of the paragraph he hints that, one day, Josephine may not be among the mouse folk ("when she dies, music...will vanish," 360) but this only convinces us that all is well with her. The various episodes and his reflections on them set Josephine's story in an eternal, safe present. To be sure, with the accumulation of episodes the reader experiences a sense of passing time. *Expressis verbis,* the narrator contradicts this impression several times: "Many believe that Josephine is becoming so insistent because she feels herself growing old... I do not believe it....For her there is no growing old" (373). Time breaks in, only three paragraphs before the last one of this novella of thirteen pages, and the reader discovers that sometime during the telling of the story Josephine disappeared: "That happened a day or two ago; but the latest is that she had disappeared, just at a time when she was supposed to sing" (375).[11] The concluding paragraphs disagree with the beginning. We conclude either that the narrator at the beginning knew about her disappearance and deceived the reader, or that he was surprised by it and does not have the omniscience he claims. In either case he has proved unreliable. This discrepancy, like others noted earlier, points to the need to look closely at the narrator as a character in conflict, and at his relationship to Josephine and the mice. Who is he, what does he represent, and what is he after? Because he is involved with Josephine and the mouse folk, we must also ask who these other actors are.

In all his works, Kafka's characters are different parts of a single self in its internal struggle. He admitted this practice for his first story, *The Judgment* (1911).[12] The Josephine story is no exception. Reading it in this manner, however, I do not wish to label psychic entities to reduce the work to a psychic allegory. What interests me in this kind of analysis is that it allows us to understand how the author views psychic dynamics, what functions he attributes to different parts of the self as they interrelate; when, how, and for what purpose they interrelate; how they assist or handicap and frustrate each other. My analysis assumes that the self is Kafka's.

The splitting Kafka describes in his tale corresponds roughly to a Freudian schema. Josephine and the mouse folk respectively represent largely unconscious id and superego functions. The narrator embodies many conscious secondary process and ego functions. In the interrelationship of these functions, Kafka describes a self whose parts are set against each other, out of phase, and ultimately mutually destructive. In delineating the split lines, tracing the lack of phasing, and forming inner dynamics into a story firm in the literary tradition of the artist story, Kafka shows us comprehensively and insightfully his failure as man and artist. By formulating this understanding artistically, he transcends it.

Josephine, Kafka, and the Primary Process

The narrator calls Josephine her people's songstress, but equivocates when defining her art (singing/piping) and her influence (good/bad). If we set aside his evaluations, and consider his description of Josephine's actions and their effects, we will understand her better as a representative of primary process. The most striking circumstance is that she hardly speaks. She, whose extravagant claims for her art the narrator makes so much of, "says very little anyhow, she is silent among the chatterers."[13] Her gestures speak all the more effectively. She announces her performances by posture alone, and whenever she assumes this posture her people come together.

As the representative of primary process Josephine is nonverbal. She exercises her art independent of time or place; by presence and sensuous appeal she demands and gets attention whenever she is aroused. To the rational narrator, she is inopportune and unpredictable. If she is not at once obeyed she becomes aggressive. She never weakens, but generates new means to win her point, whether temper tantrums or displays of exhaustion. She is never called childlike or childish, but she brings forth in the mouse folk "the same foolishness as children, senselessly, wastefully, grandiosely, irresponsibly" (369). Vain and narcissistic, she is ruthless, bent on her own enjoyment and survival. To get her way and dominate by her art, she withdraws strength "from everything in her that does not directly subserve her singing" (363), so much so that she courts death ("a cold breath blowing upon her might kill her," 363). Despite this extreme concentration on her art, nothing is said about regular practice and discipline.

Josephine's performance gives her people animal comfort, and this comfort remains the unchanging element in all performances described, "each...could relax and stretch himself at ease in the great, warm bed of the community" (370). The narrator suggests that Josephine seduces the mouse folk into this ease "when danger is most imminent" without "proper precautions...to avert dangers" (370). When the mouse folk are under her sway, all criticism stops; "opposition is possible only at a distance" (362). By seducing them into such total absorption, Josephine causes the loss of many lives. Yet, because of her delicacy (362) persistently asserted against great odds, she affects her people as a symbol of the core of their own being: "Josephine's thin piping amidst grave decisions is almost like our people's precarious existence amidst the tumult of a hostile world" (367). In her persistent struggle for recognition, Josephine uses increasingly rudimentary means from allure (374) to the omission of all technique. When these tactics go unnoticed, she pretends tears and illness. When this, too, goes unrewarded, she disappears.

In letters and diaries from 1922-1924, Kafka speaks of himself as an artist, about his creative process and its connection to libidinal life, in almost the same language he uses for Josephine. To clearly define the parallels, we must consider Kafka's writing practices as compared to Josephine's singing. Moreover, we must keep in mind that Josephine is only one aspect of Kafka the writer. She is the irrational primary process, his musical self, his inspiration, his muse. And since these states are designated as female in Kafka's and our culture, Josephine is female.[14]

It is curious that Kafka should depict all his last artist figures as performers (hunger artist, trapeze artist, singer, performing dog). After all, a writer's daily lonely struggle at his desk has little in common with a performer, who assumes poses and is in immediate contact with his audience. The choice of the performer metaphor seems less strange if we consider that all these performers, like Kafka, are shy, isolated beings who derive their art from alienation and practice it defensively in defiance of the public. Moreover, the performer metaphor stresses some important features of Kafka's art. Like a performer, Kafka practiced his art intermittently but with total absorption, in intense bursts of creative energy. This need for intensity made it impossible for him to finish long works. Considering the span of his fifteen creative years, his volume is small. For Kafka, a few months of ecstatic writing (August-December 1912, August 1914-March 1915, November 1916-April 1917, November 1921-August 1922, October 1923-March 1924) alternated with long stretches of inertia. Even though some manuscripts have been lost, Wagenbach/Pasley, dating the texts, find Kafka's productive periods intermittent: "stossweise."[15] Kafka himself blamed his need to earn a living as an insurance official. Josephine, likewise, wants to be free of the burden of having to earn a living. But when Kafka had sick leave almost constantly from 1917, he wrote no more than before. In fact, during the first four years of his illness he relinquished his artist career and he only started writing again in 1921 to save himself from what he called "a nervous condition" (L, 374).[16] Neither despair nor deathly illness nor hope of integration into a community changed his actual practice. *Josephine,* like the *Judgment* twelve years before, was the product of a single burst of creative impulse.

Josephine likes disturbances; any trouble "incites her to heighten the effectiveness of her song" (363). Likewise Kafka. His creative months coincided with his struggles to acquire a wife and family of his own. His ambivalence about marriage has been extensively treated in the critical literature since Kafka was conscious that his father was the source and subject of his writing and that writing was a way out of the competition with the father. The first three productive periods came from his involvement with Felice, the fourth from that with Milena, the fifth from Dora. His engagement to Julie brought forth *Letter to his Father.* As a child and an adult, from his earliest recollection, Kafka experienced his father as a threat, and his mother, wholly allied with the father, as his "beater during the hunt" (LF, 45)! Hence his parents appeared as one overwhelming, nurturing and punishing father to him. The oedipal problem is therefore a front for archaic issues of parental nurture and threat to self.[17] A large part of the threat was fear of desertion. The eldest child of a couple utterly devoted to each other, who had to struggle for bare survival during the early years of their marriage, infant Franz was left to negligent servants. His next two siblings did not survive this treatment and died in infancy. Insufficient early maternal care led to Kafka's lifelong search for nurture and care. Since his parents had paid him attention only when he was ill, he felt illness as one way to achieve care. All the women he became interested in were assigned the nurturer role, often with the explicit exclusion of sex (D I, 297). Because of the threat inherent in the father relationship and the weak initial mother-child bond, his sexual development remained retarded.[18] This probably contributed to Kafka's youthful looks. He comments on his childlikeness repeatedly and it is a characteristic he shares with all his heroes, including Josephine. At the same time, because of early lack of maternal care, he like the mouse folk felt he had no childhood.

Women in fact played a double role for Kafka. They could free his struggling self from the inhibitions of his restrictive parent imago, hence his preference for woman unacceptable to (Julia, Milena) or

removed from the family (Felice, Dora). Having freed him for creation, they could give him the love and esteem to support further creation and struggle against the negative parent imago. They were allies
against the authority of the father in a double sense. Josephine uses
her admirers in just this way. They assist her in performance but
she prescribes when and how they are to relate to her. Kafka likewise saw his "affairs" as purely literary ("my whole being is directed
toward literature," he warned Felice's father, LF 313) and prescribed
their dimensions.[19] They were to guarantee him the reception of supportive letters. At the same time, the support of women felt real to
him only if he granted them some measure of reality, hence, for
instance, his interest in Felice's job as typist. But the relationships
became problematical, pseudo-oedipal issues only when the women
would not stay put in their literary roles and insisted on Kafka's
erotic involvement, and thus forced him to withdraw. For him, like
Josephine, it is hard to determine whether the turmoil of his
creative/erotic life was caused by others, and he allayed it by withdrawal into writing, or whether he sought potentially disturbing people and situations to excite his creative faculty.

Like Josephine, Kafka sometimes complained that work interfered
with achieving perfection as an artist. At other times both Kafka and
the narrator see through this rationalization commenting "her work
would not at all get in the way of her singing" (372). The creative
burst remained typical of Kafka's writing as it remained characteristic of Josephine's singing. Not for him the regular discipline, daily
output, and hours of rewriting characteristic of Thomas Mann.[20]

Josephine in her performances is "wholly withdrawn and living only
in her song" (363). These spells of total immersion and creative solitude seemed to Kafka "a form of prayer" (H, 348), when he wrote
"with...coherence,...a complete opening out of the body and the soul"
(D I, 276, 1912). This self-forgetfulness was the "prime precondition
of being a writer" (L, 384). The orgiastic, sexual quality of such
intense experience in Josephine's case and his own did not escape
Kafka ("these questionable embraces...the craving for self-
enjoyment," L, 385). And from finding art an "idée fixe" (L, 431), "his
only happiness" (L, 386) it was only a short step to feeling guilt.
Kafka repeatedly expressed guilt about being cruelly neglectful of
others because of his art (L, 431). Josephine likewise is indifferent to
the slaughter of her audience by enemies (371). The connection

between intense absorption in creation, craving for support of one's narcissism, indifference to others, demonic possession and sexual gratification which Kafka found in himself and attributed to Josephine, appears most clearly in a letter to Max Brod, in which his art is both salvation and curse.[21]

> Writing is a sweet, miraculous reward. But what for? Last night it was clear to me... that it is reward for service to the devil. This descending to dark powers, this unleashing of spirits naturally bound, these questionable embraces and all the rest which takes place down below and of which one no longer knows when writing stories in the sunshine. (L, 384-385)

The primary process component of creation thus finds apt expression in the animal artist traditionally associated with demonic forces, dog, mouse, or mole. This part of the self is small, hidden, instinctual, uncontrollable, driven, sexual, undermining cohesion, alienated from others and yet seductive.

In giving herself artistically, Josephine regresses throughout the story. This regression leads to a final fusion with the spiritual matrix of her nation, so the narrator can say that she is redeemed into the "throng of the heroes of our people" (376). She merges with this matrix during each performance and emerges from it as symbol of mousehood. As an artist, she creates this matrix as a realm to be shared, but note how frail, miserable and uncaring of her this matrix is.[22] In Kafka's other works, the realm of the artist during creation appears in curious, different guises. It is a cage of deprivation in the *Hunger Artist,* the airy heights of the trapeze artist, or the mole's subterranean castle-keep. In a letter to Brod, Kafka speaks of the "airy, terrible realm" (L, 383) of a writer. Its danger (for it contains the father) seemed to him like being borne along by the hunt (D II, 202, January 1922) to the last frontiers of the mind. But this realm has its positive aspects. Its safety lies in its very lack of substance. But this lack could also appear to Kafka as being dead while alive (L, 385). Withdrawal to such a place was a hard price to pay for anger at the man who, he felt, had condemned him to live there. The son's anger against the father never entirely dissipated in his writing. The anger served as an ever-ready source of creative energy[23] and probably accounts for the cruelty he often projects on authority figures.

The artistic primary process self, by its tendency to merge into nothingness, undermines and gradually destroys the healthy self. Hence Kafka sees himself as exploring and exploiting death. "What an ordinary man occasionally wishes for, a writer like myself fantasies continually: He dies (or does not live) and continuously weeps for himself." Because he saw his existence as a writer as a game with death (L, 385), Kafka believed himself responsible for his tuberculosis. The diaries and letters are full of self-recrimination about the "childish-disgusting but successful game" (D II, 404) of feeding his own unhappiness, illness and writer's existence. The tone Kafka adopts toward this part of himself, which he calls his soul, recalls the narrator's irritated attitude to Josephine ("The soul obviously left the real ego but only became a writer, was not good for anything else; can the separation from the ego so weaken the soul?" L, 385). By 1922, in a letter to Max Brod, Kafka realized he could not redirect his drive to fusion and death. The life of a death-bound writer was one way of existence — madness was the other. The writer "must never leave his desk, if he wishes to escape madness, he must hold on to it with his very teeth" (L, 386). Josephine holds to her claims with the same desperation. Kafka saw little chance for himself, or that part of himself which was Josephine, to relinquish the death drive. The same drive appears more explicitly in the hunger artist's hungering.[24]

Kafka's intention of portraying the orientation toward death of the primary process becomes clearer if we understand the mouse as a symbol in his literary tradition and personal history. I have already referred to Josephine's piping calling to mind Mephistopheles' rat song.[25] A personal meaning of mice supplements the literary one: shortly after his tuberculosis was diagnosed and he was advised to go south for treatment, Kafka moved to the Bohemian countryside and spent the winter of 1917 on a farm with his favorite sister. When cold weather came, field mice moved into the house and Kafka panicked. The language in which he described the mouse phobia reveals that he projected on the mice his fear of his illness. In a specific reference to leaving it to "psychoanalysts...to find out where the fear comes from" (L, 207), Kafka seems to be begging to be relieved of self-deception about the seriousness of his illness. What frightened him about the mice was their "secretive appearance...together with a feeling they had undermined a hundredfold all the walls" (L, 205). The connection between undermined walls and his body eaten away by bacilli is strong and unmistakable. Kafka is describing, without knowing it, his imperceptible and irresistible drift into death. The mice phobia externalized the fear, making it tolerable because it allowed action. He sought relief by trying to exterminate the mice and by moving into his sister's room. As with all phobias, the attempts were debilitating because they prevented him from understanding his actual situation (dying of tuberculosis in a cold, damp farm) and taking appropriate action by moving south.[26] In making his last artist a mouse, Kafka transformed the phobia of his early illness and his unconscious fear of death into a conscious working through of the fear of death.

The narrator does not see Josephine's demonic drive entirely negatively and speaks of her rising, in death, "to the heights of redemption" (376). This optimism becomes clearer if we link Kafka's story to the singing creatures of Midrashic paradise. In that realm, before the fall of man, all creatures sang in praise of the Lord.[27] It is in terms of this Hebraic tradition of the mouse in paradise that we should see Josephine's demand for freedom from work, for paradise was a state traditionally associated with freedom from toil. If the mice of the story recognized the demand, they would proclaim Josephine a creature of paradise. Art viewed in this manner is a way out of mousehood. When Josephine maintains that she sings, she is maintaining that she is of paradise and mediates to the mouse folk this state, which would otherwise be lost to them. The existence of paradise in the midst of life, as a potential state of bliss, was a notion familiar to Kafka (H, 34). Josephine's song provides a temporary paradise for the people. During her performances they are "set free from the fetters of daily life;" at peace, they can dream of a lost happiness (370). From her mediatorship of these states, Josephine derives her claim to be her people's savior (366) and establishes a link to the Romantic tradition — the artist as savior. Kafka, of course, was familiar with this tradition of the German *Künstlernovelle*.

Josephine and the Mouse Folk

As a representative of the primary process, Josephine is dominated by the pleasure principle. This brings her into conflict with the mouse folk who have characteristics of the superego or, more precisely, of a precursor of superego functions or of an archaic social self.[28] At the same time, the mouse folk demonstrate what it means to be a mouse, and what it is that Josephine and the narrator wish to escape.

The relationship of Josephine to the mouse folk is of supreme importance to both. It is the only relationship either has. Josephine is their only artist and only charge; they are her only public. Without the mouse folk, Josephine goes downhill (376); without her, the mouse folk have no music. Josephine is said to have "enormous influence" (361) over the folk, but they do not listen to her demands. Though they deny her art is different from their habitual piping, they always gather around Josephine to listen. In spite of their "enthusiasm and applause" (363) Josephine believes "she is singing to deaf ears" (363) and she is quite right, they are unmusical. Nevertheless she sings for them most of her life.

Josephine wants unconditional, unlimited admiration, that is, unlimited control, but the mouse folk cannot give anything and refuse even an empathic recognition of her struggle. "The people listen to her arguments and pay no attention" (372). The "people show...their cold, judicial aspect" (372), "stony, impenetrable." Josephine's attitude is that of the small child who has a temper tantrum, but the mice are unresponsive like a father "deep in thought turning a deaf ear to a child's babble" (374). In the course of the story Josephine's demand (372) becomes a struggle for a right (373-374). Her intensification of the struggle is not matched by increased effort of the mice.

The narrator repeatedly insists on the mouse folk's paternal attitude to Josephine (372). However, since mouse children are expected to fend for themselves early, the author asks if the people are "fitted to exercise such paternal duties" (365) and answers his question affirmatively, that they perform "at least in this case, admirably." If the reader suspiciously asks what the care consists of, he finds that the people provide nothing for Josephine. They are the mass against which her voice resounds, the obstacle against which she vainly tests her strength. Unwilling to let her dominate them, they frustrate her. They neither feed nor warm her, although she gives them a symbol around which to gather in warmth and comfort.

In their all-encompassing, judicial, prohibitive role, the mouse folk's impact on Josephine seems negative only. Their impassivity increases her desperation and freezes her in opposition. Yet the struggle has a positive effect, for it makes her individual, dramatic, inspired by heroic effort. Giving her an unavoidable task, the struggle makes her strong and gives her identity. The mouse folk, lacking such challenge, have no desire to develop individuality. They are matter-of-fact, "love slyness," indulge in continuous "childish whispering and chatter" (365). Well defended against Josephine's song by sociability and toughness, they represent a self which continually utters superficial injunctions, and thus obscures other calls. Such a social self is frustrating and irritating to the sensitive, self-conscious artist because of its ubiquitous ordinariness. It is precisely this ordinariness from which Josephine escapes with her song, this incessant chatter which she silences, the continuous activities of unreflective existence which she stops, in order to give them a taste of her paradise. But she succeeds only for brief intervals. She would like to put a stop to this existence of the social self forever, hence her persistence.

Many details of the relationship between Josephine and the mouse folk reflect Kafka's relationship to his parents, both introjected and external. As Josephine remains dependent on the mouse folk, Kafka remained in his parents' home until his last year. The mouse folk's "bed of the people" (370) recalls Kafka's remarks on his parents' marriage bed (the "marriage bed of my people," L, 182). The aimless chatter of the mice reflects his complaint (D I, 114) about the family uproar at the nightly card game. Mice characteristics such as thoughtless sociability, materialism, tough shrewdness, survival ethics, were, in Kafka's mind, those of his parents. They never acknowledged a work of his: "Put it on my bedside table" (LF, 87), was his father's acknowledgement of the *Country Doctor* volume Kafka dedicated to him. So the mice ignore Josephine's art. As the strength of the mouse folk is enormous (365), so Kafka felt the strength of allied father and mother. As parent imagos they were totally negative and lacked any capacity to understand the child's physical and emotional needs (cf. the father's abuse of power in the pavlatche incident, which Kafka describes in LFa as his only precise early memory; there the father carried the feverish, complaining boy onto the balcony to get him to stop crying for water). Because of the father's total lack of empathy, competence and power appeared to the child only as abuse of both. During his life, Kafka increasingly came to see his parents as representative of modern Western Jews, against whom he set his admiration for Eastern Jews and his interest in the national movement. From the point of view of the Jewish nationalist Kafka became, the Western Jew appears superficial, yet possessed of enormous vitality, rootless, without traditions, intent on material survival. The Josephine story thus represents not a general but a very specific national-political view of Western Jews.[29]

Without the mouse folk Josephine cannot sustain life: her road must go downhill. The people, however, "continue on their way" (376). Kafka must have felt that he could not sustain his own artist self without fighting parental tyranny or seeking parental approval. He was not financially dependent on his family: like Josephine "not work-shy" (372), he provided for himself. Although he told his father, "My writing was all about you," he rejected the father's charge of emotional and physical "parasitism" (LFa, 125) by claiming that he had internalized the father's point of view and thus was sufficiently punished. At the time of writing the *Letter* Kafka accepted internalization, the attendant self-accusation and self-mistrust, as permanent conditions. By confessing this acceptance, he hoped to "reassure us both a little and make our living and our dying easier" (LFa, 125).

As appears from the story, Kafka's precondition for artistic production was to be locked into an inner struggle between Josephinean self and parental self. Josephine sings only in relation to the mouse folk. When Kafka withdrew from his various attempts to marry with the excuse that marriage would interfere with his existence as a writer, he was correct. He would not have been able to produce literature so dominated by the father figure. Social self and artist self hold each other suspended; Josephine's art is bounded by this suspense, she is driven by it and finally driven to death by it. The social self, with its silent unresponsiveness colludes with the fusion drive of the artist. In *Josephine,* the framework of suspense between artist and social self is reinforced by another, the narrator's. Until recently, his perspective has been overlooked by Kafka criticism.[30] For a Kafka character, he takes an active role, mentioning himself and his point of view nine times.

The Narrator

As an actor in the story, the narrator plays the role of the ego, standing between libidinal artistic and superego functions. Where he identifies himself as "I" he does so in terms of ego functions, of thinking (360), noticing and speaking (362,366); as an oppositional (362), impressionable (365), disbelieving (373), unknowing and unnoticing (374), observing (374), and fancying (375) part of the self. Shaping the narrator, Kafka held to a rationalist view of the ego and specifically excluded its emotional functions. The narrator defends against emotions or censors them: they have no place in consciousness and remain repressed, ego alien, restricted to Josephine and the mouse folk, keyed into their actions and outside the narrator's and Kafka's control. It should be said immediately that this blockage of emotion from expression, hence differentiation and growth, this emotional poverty and deprivation, make Kafka's art unredemptive for him.

The narrator is "half in sympathy" (362) with the mouse folk's opposition to Josephine and half in sympathy with her. When close to Josephine during performance, he becomes one of many under her sway. When "at a distance" (363) he can reason about her and judge her. He cannot feel what Josephine's music portends, but has "thought" about what it means (360). By claiming to be only half in sympathy with Josephine and referring to his rational functions only, he pretends to an objective point of view, reinforcing this pretension by continuous use of the plural, "our singer," of factual information, "we all pipe," or impersonal constructions, "There is no one but is carried away" (360). His is the pose of the omniscient chronicler.

Like Josephine, the narrator is distinct from the other mice. An intellectual interested in exploring the nature of music, mousehood, the role of art and the artist for a repressed people, he has differentiated himself from the mass. His interests parallel Kafka's early involvement with the Yiddish theater ("Speech about the Yiddish Language," 1911), his sporadic interest in aesthetic questions and philosophy, his preoccupation with the Jewish national movement, and his identification with, but partial rejection of Western intellectual Jewry. As we have seen from analyzing the story's structure, the narrator as essayist and aesthetician makes a closely reasoned argument covering, in cohesive, logical manner, all important points of a theory concerning the function of art and artist in a society.[31]

A realist who accepts the hardships of mouse existence without self-pity (it is instructive to compare his attitude to Kafka's remarks about encounters with antisemitism, cf. H 419, LM, 47-48), he shows a deep and sympathetic understanding of "mousehood" psychology, e.g., the connection between their lack of a childhood and childish-ness. It is especially instructive to compare the narrator's description of the demand for schools among the mice with Kafka's sponsor-ship of the Jewish primary school in Prague *(Letters,* 463). Like the narrator, Kafka felt that his people had to do without the ego strength resulting from an education of their own, and like the narra-tor, felt he had been deprived of childhood. The only positive expres-sion of feeling in the story, the narrator's description of "swarms of our children, merrily lisping or chirping...rolling or tumbling along... rosy with happiness" (368-369) recalls Kafka's encounter with chil-dren of Eastern Jewish immigrants at the Müritz colony (L, 436). Like Kafka himself, in the opinion of his friends Brod or Janouch, the narrator is an unassuming character dedicated to recording and speculating on Josephine and the people. He neither glorifies nor derogates himself. He is clear, concise, inventive in argument, hypotheses, and speculations regarding his subject. He has an absorbing interest in aesthetics and language, while Josephine's is restricted to music. To better understand the relationship between Josephine and the narrator, we need to look at the media, music and literature, in which they express themselves.

Kafka considered himself unmusical, distrusted the effects of music, yet made several of his artists musicians and wrote some of his most moving words about the effects of music.[32] He explained his distrust to Janouch in terms which contrast music to writing and thus elucidated the narrator's as well as Josephine's art.

> Music creates new, subtle, more complicated, and there-fore more dangerous pleasures... But poetry [that is verbal art] aims at clarifying the confusion of pleasures, at rais-ing them to consciousness,... humanizing them. Music is the multiplication of sensuous life; poetry, on the other hand, disciplines and elevates it.[33]

Kafka's distrust of music derived from an extraordinary sensitivity to sound, amounting sometimes to a phobia.[34] He described this to Janouch:

> Everything which lives reverberates. Everything which lives makes sound. We only hear part of it. We don't hear our circulation, the dying and growing of our body cells, the sounds of the chemical processes. Nevertheless, the cells of our organism, our brain, nerve and muscle fibers are

inundated by inaudible sound. They resonate with our
environment. The power of music results from this. With
music we can achieve deep resonances in our emotions.
We use musical instruments for that purpose... the builder
of musical instruments must build instruments which raise
into human consciousness otherwise inaudible and unfelt
resonances. (Janouch, 111-112)

The musician, penetrating the physical basis of life, has greater
power over men than the writer. This echoes Schopenhauer's
theories of music as an oceanic art, an objectification of will, leading
into the unindividualized life-force and hence into personal death.

The Janouch passage indicates why Kafka's sensitivity to sound
must have been painful, and music threatening. During times when he
suffered from sound sensitivity, Kafka felt helpless to stop the
sounds.[35] But a musician or builder of instruments, unlike Kafka,
understands the affective meaning system of musical language, and
how to organize emotionally meaningful sounds. He thus can make it
ego-syntonic, and control his aural receptivity. Lacking training, with
a defensive attitude, Kafka had no way to regulate the emotions
aroused by his receptivity. But he knew how to use language to control sensory or psychic stimulation, as his comments on writing show:
"writing... is a seeing of what is really taking place,... a higher type
of observation,... the more independent [of reality] it becomes, the
more obedient to its own laws of motion, the more incalculable, the
more joyful, the more ascendent its course" (D II, 212). The narrator
represents the verbal, rational, emotion controlling part of Kafka's
being as an artist. The split into several selves which Kafka
describes in diaries and stories is, in *Josephine,* not into Kafka's
usual dichotomy between artist and bourgeois, writer and lawyer,
ascetic and bridegroom, but a division into two kinds of artists.
Josephine, through music, represents the artist's primary process;
the narrator through verbal art portrays his secondary process. Both
are sufficiently individualized to enable us to recognize Kafka's own
traits in each. Only both together make up the particular kind of art
that Kafka ever more consciously produced: thus the two figures are
dependent on each other. Josephine's existence would go unnoticed if
not for the narrator, who brings her into our consciousness. But the
narrator is equally dependent on Josephine, for he has no other subject. While Josephine, being primary process, cannot and does not

recognize the narrator, he, being secondary process, can know her, but only defensively, imperfectly, with reservations. The narrator's attempt to tell her story, although it makes her live for us, is an attempt to control her by language, and to censor her. The tension between the narrator and Josephine results from his nervousness over his insufficient defenses against her tyranny. His narrative method and his treatment of Josephine as a theme are permeated by defensive strategies.

In the first paragraph of six sentences the narrator outlines the overall relations between Josephine, the mouse folk, and her art. Except for the first sentence, "Our singer is called Josephine" (360), all contain negations. This could be rephrased by saying that the narrator makes sixteen statements about his subject, thirteen of which are formulated negatively. Only three are positive statements: the singer is called Josephine, the mouse folk are cunning, Josephine loves music. The high number of negations continues in the rest of the story. Such insistence on the negative doubtless has some function. Freud's essay *On Negation* (1923) illuminates the narrator's use of negation.

> Negation...is already a lifting of repression, though not, of course, an acceptance of what is repressed. We can see how in this the intellectual function is separated from the affective process... *(Std. Ed.* 19, 236).

Negation in precisely the function Freud assigns to it is the main method used to explore a topic which causes the narrator discomfort. Questions and rhetorical questions have a function analogous to negation. But because affect remains repressed, it is a partial de-repression.

We appreciate the narrator's difficulties with his subject when we consider his first question about Josephine's art: if her singing is "in fact singing at all?" (361). Since he is a mouse and mice "are quite unmusical" (360), he cannot tell if her song is music. Like a tone-deaf person who appoints himself referee in a song contest, he lacks the means to judge. Consequently he must use secondary process means: questions, hypotheses, inference from past experience, conclusions drawn from available non-musical evidence; an awkward procedure. His limitations as rational self (he can only think, not feel) impose a severe handicap. Kafka fully exploits the potential for irony given with the narrator's limitation.

Attempting to decide whether Josephine's music is singing or piping, the narrator infers from past mousehood tradition that there is
in fact a difference between their present piping and ancient song. He
surmises that Josephine's art may be singing, but, by the means he
uses, he cannot tell. Indirect evidence compiled from observation of
Josephine's performances does not lead much farther and hence,
through several arguments and paragraphs, he vacillates between singing versus piping. Finally, he offers a third possibility, the absurd
hypothesis that her song's effect may result from "the solemn stillness enclosing her frail little voice" (362). He debates these points
through several performances and, not having found a satisfactory
answer, poses another direct question: "What drives the people to
make such exertions for Josephine's sake?" (364), a question which
gives him the chance to report his observations of Josephine's effect
and argue from this to the importance of her art for the people. He
favors the psychological interpretation that Josephine's effect results
from the people's irrationality and childishness which sometimes
makes them abandon themselves recklessly to momentary pleasure,
that is, to Josephine. After more rhetorical questions, the narrator
concludes that Josephine's art, since it affects the people, must be "a
kind of piping" (370), and that it satisfies the people precisely
because it is piping and not singing. Having stated the mouse view,
the narrator rests his questions until the penultimate paragraph.

He begins the second part of the story, treating Josephine's struggle
for recognition, by qualifying the acceptance of Josephine's art he has
just made. "But from that point it is a long, long way to Josephine's
claim that she gives us new strength." In reporting Josephine's opinion that she gives the people strength, is beyond the law, etc. he is
working from hearsay, inferences and speculation. Questions become
indirect, subjunctives increase, and sentences grow more complex and
abstract than in the first part of the narrative. (Subjunctives average
five per page in the first part, and increase to eleven in the second).
Each of Josephine's claims or actions leads to more detailed refuta-
tions. The more Josephine demands of her audience, the more
numerous are the narrator's intellectual arguments and the greater
his effort to drown her out. The second half of the narrative thus
demonstrates a key contradiction in Kafka's poetics which Walter
Sokel recently described particularly well. For Kafka, "the author
should be nothing but the medium for what wants to be expressed; but

self-reflection [the narrator] steps between the inspiration and the act [Josephine], and dams up and pollutes the flow from within."[36]

Josephine's disappearance, which comes to the reader as a complete surprise, breaks into the elaborate edifice. The paragraph reporting her loss is brief. Short phrases are joined in simple factual sentences which effectively render the narrator's shock: "Josephine has disappeared; she does not want to sing; she does not even want to be asked; this time she has left us altogether."[37] In the concluding paragraphs the narrator resumes his arguments. He surmises that Josephine left to increase her power (376) and wonders how she was able to gain the power she had over the people, when she calculates so poorly. These surmises attribute his own motives and design to Josephine and thus betray his own struggle for control and power. He does not realize that her actions do not necessarily have a deliberate, calculated purpose. His final questions, all of which define Josephine's song in terms of its having been silence, imply that her art remains as much a mystery to him as her life and disappearance. Nevertheless, by the act of naming the mystery and its possible solutions, he formulates hope for Josephine and the mouse folk: they having an "eternal history," will endure; the memory of Josephine's song cannot be lost because it had always been silent and unrealized; it will remain an ever-present, realizable potential for paradise. Josephine will become part of myth and merge into "the numberless throng of the heroes of our people" (376). He thus charts a way out of death but is silent about his own fate. Since the portrayal of Josephine was his only task, we may surmise that his existence is wiped out with her death. A historian among a people who "are no historians" (376), he and his history will be forgotten. By formulating a hope for his people, he will live on. But from another point of view, that the narrator represents a consciousness which struggles against Josephine's and the people's death drive, his end is a tragic defeat.

The struggle between the narrator and Josephine repeats the pattern of conflict between Josephine and the mouse folk. In both, one partner is impervious and impassive: the mouse folk ignore Josephine's desires; she pays no attention to the narrator. They both imagine resistance, and intensify their efforts, Josephine becoming more dramatic, the narrator more complex. This amplification is not based on communication but its absence. To remain with the musical image, Josephine's growing insistence is an outward spiral of sound waves; the narrator reacts with more resounding defenses, and one drowns out the other, since there is a point beyond which amplification cannot go. All unknowingly, the mouse folk lose Josephine; the narrator loses Josephine, and Josephine loses both mouse folk and narrator. The lack of phasing between split parts of the self, the reactive quality of the parts in interaction, the lack of communication are characteristic of Kafka's art. Yet, the three hold together because of their struggle; without it, the self would disintegrate.

The narrator's deep loneliness reflects Kafka's own. His search for answers takes place without an audience for whom a message might be intended. Unlike the practice usual in novellas, he does not say why or for whom he writes. He does not care whether he is heard. His separation from Josephine, the mouse folk, or any other possible audience is such that it does not even occur to him to complain about his lack of resonance. (The ape of *A Report to an Academy,* with no audience of his kind, has at least a human audience.) Josephine's disappearance thwarts the narrator's exploration and costs his only foothold in reality, the narrative. This is how Kafka must have experienced his own approaching death, from the vantage point he had reached as an artist. He was surprised even though he understood it and had foreseen it.

The narrator's is, of course, not the only way of conducting an exploration. He believes himself in control of his material but is carried along by the struggle between Josephinean and mouse folk selves. To escape their sway, he would have to do two things: first, he would have to admit emotion, to feel; second, he would have to designate a fixed point where his narration should lead, decide which argument to support among the many he offers. Kafka's narrator never feels, makes such a decision, nor realizes it should be made. His way of conducting his exploration gives a clue to his indecisiveness. Not having at his disposal the tools to estimate whether Josephine sings or pipes (feeling would be an appropriate tool), he spends two-thirds of his account designing and discarding tools to measure her effect before deciding, "Of course, it is a kind of piping" (370). The hesitating manner shows that his trust in his tools is very weak.

A similar difficulty of decision arises from the narrator's own medium, historiography. The narrator is historian of a people who have no tradition of recording or transmitting history. The narrator's dilemma with the media of communication is therefore double: he lacks tools to understand and transmit the message. This reflects Kafka's unease about writing in the German language. Though the family during his childhood spoke the high German of the middle class minority, the servants he was left with during first language acquisition were Czech. He did not speak German consistently until he began primary school at six. At the family's store, Yiddish was spoken in addition to the other two languages. Schooling, literary training, and family aspiration rooted Kafka in German, but he felt uncommitted to any of the three tongues. Even as late as his fortieth year, he was making a serious attempt to substitute Hebrew for them. The linguistic dilemma reflects the cultural dilemma of the rootless intellectual during dissolution of the Austro-Hungarian Empire. Just as he had insufficient mothering and therefore insufficient trust in and capacity for feeling, he had insufficient bonding to a mother tongue. The hunger artist's hungering is only another metaphor for the problem. The difficulty of his artist heroes with their media adds to their problems in making decisions and results in unredeemed lives and unredemptive art. The three parts of the self coexist in exhausting struggle. What could make the creative process curative of rifts of the self?

In the course of life, a person comes upon values and truths about existence in the world and sooner or later finds and feelingly experiences a truth that matters. This truth gives direction to the life. Committing himself to this value, the person experiences, in a cathartic breakthrough, an alignment of the parts of the self toward the same aim, a new integration. By living this truth daily, the new aim gradually and often painfully changes the habitual alignment of the parts of the self. There have been, of course, ages during which the life-giving truth is a person's unquestioned birthright, provided by family, culture, religion. Kafka's artist, like other 20th century heroes, finds no past truths to commit himself to, and would have to shape his own.[38] He would then need to commit himself to the value, choose it over all others, live it, and bear the pain of change. *Josephine,* like other Kafka stories, is an existential work whose narrator-protagonist cannot feel, refuses to make the existential choice, does not experience a moment of breakthrough which might make commitment possible, and has only poor tools for fashioning values. By imperfect intellectual measurement, he finds several truths meaningful to him, but commits himself to none. Unless he is deliberately destructive, we must assume that he has good reasons for avoiding commitment.

The narrator's indecisiveness gives him several advantages. As his self-satisfied tone suggests, inventing new hypotheses concerning Josephine's struggle affords him pleasure. As Josephine's singing is a way out of mousehood degradation and hardship, the narrator's intellectual play is a way out for him. It also protects him from feeling Josephine's insistence. Furthermore, he is by no means indifferent to the power of the other combatant, the mouse folk, whose strength seems enormous to him (365). But the mouse folk have only a restrictive function, they furnish no positive ideals or orientation. We must conclude that he is as afraid of being overpowered by the mouse folk as of being overwhelmed by Josephine. To keep the two in opposition means security from emotion for him; it also assures his superiority. He can blame Josephine, speculate about her, moralize at her expense. As long as the struggle lasts and neither side wins, he has a subject. Since there is nothing but this task to sustain him, he must not allow it to end. Kafka's 1922 words to Brod come to mind: "the writer must never leave his desk if he wishes to escape madness, he must hold onto it with his very teeth" (L, 386). Thus the narrator continues to question and hypothesize even after Josephine's disappearance. The attempt to continue beyond her life maintains his power over fictional if not real events. His indecisiveness and continued arguments imply that he desires power as Josephine wants escape from mousehood limitations. By choice or commitment he would surrender his absoluteness and boundlessness. The illusion of omnipotence in a choice not made holds him under such a spell that he does not see that for the sake of omnipotence, he is sacrificing his life. The creative process of the artist burdened by the narrator's dilemmas as well as Josephine's is doubly unredemptive. The ego elaborates defensively on the fatal conflict of id and superego and, in the attempt to be superior to it, maintains the conflict, makes it irresolvable, and hardens the rifts between parts of the self.

We can gain further insight into the psychology of Kafka's creative process by rephrasing it in terms of Kohut's self psychology. The possibility of redemption through art, although it was a perennial hope for Kafka, was one he easily abandoned. The reason may relate to his rejection of Freud's theories. Kafka was aware of the central role of the father/son issue in his work and must have suspected that he used it to define himself. The father/son struggle gave him self-cohesion and his work a purpose. The struggle and the artistic work masked the lack of self-cohesion and the pain of deprivation which the self experienced in the preoedipal development stages. Kafka felt this lack as inner emptiness, ennui, insubstantiality. A Freudian analysis would soon have revealed the emptiness beneath the screen of the quasi-oedipal struggle and might have been a self-shattering experience. The struggle and its portrayal had a protective function against total self-disintegration. Kafka must have hoped to fill the inner emptiness with his artistic children, as indicated by the story allegorizing his oeuvre: *Eleven Sons,* 1917. In reality, literary creation was powerless to fill the emptiness because he used writing as a protective screen. Writing was a defense against marriage. Since he sensed his hopes for salvation by writing were futile, he often turned against writing and could easily be diverted by another screen, illness, which allowed remedy for early childhood deprivation by regression to the orality of infancy. Illness did not allow forward development but was a limiting, regressive solution. From 1922 on, when it was clear that he might die, Kafka tried to break through screens, and that is why the problem of the artist moved into the foreground of his work.

As author of *Josephine,* Kafka is in a different position from the narrator. After all, he created all three entities of the self, the conflicts between them, and the effect of the narrator. By completing the story Kafka made a choice and confirmed it by the act, rare for him, of sending it for immediate publication. He committed himself to saying what happens to a struggle and a holding off maintained as persistently as that in his own life. The story shows his awareness that, by relinquishing his omnipotence, he could have redeemed himself.

Josephine does not say what truth might have been salutary to Kafka or to the artist generally. Kafka restricts himself to analyzing what is wrong. The work differs from his other later works on the artist figure (*The Hunger Artist, The Investigations of a Dog,* and *The Burrow)* in possessing a clearly defined, well developed representative of ego functions and in presenting a completed point of view. *Josephine* represents Kafka's realization that his early death was not inevitable. The splitting of the parts of the self in an investigation could be clarifying and lead out of fatality. A representative of the conscious functions is defined by capacity for choice. Hence the introduction of a character like the narrator represents the realization that a choice made and held to (completing the story) resolved the conflict and provided a basis for new life and themes. If the tuberculosis had not been too advanced and the insight too late, Kafka's continued artistic career would have had to explore new themes in place of the father and the rebellious son. What they might have been appears from the Utopian plan the narrator describes (reflecting Kafka's involvement with Dora Diamant and the Zionist movement) to give children longer schooling, a more carefully tended childhood and a chance for stronger ego and self development. From *the breakthrough of emotion* in this passage, the speaker's enthusiasm and pride, his reference to children "rosy with happiness... merrily lisping and chirping" (369) we glimpse other possibilities of creation.

Summing Up

With *Josephine*, Kafka places himself in the long tradition of the artist story, with which he was intimately familiar. He continued the splitting of the artist figure into parts important to the creative process, and the quest pattern characteristic of the genre. The quest fails almost totally. His artists, as mice, occupy lower existential positions than earlier figures of the tradition, are meaner and more pathetic, have less dignity and power. They reflect Kafka's artistic self-conception of painful degradation and a deep division of the self, with irreconcilable, fatal, tragic-comic contradictions. They are lonelier than even Arthur Schnitzler's or Thomas Mann's alienated artists. Like earlier artist figures, they ask for confirmation and plead for understanding, but they receive less.

The medium of Kafka's last artists is defined by absence — hungering, neither singing nor piping, telling a history although denying that time, history or historians exist, being a writer but owning no language. The Kafka artist, without a sensuous medium, creates not out of love of the world[39] but out of negation. Having no valid medium and only inappropriate receptors of communication, Kafka's artist figures have less hope of establishing contact than their predecessors. Nevertheless, none gives up, and they make the lack of a medium and the poverty of their receptors into new sources of art. Theirs is creation at the edge of nothingness. Their effort highlights the constructive thrust of the creative process.

Like other writers, Kafka sees his art as coming from the unresolved oedipal struggle. In contrast to such writers as Mörike or Schnitzler, his was a pseudo-oedipal conflict which eventually proved fatal. Kafka describes this struggle in a manner suggesting that it was frozen into a ritual repeated at intervals with variations. It is fitting that Kafka should have seen a predecessor in Grillparzer's *Poor Fiddler* (LFa, 551; 574).[40] Kafka's narrator, like Grillparzer's dramatist narrator, records the struggles of an alter ego. There are some crucial differences. Grillparzer's dramatist has other subjects than the fiddler; Kafka's narrator has only Josephine. Grillparzer's dramatist addresses a Viennese audience. Kafka's narrator has none. Grillparzer's dramatist witnesses a catharsis, a breakthrough of emotion and tears, by telling the fiddler's story (and his own) and achieves a tenuous resolution of the conflict and integration of the parts of the self. Kafka's narrator remains split off with no hope of penetrating in feeling to the conflict's core. He does not realize why he tells Josephine's story; thus cannot claim his part in it. Through most of his life, Kafka's situation was like the narrator's. Writing gave him temporary release from inner pressures, but not enough to keep him alive.

VII
KATE CHOPIN'S *THE AWAKENING*:[1]
ENGULFMENT AND DIFFUSION

Up to this point of our inquiry, we have examined the patterns of creativity which authors from the Romantics to Franz Kafka ascribe to the heroes of their narratives about artists. Upon these heroes they project fears and wishes which concern their own creativity. The problem often involves their own survival as creative persons and the work turned into a self exploration. Often they attribute to their heroes their own aesthetic practices and theories. The recurrent pattern is that of the quest as Harry Slochower has described it in his *Mythopoesis*.[2] On the quest, the artist's creative process is activated by sudden, illuminating breakthroughs, experiences which contain elements of the heroes' unresolved self or oedipal problems. These breakthrough experiences open the floodgates of the primary process, unsettle the protagonist, and by casting him into a different environment, mood, time or cast of characters, nearly shatter his self integration. The experience is mysterious, usually misunderstood, sometimes terrifying and sometimes intensely pleasurable, always startling. All artists deal with these experiences by treating some aspect of them in their art. Why authors deal thus with the return of the repressed, what ego resources they mobilize, what histories they assign to different heroes, etc., all these factors vary. But there is always a basic pattern of an oedipal (or pseudo-oedipal) conflict in which a mother figure is the inspiring muse and in which a prohibiting father figure's blessing needs to be won by the creative labor.

When we consider artist stories by women writers about women artists we should expect to find a similar pattern.[3] The nuclear oedipal problem, however, should be of the female oedipal constellation. As we should expect, it is not simply a reversal of the male pattern.[4] There is, to be sure, a fatherly muse (e.g. George Sand's Corambe).[5] And the relationship to the father is essential for the woman's identification with intellectual-spiritual goals and often the girl's only access to the education needed for artistic pursuits. Based on the rough life history of 213 women writers, Elaine Showalter in *A Literature of Their Own*, from a sociological perspective, comes to a similar conclusion: "A factor that recurs with remarkable frequency in the background of these women (writers) is the identification with, and dependence upon, the father; and either the loss of, or alienation from, the mother."[6] And, to be sure the crucial, complex, and doubly dangerous relationship in the woman artist stories is that to the mother figure/mother figures. It is on the *problem* of the mother figures in Kate Chopin's *The Awakening* that I wish to concentrate.

The Artist and the Feminist Awakening

In looking at the work of some ninety women authors in the major Western literatures, I found only a few artist stories, almost all written in this century about performing artists. Up to the present generation of German women writers, no women artist stories were written in German speaking countries. Why are there so few woman artist stories and why only of performing artists? The artist story depends on a publicly recognized professional ego identity — that of poet, painter, composer, etc. Such a *public* identity was closed to women till the turn of the century when the feminists made possible a *publicized* female identity. Moreover, the artist story deals with an intensely self-conscious ego, requires an "engagement with feeling and a cultivation of the ego."[7] Women, especially German women up to the present, were required by the culture to negate their individuality. As Kate Chopin puts it ironically, *by training* women "esteemed it a holy privilege to efface themselves as individuals" (10). The feminist writers, who did not thus negate their egos and who had sufficient self-consciousness *(e.g.* George Sand or George Eliot) probably neither could nor would expose the precious identity and undermine it by the harrowing self-doubt and threat of disintegration a writer faces in writing an artist story. Kate Chopin's *Awakening,* on many other accounts an astonishing work, is a first and most remarkable sample of the woman artist story. The coincidence of two factors may be responsible for the genre's first appearance on the American literary scene. The feminist movement was strongest in the United States during its earliest phases because of the decisive role women played in frontier society. By need the frontier woman had to develop a strong identity. In addition, in the 1880s literary life of St. Louis (as in literary America elsewhere) the tradition of the self-conscious, tormented artist of German Romanticism in its Nietzschean transformation found enough resonance to stimulate discussion of the problem of art versus life. Kate Chopin brought a further qualification to an occupation with the genre in that her French mother's family mediated the tradition of late 18th century intellectual feminism to her.[8]

Chopin indicates by the very name of her protagonist, Edna, i.e., Hebrew for rejuvenation, that the heroine experiences a regressive and revitalizing process. Her last name Pontellier (pons = bridge), is an echo of Nietzsche (man as a bridge to the overman), and suggests there is also a forward development. Edna's awakening takes place as she spends her summer vacation at the Gulf coast with her two small sons, a company of Creole friends, and her New Orleans businessman husband, who visits for weekends. Edna's awakening is, in Chopin's words, a realization of "her position in the universe as a human being" (14-15), a sensuous, emotional, and spiritual rejuvenation at age twenty-eight. The awakening leads her into a fantasy love of young Robert Lebrun, into a questioning of her role as wife, mother, and mistress of a bourgeois household, into exploring an identity of her own as an artist by studying painting, into a casual love-affair, and finally into a separation from husband, children and family. Her attempt at self-realization fails when she drowns herself by swimming out to sea.

Contrasting Mother Figures and their Effect

Throughout the narrative Edna associates with two other women. The first is a professional pianist, Mademoiselle Reisz, whose name means charm or tear, an artist whose performance arouses "a fever of enthusiasm" (27) and whose likeness to the Romantic conception of the artist as child is ironically indicated by her diminutive size and by her fondness for chocolates. She is no longer young, "a disagreeable little woman" (26), misshapen, graceless, with no taste in dress and with an artificial bunch of violets always pinned to her hair. For Edna, the author, or any woman, she is no ego ideal but an ego horror. Nevertheless, *she* is the mistress of the artist's dilemma, the successful artist who is so frequently a counter figure to the failing artist hero of artist stories.

Adele Ratignolle is the second woman, who is the mother woman Edna is not. Her name meaning "root — source" indicates that she plays an important role in Edna's awakening as root, source and mother figure. Chopin portrays her ironically as a "sensuous Madonna" (13) with "spun-gold hair,...blue eyes,...lips that pouted,...a little stout" (10). Edna's interaction with both women is essential to an insight into the sources and the failure of her attempt at human and artistic growth.[9] The splitting of the mother figure into two aspects of the maternal reveals Edna's ambivalence to mothers and corresponds to a male artist's characteristic split of the father image into a good and a bad father. Mademoiselle Reisz is a phallic mother who entices Edna into a fantasy, while Madame Ratignolle is the constraining mother.

Through two pregnancies and painful childbirths, through the daily and poor managing of a prosperous household, Edna's life has been a comfortable, somnambulist conformity to middle class southern mores, in the manner of Madame Bovary. During adolescence, to be sure, she indulged in fantasies of passionate love for unobtainable heroes, but at her marriage she resigned them, finding refuge from their "excessive and fictitious warmth" (20), in her fondness for her husband and in a dignified place in reality. Her husband, addicted to club and business, has not insisted on closeness with her and neither have her children.

Edna's reserve gradually breaks down during that relaxed summer at the shores of the gulf in the society of the Creoles with their "entire absence of prudery," their "freedom of expression" about matters of affection and sex, in their being "like one large family" (11). The relaxation of limits, the oceanic fusion with others and with nature, dominates the first section of the narrative in the ever present image of and allusions to the sea: "The voice of the sea is seductive;

never ceasing, whispering, clamoring, murmuring, inviting the soul to wander. ... The touch of the sea is sensuous, enfolding the body in its soft, close embrace" (15). The personification *(touch, embrace)* makes the sea into an all-mother. At this point of the narrative Edna is undifferentiated, vague, uncertain of her feelings, and ambivalent about what is happening to her. Expressions like "she could not have told why" (14) or she "never knew precisely what to make of it" (13) are characteristic of her.

Edna seeks for a center in all this vagueness and confusion (which we might liken to an infantile stage of undifferentiatedness) and finds it in the motherly and solid Madame Ratignolle who protects her (the incident where she warns Robert), who teaches her (the incident where she shows her how to sew for the children), who listens to her confessions (the incident where she reveals her childhood world to the older woman), and who is the subject of her first attempt to express herself artistically (the incident where she paints Adele's picture). How little Edna can differentiate herself from the mother figure appears in her failure to achieve a likeness, for to make a portrait of someone means after all to see the other as other. Edna, despite "natural aptitude" and "a certain ease and freedom" with which she handles the brushes (13), cannot produce a recognizable likeness of Adele. However, the intimacy with Madame Ratignolle over painting and confession, "the subtle bond" between the two women, "which we might as well call love" (15) *increases* Edna's openness and diffusion. At this point in the narrative it is only in connection with the sea that this openness appears as a source of danger. In the sea the soul can "lose itself...in abysses of solitude" (15).

The opening up begun by environment and by her love for Madame Ratignolle is completed by Mademoiselle Reisz who, one evening, plays some Chopin preludes for Edna. It is surely not mere chance that the author attributes the final breakthrough experience to the good offices of her namesake composer. Edna's previous experience of music has been visual, conventional allegories of emotion (that is secondary process elaborations); Mademoiselle's music tears away the veil of images, Schopenhauer's veil of Maja, and opens her to primary process: "the very passions themselves were aroused within her soul;" and now note the language which describes the music's action on her, "swaying it, lashing it, as the waves daily beat upon her splendid body" (27). Her awakened emotions and the waves of the sea fuse, and it is therefore not surprising that she, who all through the summer could not learn to swim because a "certain ungovernable dread hung about her when in the water" (28) at that evening's swimming party can trust the element, can swim and "control the working of her body and her soul" (28) in the water.[10]

Edna uses her newly found mastery in the element in a way which remains characteristic for her. Rather than stay with the group of friends cavorting in the water, she scorns their closeness. She wishes to swim to "where no woman had swum before" (28). This means Edna uses her newly found mastery and control over her body to get away from closeness with others. And she directs herself to achievement (where no woman had swum before). It is not in competition with males; her achievement is to move her away from the others who represent the family and ultimately the mother. While in the maternal element, she exploits the element to affirm herself. The case of Mademoiselle Reisz' use of art shows us that this, for the woman artist, is the successful and productive way of managing the maternal element.

The Artist as Woman

Edna diverts the energy released by her awakening into a quest for a lover, but her love for Robert quickly turns into fantasy in the Edenic dreamlike adventures of their day together after the awakening. Moreover, as his last name Lebrun indicates, with its echo of the 17th century French court painter Charles le Brun, Robert is the artistic alter ego of Edna, the representation of her artistic interest and of little importance as a character in his own right. When Robert leaves for Mexico, Edna's artistic inclination becomes independent of him and flourishes. She returns to town where she employs her energies in an exploration of her position, of her talents, and of her environment. Her earlier dabbling in sketching becomes an attempt at self-definition but also a search for and gratification of a fusion experience. It becomes an activity which parallels her swimming and is spoken of in similar language. Her artistic experience contrasts with Mademoiselle Reisz' professionalism on the one hand and with Adele Ratignolle's amateur piano practice "on account of the children" (25) on the other. Like other artist heroes, Edna is unaware that her attempts to paint like her other explorations are undertaken to make egosyntonic the emotions and sensuousness released by the awakening experience. Edna shares with Mademoiselle Reisz and with other artist figures a restlessness, intrusiveness, love of motion (physical, emotional, and intellectual) which contrasts sharply with Madame Ratignolle's placidity, and domesticity. To appreciate the difference between Edna and Mademoiselle Reisz, let us examine how the professional artist uses her artistic gift.

From the beginning of their acquaintance, Mademoiselle Reisz has played for Edna at Robert's invitation. It is to feel in touch with Robert, therefore, that Edna goes to see the pianist in town. Mademoiselle Reisz deliberately fuels the passion of the lovers. Her play with and for Edna during Edna's visits to her studio is a fine example of skill in artistic seduction and of symbolic fusion with the seduced. Let us observe the sequence in which she arranges her "play." She raises Edna's expectations about a letter she has received from Robert, hinting that the letter is all about her, yet refusing to show it. She prepares her performance by mentioning that Robert likes her rendering of Chopin's *Impromptu* and has asked her to play it for Edna. She flatters Edna, wins her trust and solicits a confession, challenges the confession and then hands the letter over and begins to play. She settles into the performance with improvisations of her own, glides into Chopin, melts the *Impromptu* "with its soulful and poignant longing" into "the quivering love notes of Isolde's song" (64), and fades back into the Chopin and rounds out with her own improvisation. Her success at emotional manipulation is confirmed for her by the tear-stained letter she finds after Edna's leaving and by Edna's return visits. Mademoiselle Reisz feeds on the lovers' fantasy, makes herself part of it by her music, and manipulates it and them.

Both Edna and Mademoiselle Reisz seek a symbolic fusion experience; Reisz, however, asserts herself in it. The difference between them appears in their respective attitudes to sea and water. Edna loves to swim once she has mastered the skill; Mademoiselle Reisz never goes to bathe all summer. Reisz has, as the narrator jokingly comments, "the natural aversion for water...believed to accompany the artistic temperament" (48). Mademoiselle Reisz, however, does use water; she uses it for boiling the chocolate with which she regales herself and Edna. But she would not dream (especially not dream) of swimming in it. The artist knows that she needs extraordinary ego resources to help her maintain mastery in the coveted fusion experience; such resources as self-assertiveness, honesty about her own (and others') motives and what she calls "the courageous soul" (63). But the artist must also have such defenses as Mademoiselle's self-limitation. She, after all, exposes herself to very limited experience — to emotional stimulation from Robert and Edna only, and that in small doses. Hers is an economical passion which she administers in narrow confines indeed while Edna's, appropriately symbolized by bird flight and sea image, is unlimited. Mademoiselle Reisz knowing the risks Edna takes, appreciates the difference between them when she says in warning, the "bird that would soar above the level plain of tradition and prejudice must have strong wings" (82). Edna cannot profit from Mademoiselle Reisz' insight because she can neither respect nor emulate her. In fact, Edna lacks a positive, purposeful human influence.

A word needs to be said of the relationships to her parents which Chopin attributes to Edna, a history which is admirably consistent with Edna's psychological liabilities. Edna is the second of three daughters whose mother died when she was quite small. Her older sister assumed the role of the mother and must have restrained her sisters in the narrow, traditional female role. She was, unable to provide her younger siblings with the warmth they needed (Edna's reserve derives from lack of mothering) and with the guidance they required (Edna's constant fighting with her younger sister speaks for lack of adult control over the children). Edna is a person still much in need of mothering and hence finds it impossible to care consistently for her own children. This need makes her susceptible to the domination of mother figures; it inspires her with a strong yearning for and yet simultaneous fear of human closeness. Edna's father was not able to compensate his daughters for their loss. He is a contradictory person. Though a stern Presbyterian, he is self-indulgent (his toddies), and interested in appearances only (his padded shoulders). Though he supports Edna's artistic inclination (it confirms his excellence as a father), he has not provided her with consistent and disciplined purpose. As appears from his gambling at the races and the resulting loss of his Kentucky farm lands, he has his own fantasy under poor control and can therefore not provide Edna with a sufficiently strong drive toward self-control and mastery.

The Woman Artist and her Opposite, the Mother

What is it then, in the events of the story, that is responsible for Edna's inability to deal with the awakening experience? Let us return to the beginning of Edna's awakening and her relationship to the maternal Madame Ratignolle, of whom, by the way, she *sees* more in the novel than of any other character (nine times to Robert's eight). The themes of Madame's pregnancy and impending delivery dominate the novel as much as Edna's self-realization. The growth of the child in the womb is paralleled by the increase in Edna's sense of self, independence and expressiveness. The birth of the child coincides with the death of Edna's self. Just before the birth, Edna seemingly is at the height of her powers; she has won Robert (her initiative), she has won commissions for paintings (103), and she has claimed the right to her own person. "I give myself where I choose" (107), she tells Robert. Nevertheless, in actuality she has grown increasingly isolated, with the departure of her father, her husband and her children. She is therefore all the more sensitive and exposed to the only tie with reality which she has, namely with Madame Ratignolle. Kate Chopin depicts with fine psychological perceptiveness this gradual loss of anchoring in the social reality which is characteristic of the life experience of a suicide.

Edna *is* tied to Madame Ratignolle. How strongly so appears from her immediate response to the latter's call to be with her during the impending delivery of her fourth child. Edna goes, even though she is called from a long awaited meeting with Robert, a meeting she does not want to leave. Once at the Ratignolle's she feels useless, even in the way, yet she does not return to Robert. And a long and torturous delivery it is. Unlike Madame Ratignolle who obviously luxuriates in her pregnancies, Edna, having been unawakened emotionally during her marriage, has not felt the union and fusion experience of conception and pregnancy, has not felt biological creativity, nor the joy over a child born. She has only experienced, during her deliveries, pain, stupor, anesthesia, and an awakening to an alien life to be cared for. She states her detachment candidly. A "new life...added to the great unnumbered multitude of souls that come and go" (109), she muses about the children she has given life to. Madame Ratignolle insists all through the delivery that Edna stay. We know from a conversation of the two women on the preceding day, that Madame disapproves of

Edna's bid for freedom and wishes to recall her to her duty. Her making Edna stay through the birth ordeal and her twice repeated, "Think of the children" (109) at its end are intended as an object lesson to Edna, an object lesson that says to Edna: This is what it means to be a woman: pain and suffering and sacrifice for the children. This at least is how Edna understands it when she accepts the lesson "like a death wound" (110).

To experience birth is, of course, in a sense to experience the original trauma of rejection and separation. It is in this sense that Edna experiences Madame Ratignolle's words: they are a total rejection of the artist Edna has become and wants to be. Given Edna's experience of childbearing, unrewarding as it has been, Madame's having her watch the "scene [of] torture" (109) and then condemn her to that role amounts to a deathblow. Edna loses, at the Ratignolle childbirth, the mother who was the source of her awakening. With having renounced her children earlier and with Robert (who represents her art) being gone when she returns to her own quarters, Edna is left without recourse to deal with her death wound. Hence her lapse into shock, for during the last pages of the novella she has ceased to feel. She retreats ever deeper into fantasy, into a fantasy in which the ocean represents the unlimited and unlimiting mother (hence the narrator's repetition of the earlier sentence evoking the enticement of the element, the "touch of the sea is sensuous, enfolding the body in its soft, close embrace," 113). Lost in this fantasy, Edna does not feel the cold of the water but only the "soft embrace" she wishes to feel.

There is, of course, and that is much like in other artist stories, a third artist in the story, namely the author-narrator. Her perspective is omniscient. She is a distinct character, who tells of her sympathies (they are with Edna), who expends her irony on all characters, and who identifies mostly with Edna. The narrator is conscious of the literary tradition of the artist story, of Schopenhauer, Wagner, and Nietzsche,[11] of contemporary feminism, of the historical situation of the Reconstructionist South.[12] But above all, she is in complete control of her craft. Since she contains both artists of the story, she triumphs over the limitations of the one and the tragic downfall of the other.

The Author and her Protagonist

Kate Chopin's own situation as an artist was like Edna's and yet very different. Like Edna, Kate was married and had children. Unlike Edna, Kate Chopin was a resourceful person, taking to writing after her husband's death with the intent to supplement family income and to counteract depression.[13] Unlike Edna, Kate had a strong and positive father identification, with a father who died when she was a precocious five year old. The memory of her father was kept alive by the kind of instruction in literature and thought which she was given by her French maternal great-grandmother. Like Edna, Kate Chopin, during the years of her marriage, concentrated on the life of her family. Unlike Edna, Kate maintained a strong and steady commitment to intellectual activities and writing. Devotion to school, to writing and to intellectual pursuits freed Kate from the depressions she suffered in her teens after the loss of her great-grandmother and her favorite brother. In her thirties, after the deaths of her husband and her mother, she once again turned to writing, participated in the intellectual life of St. Louis, and published steadily. During the 1890's she built up a considerable reputation as an author and there is in her stories from 1889-1899 a gradual gain in narrative mastery and in boldness of theme. Increasingly she wrote from a frank, sensual and even sexual female perspective. At its publication in 1899, *The Awakening,* with its outspoken and sympathetic portrayal of a woman's relinquishment of her role as mother and wife to develop herself as an artist, met with general condemnation as being morbid and obscene. Personal rejection by friends and acquaintances added to the injury. Nevertheless, Kate Chopin continued with some writing but — and this is the shame — it was writing with the spirit gone out of it, a few stories for adolescent girls' magazines like "Charlie." Early and repeated loss made Kate Chopin sensitive to the rejection of her reading public. The severity of their judgment silenced her independent voice.[14] She died a few years later, in 1905, at fifty-two, of a brain hemorrhage. In a sense, Kate Chopin's readers did to her (even though less dramatically) what Madame Ratignolle did to Edna.

Male and Female Artists

Let us provisionally note some differences between artist stories by male writers and Kate Chopin. Different roles are played by parental figures in the quest. For male heroes, the key incident of the story is an offense against the male authority figure. The heroine, in contrast, is constrained by a female authority figure, or caused to regress. There is greater preoccupation by the woman artist with fusion and symbolic fusion experience; this is what the female artist seeks in creativity and this is what she seeks to master. There is greater danger to the woman artist of passivity and regression. As we have seen at the beginning of our essay, the heroine begins (for Kate Chopin) with a weak ego and sense of self. She is easily tempted into fantasy and unreality (via Mademoiselle Reisz), or her ego's drive to self-realization, its self-directed forward drive, is easily curtailed as it is by Madame Ratignolle, and the ego driven back to earlier preoedipal stages.[15] Without internal and external checks against the backward regressive movement initiated by the constraining mother, the constraining mother becomes the engulfing mother. Under her dominion, form, expression, art, consciousness and self are dissolved and in her as oceanic mother life itself ceases. There is another difference; the male artist also seeks fusion experience with the maternal element but he sees it his main task to gain mastery over and to differentiate himself from a father. And his work of art is a symbolic recompense, an atonement to the father for his desire for merging. The woman's work of art as seen by Chopin is neither an atonement nor a recompense. It is an attempt to transcend the fusion experience and therefore its dangers by embodying it in form and by expressing it; it is an attempt to transcend the constraining and engulfing mother. The dangers which men and women writers encounter in their quest are different. The male artist encounters a violent father figure who threatens to punish his transgression violently and who sets clear and decisive limits. As punishing superego, the threatening father can and often does destroy the artist son. The constraining mother of the woman artist story is the equivalent of the threatening father but her anger at the daughter's striving is not overtly violent nor are the limits she sets clearly defined. Her diffuse anger leads to silence, negation of self, depression. Finally, in transcending the fusion experience the artist-son is helped by his identification with the father as representative of mastery, achievement in reality, forward direction. This identification is supported by both parents and the culture. A woman artist also needs identification with a representative of mastery to transcend the fusion experience, but it is an identification which neither the mother nor the culture easily tolerates. Yet this is what she needs if she is to deal successfully as an artist with her artistic capacity for diffusion of ego boundaries. She fails as an artist, as Edna does, if she does not have such an identification and support. To have such a strong and positive father identification and to seek such support even in adult life from older males was Kate Chopin's own androgynous solution to the woman artist dilemma. Mademoiselle Reisz', the phallic woman's solution, is another, less attractive possibility for safety from the engulfing mother; it is bought at the price of severe self-limitation and restriction of life. There are of course other possibilities of dealing with artistic experience by women and we will develop these from the analysis of another more recent woman artist story, Sylvia Plath's *The Bell Jar*. The existence of mother-daughter teams of artists like Mary Woolstonecraft-Shelley and Mary Shelley or like Sophie de la Roche who raised Bettina Brentano makes us hope that mothers who do not restrain their daughters from spiritual explorations do not hold the terror of the engulfing mother.

VIII
SYLVIA PLATH'S *THE BELL JAR:*
THE MALIGNANT SYMBIOSIS[1]

Kate Chopin's encounter with a hostile public over her novel and the effect of this rejection on her production shows how powerful the connection between work and author in and beyond creation may be in an artist. We have observed this connection and the effects of rejection of works on heroes and authors alike. We have also observed that, in the attempt to master ego-threatening materials, authors adopt a point of view separate from plot and hero. This adoption of a reference point can be the fiction of an autobiographer, or of an impersonal, omniscient narrator (Mörike) or of a narrator with a restricted perspective (Büchner), or of an editor and omniscient observer (Hoffmann). The reference point can be achieved by balancing characters or narrative elements (e.g., chapters, settings, key metaphors) against each other. Almost all authors play with point of view and achieve a considerable degree of complexity and irony by means of point of view. And this irony appears to be in the service of ego control of the material. We have also noted that the struggle with point of view is by no means always resolved. In Kate Chopin's *Awakening* character balancing and juxtapositions of locale and metaphors are ineffective in the final pages of the novel to convince us of the separation between heroine and author. In the lyrical passages which evoke the yearning for oceanic merger, the author herself appears to merge into the heroine. We may speculate that the rejection of the *Awakening* affected Kate Chopin so fatally because the relationship between heroine and author remained symbiotic beyond the creation of the work. How fearful such incomplete separation from the work can remain for an author we saw in Mörike's life and in his inability to produce further work. The questions of the struggle with point of view, of the separation from the finished work and of the influence of the finished work on the author draws our attention to the question of the work of art as a transitional object.[2]

The childlike artist, open as he is to breakthroughs of the primary process and hence to disruption of ego boundaries and the cohesion of the self, treats his materials (themes, form, medium, etc.) as transitional objects with which he plays, into which he invests, on which he projects and discharges libidinal and aggressive energies. Unlike the child, however, some artists (e.g., Hoffmann's Nathanael) are unwilling to discard the transitional object (completed works) once ego structures are reformed or object relationships re-established after a creative breakthrough. For the sake of remaining creative he may create havoc in his own and other lives. He may feel that he must let (voluntarily and/or involuntarily) creative energies flow freely between himself and his medium and/or work and never totally dedicate his energies to human relations. This withholding may make the artist appear cold, distant, manipulative, weak, unstable in his human relationships, although he may be extremely dependent on them. In addition, since his ego and self boundaries are hazy or fragmentary, he cannot tell where object relations end and where transitional objects and his invested energies begin. Therefore he may use others as mere means (the artist as exploiter; the power theme), but he may also be vulnerable to exploitative use by others and may imagine that he is so used. In all this flux, fear for the cohesion of his self may drive him (depending on his personal early history) from clinging to others to turning in on himself even while his energies remain freely flowing. It is early in his life that the firmest bond of his existence is established to a transitional object which gradually through environmental and parental influence becomes weighted with intellectual/emotional/cultural freight. The transitional object then becomes the center of his life, he structures his self (ego as well as libidinal/aggressive energies) as well as objects (persons meaningful to him) around the transitional object, i.e., his art. Hence the reception of the work of art by meaningful others (object relations) as well as feeling about the self (from self-esteem to ego weakness) will influence not only the shaping and manipulating of the transitional object (i.e., creation) but also its perception during and after creation. And since energies in the artist remain volatile, the created work remains in living interchange with its author, a Pygmalion if you will.

In all of us libidinal/aggressive energies are inextricably mixed. In fact, these energies crystallize into libidinal and into aggressive drives only in the course of human development. In states of deep regression, if the boundaries between self and transitional object blur, undifferentiated energies will ebb back into the artist's self, and the earlier the developmental stage from which the artist draws, the more undifferentiated they will be. A created work may therefore have a salutary as well as a destructive effect on its creator in regression. Sylvia Plath's novel *The Bell Jar* will occupy us in a further exploration of the woman artist and the role of the work of art as a transitional object. Plath's novel lends itself particularly well for this purpose, since the work became the receptacle of her anger against parental figures and expressly deals with her poet heroine's recovery from a suicidal crisis. She herself intended the work to have a therapeutic function, to help her, as she wrote, "to free myself from the past."[3] The pseudonym she chose for the novel (Victoria Lucas) indicates clearly that she thought that this purpose had been accomplished. Nevertheless the completed work did not contain the anger sufficiently, for shortly after the publication of her novel she killed herself at age thirty. Why the work in her particular case failed its therapeutic purpose becomes another of our tasks in this chapter. The task is all the more urgent as several critics maintain that her "suicidal art" endangered her and carried her too far into inner conflicts.[4] Sylvia Plath thus also becomes a good test case for an investigation of the danger of art as a tool in self-exploration and of the romanticized myth of the artist as a sacrificial victim to creation and hence to culture.

Autobiography and the Narrator

The Bell Jar is largely autobiographical. Sylvia's father, like that of her heroine Esther, died when she was nine. Like Esther, Sylvia spent the summer of 1953 in an apprenticeship with a women's journal in New York. Like Esther, Sylvia was confused and appalled by the city and failed to meet its challenge (e.g., *Letters Home,* 125-135).[5] Like Esther, Sylvia felt torn over the choice of having a career or being a woman; one option excluded the other. For both there were doubts about their adequacy as intellectual achievers and as women. Both returned from New York to the suburbs in depression. Sylvia's suicide attempt resembles Esther's down to the very clippings from the daily press. Both recovered from the depression in an asylum, being given psychotherapy and shock treatments. Both returned to college for the second semester of the school year.

The Bell Jar was long in the making. Plans for a novel on the subject of a student-poet's breakdown and recovery go back at least as far as the summer after the events (1954). Sylvia appears to have mentioned versions of it when she left Cambridge University, England, after her Fulbright years there (1955-1957).[6] She worked on the novel from May 1961 on, when she also applied for a fellowship to complete a novel *(Letters Home,* 491). She mentions it as largely finished in a letter to her mother of November 1961 *(Letters Home,* 513) and sent the completed manuscript to a London publisher by August 1962. We do not know what problems Sylvia had with composition, but it can hardly have been a difficulty with disciplined writing and sustained effort. She had after all been publishing fiction since high school.

We observed that in many of the authors we dealt with, the struggle with writing the story is a struggle with structure and point of view. As the work is an attempt by author and character alike to master unresolved conflicts by symbolic resolution, the difficulty for the author is to find a reference point beyond the conflict from which it can be resolved. As one device to indicate an order beyond the events (and hence an author who orders them), Sylvia Plath uses recurrent metaphors as well as splitting and paralleling of characters. For instance, the bell jar of the title appears in regular intervals in the novel; or the novel begins with an ominous reference to the electrocution of the Rosenbergs and ends, after the deadly potential of electric shock has been explored and gradually been transformed to a relief-giving significance, with a reference to the beneficial shock treatments which Esther has received. Each section of the novel is presided over by a different mother figure. The sections dealing with New York feature the relationship to Jay Cee, the successful and ugly editor at the journal. The section dealing with Esther's immediate past before coming to New York is dominated by Mrs. Willard, her boyfriend's mother. Esther's return home to the suburbs moves Esther's own mother into the center. During her illness and recovery, Esther's patroness, Mrs. Guinnea, and her psychiatrist, Dr. Nolan, move into the foreground. During the New York section, the American girl appears in several split off forms. One form is the intellectual New Englander, Esther; others are the sophisticated and decadent Southerner, Doreen; the Midwestern farm girl, Betsy, and the urban, vacuous and deadly hat maker, Hilda ("I'm so glad they're going to die," 82). In the final sections of the novel, Plath again splits off Esther's alter egos. Esther's anger against mothers is lobotomized in the figure of Valerie, who stays behind at the asylum, and is eliminated with the figure of Joan, who commits suicide. By paralleling and splitting off characters, devices of which we have mentioned only a few examples, Plath achieves a tightly controlled plot. All characters and incidents of the New York and suburban sections work towards the central suicide crisis. Esther's circle of life in these sections grows ever more constricted. In the asylum sections, Plath describes more briefly a gradual widening out again of Esther's circle of life.

Sylvia Plath also uses a narrator as a device to establish distance from the conflict. In the finished novel, the point of view of Esther, the heroine, is seemingly clearly differentiated from that of the narrator. The events of summer 1953 are reported in the past tense. Esther's major problems have been resolved by the narrator of 1961. Although Esther, at the end of the novel, wonders "who would marry me now that I'd been where I had been" — namely at the asylum — (197), the narrator has a baby and thus presumably is married (3). Although the heroine, whose main symptom was an inability to write and express herself, at the end of the novel has not yet resumed writing, the narrator has no difficulties with her story. Occasionally, at the beginning of the novel, the narrator falters with an "I guess" or "I think" about the accuracy of her impressions then (e.g., "I think the floor was pine-paneled, too," 12). But such uncertainties are minor, and they stop after chapter four. From then on, the narrator recounts in detail, without faltering and in the past tense.

The narrator, then, resolved Esther's problems about writing and her doubts about her role as a female. Her use of the present tense for a few characteristics of herself now establishes a link with the Esther of the past and the events of her breakdown, and a significant link it is. Then as now, Esther is appalled by *thinking* about violence and suffering violent death. ("The idea of being electrocuted makes me sick," 1). Then and now, she is jealous of "girls...with wealthy parents" (3). Then and now, she is demoralized when two people, a man and a woman, occupy themselves with each other, and she feels insignificant to the point of disappearing out of life (14). Now as then, she reacts to emotional trouble by withdrawing to a hot bath (17). Now as then, she loves food "more than just about anything else" (20). What emerges from this listing of stable characteristics is a person troubled and concerned by violence and death, with a wish to be taken care of by parents, not at ease about her relationships to the other sex, with a strongly developed orality and with a tendency to withdraw when troubled and to feel fully herself only when thus regressed. In fact, the longest and most empathic passage in the present tense in the book comments on this love of hot baths, "I never feel so much myself as when I'm in a hot bath... I feel about a hot bath the way...religious people feel about holy water" (17). These characteristics spell a weak ego with few and questionable coping strengths. The weaknesses are those that played a significant role in Esther's breakdown in the first place. At closer scrutiny, the narrator's solutions to the woman and career questions reveal themselves as superficial.

This conclusion means that Esther's and the narrator's points of view about events are only superficially different and that the device of the narrator does not really introduce a point of view beyond the events of the novel. What makes Sylvia Plath's novel so relevant to our purpose, despite (or rather because of) the lack of the differentiation between heroine and author is that it shows so clearly the reasons for the failure of the creative function in the heroine/author and the failure to work through a life crisis using a work of art. By observing the interactions in the novel, we can come to understand why the heroine fails to resolve her conflicts and why Sylvia Plath does not understand the meaning of her heroine's dilemmas. What then is the kind of world her heroine lives in and what are her conflicts?

The World of the Mothers

The Bell Jar of the title symbolically represents the mother's world — .the America of the 50s. It is a sterile, hygienic, mechanized world in which women in test kitchens in "flawless makeup of a uniform peach-pie color" prepare "technicolor meals" (21). It is a world of self-alienating practicality in which only money and achievement count. A measure of Esther's hunger for living sustenance appears in her insatiable appetite ("No matter how much I eat, I never put on weight," 20), an appetite that cannot be satisfied by "the richest, most expensive dishes." Esther's mother (like all mother figures in the novel) is a dominant woman, achievement-oriented, without warmth or love. She teaches shorthand in a city college (as did Plath's mother). She has been left unprovided for at the death of her professor husband, and she resents having to work. Hers are the values of the middle-class educated American — progressive, rationalistic, success-crazed. She scorns religion as much as feeling. Having found salvation from insecurity and loss in hard work, she believes activity is a cure for everything. "The cure for thinking too much about yourself" is "helping somebody...worse off than you" (132), she advises her troubled daughter. Rationalizations assist her in denying feeling. At her husband's death she "had just smiled and said what a merciful thing it was for him he had died, because if he had lived he would have been crippled and an invalid for life" (137). With denials like these she forces her children to repress their grief and eliminate the father from their life. In fact, she denies any emotion that might interfere with her upward drive and middle-class notion of propriety. Her response to Esther's mental illness is characteristic. "We'll act as if all this were a bad dream" (193) she tells Esther on her release from the mental hospital.

It is not only a feeling response which Esther misses from her mother, it is any kind of response to her as a separate person with needs and gifts of her own. The mother simply does not *see her*. When Esther returns from New York, for instance, her cheeks are bloodstained and she is wearing another girl's clothes. Her mother's only question, " Why lovey, what's happened to your face?" is satisfied with a brief "Cut myself" (93) and a silent withdrawal into the back seat of the car. The mother continues oblivious to her daughter's distress. Though she presumably knows Esther's ambition to be a writer, she tells her, turning "her back," "you didn't make that writing course" (93). She has no comprehension of a hope dashed, of "a bright, safe bridge over the dull gulf of the summer ...plummet[ed] into the gap," as the disappointment feels to Esther. Esther's mother is simply unable to reflect back to Esther a disappointment — or any feeling or reality.[7] Esther's reaction is instantaneous ("The air punched out of my stomach," 93) and she cannot acknowledge that she had a hope in the first place. "I had expected it," she concludes. But it is not only such confirmation which Esther lacks. As Mrs. Greenwood's oblivion to her daughter's rudeness suggests, she never insists on anything with Esther. Rather than demand, for instance, that her daughter get dressed that summer, she, as Esther sneers, would never "tell me to do anything. She would only reason with me sweetly" (99). To confront Esther, to draw a feeling response from her, to confirm or to disillusion an expectation, is simply too much for her. We can gather from this incident and others like it that Esther was never given either confirmation of herself or provided guidance. She thus was expected to take care of an important task of parenting on her own, namely the provision of outer and inner structure. Therefore since her mother has not engaged her in an interrelation which builds such structures, Esther lacks the sense of self acquired in a living human interchange. The frailty of her self appears in her states of fusion into events or into other persons, a fusion which further debilitates the self. Thus when on returning home she lives in her mother's old nightgown, she acts out a fusion with the mother literally. Simultaneously, she is furious and disgusted that the mother permits the merging.

In fact, Mrs. Greenwood thrives on her fusion and does not permit Esther's differentiation from her. Her characteristic words are "We'll" (193) where *she* wants something. A reflection on Esther's fear/anger at the mother and the mother's world appears in her inability to learn the mother's (and father's) language, namely German.[8] German appears to her "dense, black, barbed-wire letters" (27) and shorthand (the mother's skill) threatens her with getting caught in jobs she does not want (100). Esther thus protects herself against fusion with the mother by her rebellious stance. At the same time,

Esther attempts to use the rebellious stance to provoke the mother and force her into some sort of confrontation which might help her break through the angry symbiotic relationship.

We have seen in our chapter on Kate Chopin that, in a woman writer's life more than a man's, a representative of power and competency, a father or an idealizable mother, an idealized parent imago, provides the child with the later capacity to be guided by ideals and to develop those ego capacities which we designate as secondary process — thought, rationality, memory, self-reflection. They must be especially strong for the creative person because the constant pull of the primary process needs a strong counter force. The child must be able to admire the adult and must be able to merge into him/her and to share in his/her power. In Esther's present and past relationships to her mother there is not a trace of respect or admiration, which means that the mother either never fulfilled that function in her daughter's psychic life or disappointed the child's need for idealization. Esther has some identification with her father as a college professor and intellectual, and this provides her with the rudiments of a counter world to her mother's engulfing and sterile world. But as the mother has never let her grieve for the father, her image of him remains general and vague. Both his life and his death "had always seemed unreal to me" (135). Characteristically, she cannot find her father's grave when she goes looking for it.

Her search for a father, for sustaining values, forms her last actions before the suicide. At this point she wants to return to the family's Catholic faith just to be able to "throw myself at this priest's feet and say, 'O Father, help me'" (135). Fearing to be rejected ("people had begun to look at me in a funny way"), she goes to her father's graveyard instead. She has hoped to find his grave in the old section of the cemetery, but it is in the new, crowded, cemented-over section where the graves are dotted with plastic flowers. Her father's grave is bare, its headstone of pink mottled marble, without inscription except for his name and dates. The pink associates her dead father with the childish, babyish, ineffective father of her boyfriend; the plastic flowers come from the world of her mother. Most significant is the lack of inscription — his name being his only legacy to her. When she weeps, leaning her head against the cold marble of the headstone, she does not grieve for a loss but for all that she never received, for the emptiness in her. That is why the weeping brings no relief, weakens her, and prepares her for suicide.

In the artist's early life, there are of course many other figures, aside from actual parents, who serve as parental figures or mentors who can nurture, empathize and give ideals. In his later life, the artist will look for support from similar figures during creative spells and crises. Esther's mentors in the present intellectual world, however, have the same weaknesses as her mother. Esther knows that she attracts unfulfilled older women who want to be her mentors, but none offers her sustenance for her own sake. Her English professor assigns her a thesis on a book Esther has not even read yet. But the professor is "very excited about my thesis" (28). Her patron, Mrs. Guinnea, her "money mother", will only come to her rescue if trouble with writing is the symptom of her breakdown, because these were Mrs. Guinnea's symptoms in her breakdown. The editor at the New York journal, *J C* (an ironic savior figure) is the only mother figure whose influence Esther craves and recognizes as good: "I wished I had a mother like Jay Cee. Then I'd know what to do" (32). Jay Cee gives her definite tasks, makes her keep regular hours, and tells her what she ought to learn — and Jay Cee *knows* herself what she tells Esther to learn (e.g., Jay Cee speaks several languages and tells Esther to learn languages).

Significantly, Jay Cee's is the only firmness Esther encounters and it is in an interview with her that Esther realizes the insubstantiality of her life goals. To Jay Cee's inquiry "What do you have in mind after you graduate?" she answers to her own surprise "I don't really know" (26-27) even though before that she never felt any doubt about becoming professor, editor, poet. But Jay Cee does not know Esther's weakness and hence can have no idea of the disastrous effect of her well-meant attempt to rally Esther's interest in her job. Nor would she be capable of helping Esther, as becomes clear later. Esther's need to define herself, her lack of identity, and Jay Cee's failure are most obvious in the satiric-tragic photography scene. All the other girls at the magazine know the symbolic costumes they want to be photographed in, but Esther has tried to avoid having her picture taken. She is afraid that "if anybody spoke to me...I'd cry for a week" (82). The effect when she finally does cry is disastrous. In fear of her tears, everyone vanishes. "Jay Cee had vanished as well. I felt limp and betrayed, like the skin shed by a terrible animal. It was a relief to be free of the animal, but it seemed to have taken my spirit with it" (83). Like her mother, Jay Cee cannot bear anything but pleasant emotions, work, and superficiality, for her answer to Esther when she finally returns is "Have a good read" (84).

The list of negative role models would be incomplete without the caricature of the happily married professor's wife, Mrs. Willard, mother of Esther's boyfriend. She fully expects Esther to make herself her son's doormat, as she has made herself her husband's. "What a man is is an arrow into the future and what a women is is the place the arrow shoots off from" (58), she perverts Nietzsche. The problem of Mrs. Willard's theory and practice is that her "sacrifice" of herself keeps both son and husband in childlike bondage.

The lack of guidance by and sustenance from parental figures and mentors is generalized by Sylvia Plath into a deficiency of the culture. There exist in it no strong adult figures, neither men nor women. Esther's family is an immigrant family which has preserved no values from the old country, Germany; parents and grandparents having been stripped of even its language as a result of World War I. The university environment exists in name only. Both the New England transcendentalist and the native American revolutionary tradition are lost to Esther. Instead of intellectual values, her college offers her Mrs. Guinnea — with books so trashy the college library won't have them. Instead of being educated at her college, Esther is left to her own devices. She has been judged especially gifted, and consequently she is not even given basic courses. She is expected to write a thesis on Joyce without knowledge of English or any other literature. Just as Esther's father remains a shadowy figure whose grave Esther barely finds, so too, the cultural tradition is almost lost. Its fragments (memorized physics formulae, bits of botany, Dylan Thomas — "I had been so free I'd spent most of my time on Dylan Thomas," 102) handicap rather than help her, for they prevent her from recognizing her ignorance and learning anything sustaining. Plath's is an eloquent comment on the failure of upper middle class education and on the writer's desperate need for personal and cultural continuity.

The Woman Artist's Response to the Mother's World

Esther is the true daughter of her mother in that she has absorbed the mother's striving for success. She wins acceptance by a perfect record in school and by winning every available prize. Yet, Esther expresses her rebellion to the mother's world in the very striving. To the mother's practical orientation, Esther opposes her career goals of an English professor and poet. She makes a point of not acquiring secretarial skills. And since she wins prizes and scholarships, as did Sylvia herself, the mother cannot really object to the "impractical" career. Esther's career choice is only one facet of her rebellion against her mother. She has learned to tyrannize over her mother by threatening to expose her rationalizations and denials. In fact, what she wants (and never gets) from the mother (and the entire world of mothers and mentors, mid-twentieth century America) is a feeling response to herself as a person. By forcing a feeling response she hopes to define herself. Since the mothers, however, do not provide a firm basis against which she can delineate herself, she remains in a symbiotic relationship to them, a symbiosis of provocation.

It is Esther's insistence on a feeling response that makes her a poet. And since it is especially negative emotion which the mother denies and forces her to deny, Esther's (and Sylvia Plath's) poetic specialty becomes the exploration of a negative world, of anger, violence, sordidness, hurt, suicide and death. Unlike the other girls in the novel, Esther is adventurous, active, on the move. She explores New York City, where she attempts to establish herself away from the mother. New York can be experienced from the mother's point of view, as is illustrated by the other girls, who are chaperoned around and see only what the mother's world wants to show them. What Esther discovers in the city is a non middle-class world, the odd, unusual, bizarre, violent. She comments, "I liked looking on at other people in crucial situations. If there was a road accident or a street fight or a baby pickled in a laboratory jar for me to look at, I'd stop and look so hard I never forgot it" (10-11). She watches without showing emotion so as not to interrupt what she observes ("even when they surprised me or made me sick I never let on," 11). Not allowing herself to show emotion about what she sees, she remains an observer, excluded and alienated. Because of her non-involvement, she relishes a sense of superiority. But it is difficult for her to maintain a sense of self in her observer's position and she has the sensation of shrinking "to a small black dot against... that pine paneling" (14).

Esther's observer's stance is the psychic equivalent of her mother's denial. Just as her mother refuses to feel the pain of her husband's death or face her anger because he left her unprovided for, Esther refuses to feel the import of what she observes. Just as Mrs. Greenwood escapes responsibility by denial, Esther, by detachment, avoids involvement. Esther never attempts to understand anything in depth. Rather than think through the problems in her physics course, Esther memorizes them. Instead of getting involved with her contemporaries at the asylum, Esther scorns them as deviant. By warding them off, she unconsciously seeks to fend off her own illness. What she actually does by her lack of empathy, though, is to avoid understanding herself and her own illness. She never tries to understand why she wished to die, but projects the wish and illness on others — her friend Joan, for instance. She does not allow herself to get close to a person, experience or problem — to get through surface word or sensation to feeling and significance. She is isolated (and knows it) before her suicide attempt, and she remains isolated afterward.

The most telling episode concerning a mechanical, empty, and formal going through of an experience merely to have had it, of her uninvolved stance, is her first sexual encounter. What she wants from Irwin, who is fittingly a mathematics professor, is a defloration. "I wanted somebody I didn't know and wouldn't go on knowing — a kind of impersonal, priestlike official, as in the tales of tribal rites" (186). Defloration, bleeding, and obstetrical intervention is all she gets from the experience, at the end of which she is glad that "Irwin's voice had meant nothing to me" (198). She is totally unaware (and so is Sylvia Plath) that she cheats herself by her detachment and cannot gain anything. She never can give of herself, learn, or resolve an issue. In this respect, her avoidance of feeling is as strong as her mother's denial of it. The other side of her detachment (one she fears and continues to fear) is the ever-threatening descent of the bell jar of isolation, alienation, distortion of feeling and perception, as well as the complete loss of self in emptiness. The angry symbiosis to the mother's world and her detachment supplement each other in a tight structure which defends her insubstantial self from being swallowed up.

The Regression into the Engulfing Symbiosis

Esther is all right as long as she lives in the familiar academic world, and does not expose her uninvolved stance to serious challenge. New York and the first trial job in the commercial writing world are the challenges which break through the defense. Sylvia Plath finds impressive, and yet simple, everyday objects to evoke the mother's world, while delineating Esther's drift into confusion, isolation, panic and regression. Simultaneously she satirizes effectively the American world of the fifties with its aggressive materialism, its sumptuous ladies' journals, its plastic surfaces and its fake good times. The difficulties involved in photographing apple pie and ice cream for advertising lend themselves nicely to a comment on what happens to homely values under Madison Avenue's glare. The culture is seen as literally poisonous to its young in the incident of the girls' ptomaine poisoning at the journal's crab meat luncheon.

Esther drifts in the city from the start of her stay there. "I just bumped from my hotel to work" (2), she comments. She moves around rebelliously, but her rebellion is not generated by herself. The decadent and elegant Southerner Doreen, who wants to expose the journal's middle-class vacuousness, impels it. But since it is not Esther's rebellion but Doreen's, the adventures with her remain unsatisfying to Esther. Three incidents stand out during which her frail self-worth crumbles and her brittle integrity disintegrates. Significantly, in all three she is alone with another person, who acts other than she has expected or planned. When Jay Cee surprises her with the question what she wants to be, Esther shocks herself by replying "I don't really know" (27). The shock is that she has neither convictions nor goals of her own. When she plans to seduce the Russian interpreter, Konstantin, symbol of competence, she finds him pleasantly ignoring her seduction. When she plays with the South American woman hater Marco, she finds herself being beaten and almost raped. The defenses against experience which had worked in her familiar world and with familiar people (note that the two men are foreigners) don't protect her in the New York world. In the course of the stay, the city turns into a devouring animal. As a symbolic sacrificial offering, Esther before leave-taking feeds it her expensive city wardrobe, "scraps were ferried off" (from the hotel roof) "to settle here, there,...in the dark heart of New York" (91).

The gesture of appeasement is in vain. She returns numbly to the suburbs and her mother's house, there to be assaulted by a last decisive blow: she is not accepted by a famous writer into his creative writing class at Harvard, an acceptance she had counted on.

At home, the bell jar descends. She turns down other chances to leave (another summer school course, a friend's invitation, etc.) and the suburb now literally closes around her like a womb. There are, of course, many ways out. But, unable to speak to anyone about her New York failures and the Harvard rejection and their true meaning, she cuts off all ways out. And the true meaning of New York and Harvard had of course been her rebellion against the mother and her world, the rebellion which until that time had always been rewarded with prizes and teacher's approval. Not being able to go forward, therefore, Esther retreats more and more into infantile existence (she no longer washes, cares for herself, does not get dressed).

It is to get her relief from insomnia that the family doctor sends her to a psychiatrist, aptly named Dr. Gordon, as he is to resolve the Gordian knot of her mind. Esther shows that she has a good understanding of her existential situation when she imagines in the waiting room what she will say to him (i.e., that she feels herself "stuffed farther and farther into a black, airless sack with no way out"). She knows that by herself she can no longer reverse her regression and she is frightened of it, as well she should be. She imagines, as she waits, the kind of father figure who could help her in her situation. He would help her "find words to tell him how I was so scared." He is "a kind, ugly, intuitive man" with "an encouraging way" who would explain to her the meaning of her fear and "would help me, step by step, to be myself again" (105). What she needs and knows she needs is a person who responds to her warmly and empathically as a unique being, a father who gives her goals to live for.

Dr. Gordon has none of these qualities. In every respect, he represents the mother's plastic world. His "features were so perfect he was almost pretty," she describes him, with "eyelashes...so long...they looked artificial. Black plastic reeds fringing two green, glacial pools" (105). His waiting room feels safe but only because it has no windows and is lit and aired artificially. Doctor Gordon is ensconced behind "an acre of highly polished desk," defended behind a family portrait of Nixonian Checkers vintage (husband, wife, two children, dog) and screens himself from her voice by his nervously tapping pencil. Rather than tell him what she fears and feels, she is so alienated by his defenses that she enumerates, in an angry and flat voice, a few of her symptoms and withholds the ones that frighten her most. Mimicking his lack of humanity, she plays tricks on him "while he thought he was so smart" (107). His first and only response to her misses completely who she is and what she feels. In an attempt to rally what is healthy in her, namely her being a college student, he asks the name of her college and then reminisces about the "pretty bunch of girls" (107) he knew there as WACS or WAVES. He seems offended that she does not remember that a WAC/WAVE station was at her college (she was eight or ten at the time), a sign that he expects her to be and to remember what he thinks is normal.

After seeing her for a few minutes one more time a week later, he decides to give her shock treatment. He treats her as a mechanism that has somehow gone awry and that can be fixed by shocking it into shape. This is what he has done to the persons who populate his clinic and of whom Esther observes that they are "shop dummies, painted to resemble people" (116). In her mother's world there are for Esther these two possibilities: She is either left to her own devices in a lush, artificial, amorphous, confusing environment or she is violently punished and the little selfhood she has developed in rebellion against the first option is shattered. "I wondered what terrible thing it was that I had done" (118).[9] The doctor's question after the shock brings home to her what she should remember and be. "They had a WAC station up there, didn't they" (118)?

As the mother's world will not help her "to be myself again" (105) she feels that she has no other option but to die. During the next few days, in ever more desperate attempts, she tries to take her life. At the same time, she still searches for a father or for some sustaining memory. Hence for several of her suicide attempts, she returns to the place of her early childhood. And in none of them does she find anything supportive or of worth. It is therefore entirely fitting that she should end the regression in her final and thorough suicide attempt by taking sleeping pills as she lies buried in a hole in the cellar of her mother's house, that is, she wants to die in the bowels of the very mother earth that has shattered and rejected her.

Creation as a Way Out and its Failure

Before beginning her quest for death, Esther attempts to help herself by what she can do best, namely, write. There is no doubt that her devotion to poetry and a future writer's career is that of the budding professional. At college, when other students followed the lectures, she sat in the classroom "and wrote page after page of villanelles and sonnets" (30). When it comes to choices between people and poems, her mind is made up: "I reckon a good poem lasts a whole lot longer than a hundred of those people put together" (46). As a paralysis of her ability to act descends, she does not mind so much that she cannot eat, sleep, or swallow; what she does mind is that she cannot write and read.

The entire incident of attempting to save herself by writing focuses on the heart of her dilemma. She begins after the Harvard rejection and after having rejected her boyfriend by a trumped up dear-John-letter. That is to say: she begins without support from an admired parental agency and without personal integrity. Her inspiration is clearly anger: "Then I decided I would spend the summer writing a novel. That would fix a lot of people" (98). As she begins to write, she experiences herself as alienated from herself, seeing herself from "another, distanced mind", "small as a doll in a doll's house" (98). The reference to Ibsen places Esther in the tradition of the woman struggling against an environment that is hostile to self-development. The self-observing stance, however, blocks off the feeling about to emerge. Hence, the few words she manages to get on paper record symptoms of her condition. The first sentence symbolically contains all the clues for understanding why she fails, clues that she cannot pick up without facing her total emotional dependence on her mother, her passivity, and the strength of her anger at her. "Elaine sat on the breezeway in an old yellow nightgown of her mother's waiting for something to happen" (98). The next few sentences record her heroine's sensations ("sweltering morning") and the effect of these sensations ("Inertia oozed like molasses through Elaine's limbs," 99). Esther knows in a literary sense that her heroine is herself ("six letters in Esther, too," 98) but she blocks out the meaning of what she records (e.g., "nightgown of her mother's" — dependence; "waiting" — passivity; refusal to get dressed — plea for her mother's attention). Esther's novel, being about passivity, cannot get going beyond the first two sentences. What does happen is the mother's arrival back from work at three in the afternoon.

The exchange between mother and daughter draws the reader's attention to the question why the mother has such a deadening effect on the daughter. Sweet as the "molasses" of "inertia", Esther's mother inquires, "Why, honey, don't you want to get dressed?" (99), contents herself with a curt evasion, cleans up after her daughter, and prepares everything for supper. Neither the troubled behavior of the girl nor her spoiled-brat refusal to move are acknowledged. The reader is justified in wondering why the mother tolerates such behavior. What becomes abundantly clear is her stubborn refusal to read the daughter's signals and her denial that anything is amiss. The daughter's messages, however, including the entire incident of beginning to write a novel, are intended for the mother. Since the mother refuses to read them, the daughter resorts to ever more extreme symptoms and measures for attention and help. The first is that the novel remains incomplete. Next she loses the very ability to control her hand for writing. The final one is her suicide attempt. The anger that could be drained off into work (writing, setting the table) remains with the daughter to poison and finally destroy her. Apparently the mother never exercised parental control and is cowed by Esther's overbearing (e.g., "I haven't got time," 99). The book never answers the question why the mother failed to respond to the child. Since she provokes and tolerates Esther's rudeness, we must assume that it represents her own unacknowledged anger.

The Resolution and its Flaws

The solution to the impasse between mother and daughter appears in the third part of the novel, which deals with Esther's stay in a psychiatric hospital. It is a mechanical and superficial solution. Esther is physically separated from the mother. In the safety of the hospital, she can express some of her anger, hence suicidal thoughts abate. Angry behavior, however, has consequences and is not tolerated by the rules of the hospital. An understanding therapist allows her to express her anger at her mother symbolically without rejecting her. Electroshock treatments break up old thought patterns ("I tried to think what I had loved knives for, but my mind slipped from the noose of the thought," 176). Her therapist encourages her moves towards independence from the mother and allows her to work out adolescent inhibitions about sex. But, and this is essential, the transformation remains external. Esther is not given enough time to internalize the sounder relationship with the therapist (the four to five months in the asylum are simply not long enough), nor is she made to confront her feelings and taught to understand the meaning of her illness. She scorns such attempts by her friend Joan and shows them as useless to prevent Joan's suicide. Consequently, she never works through the relationship to her parents. She is not taught to relate to others with feeling and remains as alienated from her contemporaries at the asylum as from her sexual partner, Irwin.

At the end of the novel, Esther has not even begun to build, out of present relationships to others, those "transmuting internalizations"[10] out of which a person shapes her own future emotional world. All interactions and all learning experiences remain external and mechanical (shock treatment, physical separation, birth control device). As she leaves the safety of the hospital, she is rightfully "scared" when she wonders "How did I know that someday...the bell jar...wouldn't descend again" (197)? Her inner resources for handling future crises are small indeed. This appears from the very language she uses concerning her treatment and hopes. "I had hoped, at my departure, I would feel sure and knowledgeable about everything that lay ahead — after all, I had been 'analyzed'" (199). She may have been analyzed (note the passive), but she has neither internalized her therapist's interaction with her nor gained any insight. She remains detached and is not even aware of her own need to escape feeling. As a poet, she has not retrieved the tool of writing. A future descent of the bell jar (that is any stress by anger, loss, or rejection) will find her poorly prepared to cope.

Esther and Sylvia

Esther's lack of internal psychic structure is also Sylvia's. There is ample reason for it in Sylvia's development and background. Sylvia's father was her mother's senior by some twenty years; in fact he was her professor in the M.A. program at Boston University. Both parents had come to the U.S. as children, the father from Prussia, the mother from Austria. The couple devoted the first years of their marriage, until Sylvia was three, to the father's biological publications, the mother serving as bibliographer-secretary and renouncing her own studies in literature. As the father did not teach in his own field, biology, but rather in German, Sylvia's mother also graded all examination papers for her husband. In spite of doing a considerable part of the work, she was expected to be, and was, submissive to her husband in everything (cf. *Letters Home,* and Aurelia's own biography, 13-14), although, as she comments, "It was not in my nature." This must have produced anger and resentment, which were never openly acknowledged. Moreover, since the father claimed so much attention, it is unlikely that the child received much. What little she got was lessened when a brother was born, when she was three. At that time, in any case, her mother reports her turning to letters and reading. Most likely, the precocity and reasonableness expected of children in a household of academic parents was extreme in the Plath household.

When Sylvia was four, her father's terminal illness began, a five year long semi-invalidism from undiagnosed and untreated diabetes, the result of the father's distrust of doctors. Sylvia's father was therefore psychically absent even before his death when she was nine. The mother, busy with her ill husband, helping him with his work, tending to the younger brother's illnesses and more pressing needs, must have given the older child hardly more than the encouragement to intellectual pursuits already provided by the father; for the rest she expected reasonable conformance. Moreover, she appears to have used the daughter's intellectual play for her own ends, *e.g.,* to control and keep Sylvia quiet with story telling or poetry writing. Hence Sylvia's occupation with transitional objects, play and reading, was not originally for her growth but served the mother's purposes. Esther's need to give herself directions was probably Sylvia's situation as well. And so was the symbiotic relationship with the mother. Forced to interrupt her own education when she married a much older man, Aurelia Plath expected to live out her ambitions through her daughter and brought Sylvia up to relate to her through her intellectual pursuits. This remained the case when the mother worked for a living for the family after the father's death. Sylvia fulfilled her own need for growth through her poetic work in part *(e.g.,* the expression of anger); but in part she used her art to maintain the original relationship to the mother by winning prizes, by writing commercial, eminently successful fiction, and by including her mother in her success story, à la *Ladies Home Journal* (the *Letters Home* are an eloquent testimony to her loyalty).

Sylvia's escape from the mother was external, as was Esther's — at first it was via academia and finally via marriage and exile to England. Her attraction as a poet to violent subject matter, to an aggressive satire of the mother's world, and to death and suicide makes sense because her poetry was an assault on the mother's denial. This being the case, however, the very pursuit of writing maintained the angry symbiosis. Sylvia's poem "The Disquieting Muses" portrays this tie between the mother and her world and her own art.[11] Using the framework of the fairy tale of Snow White, the poet asks, "Mother, mother, what illbred aunt / Or what disfigured and unsightly / Cousin did you so unwisely keep / Unasked to my christening, that she / Sent these ladies" (5), muses that are "dismal-headed," "Mouthless, eyeless," "take away light," "in gowns of stone, / Faces blank" (60). It is the mother's refusal to acknowledge the world of ugliness and suffering which gets the daughter stuck with such muses. The mother belongs to a world of fairy tales where "witches always, always / Got baked into gingerbread." This making the world harmless with "cookies and Ovaltine" (59) does not work for the daughter. She is "heavy-footed" and tone-deaf because of her "dismal-headed" muses. She promises at the end of the poem that she will not leave "the kingdom you bore me to," and thus affirms the tie of anger with the mother.

Sylvia's insight into the reasons for her anger is hardly greater than that of her heroine, Esther. Like Esther, she records phenomena, orders them formally, almost mechanically, and gives us the semblance of a resolution. At the end of the novel, all loose ends are nicely tied up, *e.g.,* the alter egos of Esther's illness are killed off (Joan) or left behind in the asylum (Valerie) when Esther's "new, normal personality" (184) marches back to school. This formal completion brings into all the sharper relief the unresolved problems of alienation, denial, and unacknowledged anger. Sylvia Plath's publishing the story under a pseudonym (Victoria Lucas) once again confirms our analysis. The author sees herself victorious over her subject matter, as was Esther over her mental illness, hence her first name, Victoria.

Though she can illuminate her conflict, she cannot openly show her anger and affirm her victory, hence the last name, Lucas.

Sylvia Plath wrote the novel when she appeared to have emancipated herself from the mother's world: She lived in England, she was happily married to a fellow poet, and she had a child and was expecting another. In fact, at that time, from May 1961 to early 1962, her success was at its apex and she herself a modern super-woman who looked like Marilyn Monroe but was Mother Eve, who wrote like Emily Dickinson but looked after her own and her husband's publishing interests like Claire Booth Luce. The tie to the mother was as strong as ever, though, as appears from a visit of the mother's to England, from Sylvia's acceptance of the mother's help with financing their house, and from her letters home. The following, for instance, are hardly the words of a poet who has rejected American materialism. "Today came a big Christmas parcel from you with the two *Ladies' Home Journal* magazines which I fell upon with joy — that magazine has so much Americana, I love it. Look forward to ... trying the luscious recipes" (515, December 7, 1961).

A few months after the novel was completed, the world of married perfection that she praises in the letters to her mother disintegrated. Her husband abandoned her, and she was left to struggle with the two children, as her mother had been with her and her brother after their father's death. The almost identical situation must have brought back fears and angers of the past. Yet the letters report neither anger, nor hurt, nor grief, nor fear, but only a concern with mastering the external situation — baby sitters, the move back to London from the country, keeping warm during the exceptional cold of that winter, and maintaining a work schedule. She denied loss, grief and anger as much as her mother did hers years back. From the last breakdown, she appears to have learned that in times of crisis she could not be together with the mother, and hence she refused the invitation to return home, and refused her mother's presence in England. At the same time she pleaded with the mother to send others to help. Meanwhile the anger at mother and husband flowed into the poems and produced a rich harvest indeed. In fact, as a poet she felt she had never been better. The world she writes about, though, is dead and she is back in the bell jar without feeling for herself or others ("in this glass capsule," *Poppies in July)*. Her blood flows out as poetry ("The blood jet is poetry, / There is no stopping it,")[12] and she herself is Medea who has killed her children before dying herself ("Each dead child coiled.../ She has folded / Them back into her body,").[13]

Sylvia Plath used her work as a poet to differentiate herself from the mother and the mother's world in rebellion. By so doing, she explored the underside of her mother's and her own American world of the 1950s. In so doing, she joined the American tradition of the actual or spiritual exile writer and intellectual who opposes the optimistic, success-oriented and pragmatic mainstream of the culture. She did not attempt (nor probably could she have done so) to understand, through her art, as some writers do, the causes of and the meaning of her rebellion. Consequently she never separated her own world from the mother's and remained, with all her rebelliousness, tied to the mother's world. She therefore failed to free herself through her work much like her heroine failed to free herself from the mother in hers. As a writer as much as a woman she never succeeded in establishing an emotional world of her own. Curiously enough her mother sees this. "Throughout her prose and poetry, Sylvia fused parts of my life with hers" *(Letters Home,* 3). The world of Sylvia's marriage and exile was an external structure of separateness. When it crumbled with her husband's leaving her, she had no emotional resources to deal with loss and grief (old and new) except by denial and rationalization or by pouring the anger into poetry.

We have little testimony except for a few poems about what happened during the last days of her life. The acute danger to her life arose when this work of anger, the novel and the poetry, gained acceptance from a wide public. In a letter to Harper and Row's before the first publication of the novel in America her mother comments that Sylvia feared the possibility of the novel's success *(Bell Jar,* A Biographical Note, 215). Although the comment appears more in the nature of a projection on the mother's part, the pseudonym and the secrecy which Sylvia maintained to the family confirms Mrs. Plath's testimony, even though the object of the fear would be somewhat different from what her mother might believe. She, in any case, thought Sylvia feared hurting family and friends who had helped her during her first breakdown by her unfavorable and "untrue" picture of them in the book. The success of the work meant for Sylvia, as it did for Esther, that no limit would be set to her anger by those who she still hoped might have some power to check it. If they accepted her anger, then it would flow freely and drown out the whole world for her. This seems to be the meaning of her last poems where Dame Kindness, a mother figure who "is so nice!" (82) applies sugar poultices, picks up pieces sweetly without acknowledging that the poet is killing herself ("The blood jet is poetry, / There is no stopping it"). If there is no resistance to her anger destroying herself and her world, then all that will be left are pieces, the pieces which her little son Nicholas in "Balloon" holds in his fists after he has bitten through a balloon. The child becomes the destroyer of an insubstantial world that leaves nothing behind ("clear as water," 80) but "A red / Shred in his little fist" (80). If even the child is a destroyer, there is no way out except by destroying the destroyer, that is herself and the children. Hence she appears as dead and perfected, wearing "the smile of accomplishment" (84) at having taken back the life she created. The suicide is accordingly the attempt to stop the outflow of anger. Her art, the transitional object, could not help her because it blurred the insufficient boundaries between herself and the world. Her being lost in an omnipotence fantasy with its frightful consequences for her personal existence links Sylvia Plath to Hoffmann's and Büchner's suicidal heroes.

Sylvia Plath, like her heroine Esther, lacked resilient psychic internalized structures to withstand the regressive pull from the creative process. This lack of firm structures appears in her work as engulfing mother figures, as a materialistic, tempting and tantalizing culture without substance, as absent, dead, infantile fathers, as weak, boyish, and treacherous male contemporaries. In a world populated by such figures, genuine encounter and genuine struggle are difficult, if not impossible. The transitional object or work with art cannot itself establish the limits of an independent world unless the creator has some internalized and external structures, values to work with. If she does not, as Sylvia did not, the work remains either purely imitative and derivative (as Sylvia's was during her teens when she published in the commercial press) or reactive and symptomatic of her anger (as it was during her exile).

Summing Up

The difficulties Edna, Esther and Sylvia encounter in the throes of creation raise some interesting questions about women artists. Does the major struggle in creation for women writers occur with the mother? Do they need a strong and positive identification with the father? Is there for women writers (unlike for male writers) no struggle with a father figure? Is the struggle of the woman writer with mother figures as complex and above all as diffuse as it is for Esther? The male writer's struggle with his father is simpler and more straightforward, as reflected in *Oedipus* by the quickness of the father's death by a stroke of the sword. Does the struggle with the mother figure in creation appear in as many and subtle forms for other women writers as it does for Plath and Chopin? Does the mother therefore split into as many figures for women writers as it does for Plath and Chopin? In the folk tale, for instance, the split seems simpler. The folk tale in fact provides insight into the nature of healthy splitting and mother/daughter encounter. The stepmother, who at the end of the tale is killed off, is always the oral mother *(e.g.,* the witch's edible house, the stepmother's poisoned apple or comb). She is the mother whose engulfment the daughter needs to transcend. The fairy godmother (or helpful animal or tree) is the mother of a later stage of psychic development. She appears when the child is deserted — that is when the child has separated from the oral mother and is in conflict with the oedipal mother. She assists the child in a task (Frau Holle) or in getting a mate (Cinderella).[14] She never stays and she does not make the child stay with her. She does not take the child's labor away, but lets the child test herself against real obstacles. This mother seems to be a figure of latency. Is it the woman artist's problem that this latency mother does not sufficiently protect her against the combination oral/oedipal mother and merges too easily into them?

We have seen that the reaction to the work by parental figures of both sexes is important to the artist's own acceptance of his work as valid. The confirmation completes the process of creation, for it guarantees that the problems reenacted in the work can be dismissed, and the new world of the author, the created object, can safely be given to an audience's treasuring and safekeeping. Audience reception of this kind can be as strength-giving an experience as it is for

Mörike's Mozart. If it is negative, as it was for Kate Chopin, its effect on the artist's continued career can be devastating, as appears from the trivial stories she wrote after the shattering reviews of *Awakening*. A critical, belittling, and negative reception of a work of art by the public still is more likely for a female artist in our society than it is for the male artist. Does this social fact exacerbate the woman writer's psychic liabilities which we discussed? Is the woman writer also more affected by public reaction, both positive and negative? In Sylvia Plath's case, we have a negative reaction to a positive audience response. If the audience confirms a work the author knows to be dangerous to her (a work of anger or destructiveness) then the emotions expressed are felt to flood the world and must ultimately return to visit their creator — that is, the creator remains open to the harmful emotions of the work. In that case, the work becomes endowed with demonic features, it retaliates and wreaks havoc in the life of its creator. This seems to have been the way Sylvia Plath experienced her completed work. By using the concept of the transitional object we have delineated more closely the reciprocal relationship between the artist and her work.

Sylvia Plath's suicide and her last poems have been idealized as a deliberate journey into madness and death to enrich our culture by these dark dimensions so often denied in our technological "plastic" world. They have also been rejected as a glorification of violence and death. The question whether art can be therapeutic and health-giving has been attached to evaluations of her life and work.[15] There is probably little doubt that Sylvia Plath herself would have seen herself in the martyr's role, a Lady Lazarus whose savior failed to arrive on time. *The Bell Jar* is not a deliberately destructive work nor a glorification of suicide. It is a failed attempt at self-cure. Her last poems are a chilling testimony of the force of human anger and a deliberate praise of death. There is no doubt in my mind that the darkness of her world and poetry faithfully reflects her biographical situation. But her use of her art shows writing *per se* is a tool that can be used for good and for ill. From our stories about artists we can gather how a given artist uses this tool at various times in life, how he wants it used, how conscious he is of the possibilities of its use. We can also gather something about why one artist uses it this way and another that way and when in his development he began using it in a given manner. And sometimes we can even reconstruct why just this tool of writing was developed and not another. Sylvia Plath can teach us something about regret and grief that she was not given sustenance enough to use her gift for observation and the word on behalf of life.

IX
THE ANATOMY OF THE LITERARY MUSE

The creative process of the writer as described in the artist story of our day embodies the important processes of the writer's psychosocial development. Now that we have detailed seven creative processes, let us outline the phases (e.g., varieties of interaction with parental figures, etc.) which they share and the developmental histories which underlie them. Moreover, we will relate the writer's life patterns (especially the pattern of the earliest symbiotic relationship that conditions the succeeding stages) to the style of the artist's creativity (i.e., the response patterns to the symbiosis). Since in our tales these two kinds of patterns are interlinked with the description of the phases of the creative process, our discussion will move back and forth between the phases of the process and the autobiographical and stylistic patterns.

A few words of caution may be in order at this point. All generalizations in this chapter refer to the seven authors whom we discussed and to three about whom I published elsewhere, namely Franz Grillparzer, Arthur Schnitzler and Thomas Mann (introduction, footnote 2). In each of the chapters, we drew a distinction between the author and his characters and showed what aspects of an author individual characters represent. The characters whose lives we parallel to those of individual authors in this chapter, are aspects which represent the author's insights into artistic psychology. Finally, a word to those scholars who are worried that psychological studies like mine do not allow them to distinguish a work like Kafka's, for instance, from the scribblings of a psychotic. Literary quality is the result of all the processes which we will discuss in this chapter — and there may well be more. These processes occur in characteristic patterns individual to each author. In a long apprenticeship, the creative writer *learns to coordinate* these processes so that they work well for him and not at cross-purposes. In the literary work of the psychotic, on the other hand, the various processes involved in creation are poorly coordinated or at cross-purposes with each other. In the mental patient, the judicious use of these processes is missing; so are the persistence over years in their most effective coordination for a specific purpose, and the capacity for sustained attention. Quality in psychotic writing (and it does occur) is a chance product; it is not chance for the seasoned writer.

The Discrepancy Experience and Diffusion/Disruption of Ego Boundaries

Approximately at the beginning of every artist novella we can observe the intrusion of a new dimension into the life of the artist, a disturbance of his equilibrium, a disruption of ego boundaries,[1] a subjective crisis experience that triggers the chain of events related to the production of a work (e.g., the appearance of the eyeglass seller in Hoffmann's tale). The protagonist is often away from home, on the move, on a journey. His life is in transition. At the time they wrote these works, the authors we discussed were, or felt themselves to be, in transition. In fact, most of them equate periods of creativity with periods of crisis in life circumstances, change of mood, habits, and values. Several of the authors could write only in periods of transition (e.g., Mörike), others responded to critical changes in life circumstance by the works we analyzed (Hoffmann, Büchner). Their tales therefore reflect the process of working through a transition.

During development, the periods of special disequilibrium of ego boundaries occur in transitional phases between developmental stages, between the earliest symbiotic, the oedipal, pubertal, and young adulthood periods. Crises during the latter (oedipal etc.) repeat crises of the former (symbiotic etc.). During periods of crises conflicts with and breaking away from earlier familial relationships, because of increased psychic and social pressures, bring about a high volatility of ego boundaries; hence the possibility for increased creativity and for increased vulnerability to pathological resolutions of the growth- and transitional crises. Thus all our stories portray the protagonist during acutely stressful periods. On the surface, the problems which initiate the crisis appear in all stories as variations of oedipal problems. The narrative portrays, in one way or another, the oedipal triad (the prototype of all human social relationships, after all) in which the hero relates ambivalently to parental figures. The hero encounters a male figure of authority and a female symbol of love, his muse. The relationship for the female artist is reversed: she encounters a female authority figure and a male muse. Some writers are conscious of the importance of the oedipal situation (Mann, Schnitzler); others are unconscious of it (Hoffmann, Mörike, Grillparzer, Stifter). Still others misperceive its importance (Kafka, Plath). The oedipal problem is so essential to the portrayal of literary creativity that it appears in rudimentary form even for a character as pathological as Lenz, whose psyche is so fragmented that it seems incapable of stable object recognition and hence of oedipal relationships. Below the oedipal surface, however, we can always discern the writers' struggles with archaic, symbiotic issues and it is with these that we are concerned in this chapter.

The metaphor of the journey, the roles of the student, explorer, traveller in our tales draws our attention to another aspect of the creative person's experience.[2] On a journey, circumscribed routines are suspended and the traveller opens up to new encounters by which to grow. The journey during the openness of ego boundaries has therefore the important function of providing material for growth. In the desire to incorporate experience, the protagonist may well seem like a sponge in that she absorbs her surroundings, encountered persons, etc. into herself. Plath's Esther, for instance, avidly scrutinizes the city as potential subject for creation. Male and female creators are equally avid explorers.

The loss of defined ego boundaries as a result of the triggering discrepancy experience is suggested by a plenitude of metaphors of change, fluidity and transformation: water, sound, air, liquids, and all kinds of fragmentations, breaks, and discontinuities. This instability of the ego is most pronounced in the schizophrenic Lenz. It is because of this diffusion, fragmentation and volatility of the ego and its functions that the creative state has been linked to schizophrenia. The diffusion and/or breaking of ego boundaries occurs in all tales, and it occasions in the heroes/heroines all kinds of feeling responses. It may cause panic as it does when Hoffmann's Nathanael sees the eyeglass dealer or it may feel as a threat to life, as it does to Edna in Chopin's *Awakening*. In some protagonists it may generate exhilaration as it does in Mörike's Mozart. And for some like Lenz, the fear may be so overwhelming that they escape from it into hallucination. It is the feeling dimension which is important here. The discrepancy experience temporarily casts the protagonists into a totally subjective reality in which all phenomena are interpreted only in relation to their meaning and importance to the protagonist's self. External reality exists; in fact its sensuousness freely flows into him. But it does so only insofar as it relates to the protagonist's needs, feelings and desires. The protagonist is now in a primary process world.[3] All authors attribute various degrees of the uncanny[4] and of mystery to the discrepancy experience because of its suddenness, because of its alogical primary process qualities, and because of their own unusual responses. And finally, they tend to retain the state of fluid ego boundaries despite their fears about its uncertainties. This state is what we have repeatedly described as regression and childlikeness.

In the state of loss of ego boundaries, the protagonists feel driven, in motion, in the flow of time, at worst being whirled about. For Hoffmann's Nathanael, the motion is a rapid whirl whose fiery circles spiral inwards and whose violent climax comes with his suicidal leap into the midst of these circles. In Mörike's Mozart novella, the pull is concentric as it is in Hoffmann's tale, but it is gradual, with retarding and eccentric phases. At the end of the tale, eccentric and concentric movement are in a delicate balance. Together with the fluidity of the spatial dimension, there is often a backward and forward flow in time — back to Mozart's childhood, to the courtly culture of 17th century France, to archaic and infantile imagery and forward to success with his art and death.

The drifting about which the protagonist experiences in the state of ego diffusion seems aimless at the beginning of the story. We noted in Mozart's wanderings, as he enjoys and scans the countryside, a gradual narrowing down (open road, valley, village, park, pavilion, etc.). Mozart seems to find his way to the place of inspiration like a sleepwalker. When the discrepancy experience actually occurs, the protagonists' attention focuses on a particular narrowed down segment of the world and they continue in their explorations in a more focused way. From the moment Mozart feels threatened about the broken-off orange, he explores the world in ever new ways which relate to the broken-off orange. The creative person's keen sensorium and capacity to observe telling detail now come into full play. These external stimuli link up with emotionally charged remembrances. Diffusion and the breaking of ego boundaries have slightly different functions, although they may occur so closely together that it is difficult to tell them apart. Diffusion is a kind of non-centered scanning of the total environment. The breaking of ego boundaries focuses the scanning on a particular object. Then the cycle is repeated.

In the imagery of our tales, we have noted in all tales the regressive tendency towards oral, early infantile, incorporative modes, and to maternal embedding elements. These indicate a yearning for fusion and symbiosis with a creative matrix. In fact, in the flux of the journey, the hero is shown in a supportive situation, a holiday environment, a natural or social matrix. Through the ebb and flow of his creative moments, the artist lives in relationship to a supportive environment. Creation, though often solitary and always forward driving, is nevertheless seen as a *relational* act. It is done with a medium, within a specified, often an enclosed space (a *Spielraum*, a play space), for a specific person or audience, within a given tradition, supported by friends, mentors, maternal and paternal figures, models, institutions of all sorts. Even forces antagonistic to the artist serve as part of the limiting and defining environment. The fluidity of the ego boundaries in the creative state and the hero's/author's symbiosis with a nurturer are importantly related. In fact, how a creative person deals with ego diffusion/fragmentation/fluidity depends on the experience of the symbiosis and on the emergence from the symbiosis and the patterns of adaptation to reality learned there.

Every one of our narratives centers around an experience of the protagonist which endangers his self-cohesion or ego integration. A secure and firmly established ego might simply dismiss such an experience. An ego too easily threatened by disintegration might quickly establish such defenses as would stall further stimulation and deny or repress the disruption. The creative person's response is neither a quick integration of the disruptive stimuli nor a defensive closure against them. For all writers, the protagonist's creative process seeks to establish an integration of the disruptive stimuli by a change of the ego structures and a widening of the ego.

Symbiotic States

Let us compare the discrepancy experience to an infant's startle response. If the mother/infant relationship is a comfortable one, the startled infant will derive comfort and security from the mother. She will share with the infant her security with her own self. A good and comfortable symbiosis experience during the first year of life dissolves the child's fear of sudden self-disintegration.[5] The mother's self-assured backing allows the child to venture forth from the symbiosis, to let go of her to look, explore, or play. As the infant explores actively in the feeding situation, seeks the breast, clings to it, lets go of it to fall asleep or to play,[6] he achieves some, even if very limited, control over having his needs satisfied. By moving out of the symbiosis in phase appropriate activity and by returning to it when stressed, the infant gradually gains an ever increasing control over his actions and the ever increasing ability to differentiate between his own actions, body ego, perceptions, capacities and those of others. He integrates his activities, wishes, and needs safely into inner structure and feels them as ego-syntonic (doing this, feeling this, having this need defines me). Additionally and importantly, the mother structures the patterns of the infant's perceptions and behaviors in her interactions with him. She directs the infant's attention, establishes a common focus, indicates segments of processes, marks their beginnings and endings and by so doing in daily intercourse gives discernible contours to the infant's experience and thereby makes learning possible. The child's later and fast acquisition of symbolic and linguistic structures, often thought to be innate, is based on preverbal patterns of perception and action learned in interaction with the mother and the early primary group.[7] One unconscious source of later language and style resides here. A good and realistic symbiosis which is resolved gradually and nontraumatically thus builds all ego capacities; especially important for our purposes, such functions as ego boundaries, and the integrative functions of language and other symbolic capacities. For the resolution of the symbiosis to occur, the mother must have empathy for, approve and encourage the child's wish to grow, to learn and to become different from her, even while providing safe returns to the symbiosis. For the child to develop ego capacities as well as ego boundaries (when it is safe to explore and when help or care is needed), the mother must be able to let the child progress and regress according to the contingencies of the occasion and the child's unique needs, gifts, and inclinations.

Because of the inevitable shortcomings of the symbiotic relationship and because of the infant's inevitably unsatisfied omnipotence longings, most people feel a lifelong yearning for the reexperience of a satisfying symbiotic relationship. This yearning appears prominently in the creative person's make-up. The wish for fusion and merging drives all our authors, but appears especially strong in the works of male authors. Maybe because male children in Western societies are excluded sooner from the symbiotic relationship than are female children and/or because the mother/son relationship is sexualized earlier than the oedipal period, the longings for and fear of merging and fusion, as far as our writers are concerned, dominate the males more than they do the females.[8] We can observe that writers of both sexes seek symbiotic and fusion experiences during the creative process. But male artists seek to resolve an insufficient or sexualized symbiosis, while female writers tend to seek to resolve a too stifling symbiosis.

A symbiosis problem is central to the psychology of all our authors and their protagonists. The common problem resulting from the symbiosis is an irritability and vulnerability of the ego boundaries (inner and outer), and various difficulties with ego-integration (i.e., with expressive functions). For the rest, the symbiosis problem affects different ego functions for each in many individual patterns. The keen sensorium and the special perceptiveness and sensitivity that all our authors report for the protagonists and share with them during their creative periods appear to be related to the symbiotic problem. At the core of the symbiosis of all our authors was a conflict. They were all first, last, at any rate special children to their mothers, in whom the mothers had a significant ego investment, and with whom they felt a closer emotional tie than with their other children. This special maternal investment provided them with some greater than ordinary ego strength (especially in regard to narcissism, identity, aggression).[9] At the same time, the mothers were especially uneasy, guilty, angry, depriving, inappropriate in response to and demand on these creative children. Kate Chopin's mother, for instance, was a child-bride to a widower with children, hence barely coping herself, not yet able to provide the child a comfortable symbiosis. Kafka's mother was too sporadic in her attention, too unavailable at times, too smothering at others (she herself had been deprived of her mother). Grillparzer's was chaotic in anger and love. Each mother expected the special child to be more responsible, to achieve more, or be closer to her than her other children. None of these mothers received the kind of support from father, family, and social environment to permit her a comfortable symbiosis with the child. Sylvia Plath's father, for instance, was too much in need of mothering himself to allow his wife to give mothering to the child (cf. Chapter 8). Kafka's mother during his early childhood assisted the father in his struggles to get ahead economically. The father's need had precedence over the child's. Hoffmann's father was notoriously unreliable, and Mörike's, Mann's and Büchner's were preoccupied with their professional lives and hence removed from mother and child. In fact, stress in the families of all our authors was considerable and forced the special child to assume responsibility early.

It is shocking to observe the tragedies in the lives of our writers, the damage they incurred, the hardships they experienced, the mental and physical illnesses they suffered, and their conflicts with families and relations. Seven out of ten lost their fathers before the end of adolescence. Of the seven, five experienced long disruptions of family life before and after the father's death, because of long illness (Mörike, Plath), divorce (Hoffmann), financial crises (Mann), or war (Grillparzer, Chopin). Although Grillparzer's father did not die until the boy was eighteen, his parents' quarrels and economic crises disrupted his whole childhood. After suffering the loss of the father, Mörike, Stifter and Mann were separated from their families. Many writers lost important siblings or supportive grandparents as children and adolescents (Mörike, Stifter, Chopin, Hoffmann, Kafka). The parents of Hoffmann, Grillparzer, Mörike, Plath were severely disturbed and in conflict with each other. Schnitzler's and Kafka's families, of the Jewish minority and upwardly mobile, were under considerable social and/or economic stress. All the writers who kept their fathers into adolescence (Mann, Grillparzer) or who did not lose them

(Schnitzler, Kafka, Büchner) were in severe conflict with them. Yet, in their severely disturbed families, our writers were the healthiest and most successful members.[10]

Because the symbiosis for most of our authors was troubled, and the mothers not particularly helpful, the task of differentiation from the mother and the early environment for our writers was fraught with difficulties. On the whole, the tasks of the women authors involved the breaking through a too close symbiotic identification with the mother, often an exploitation by her, or her too close hold on the child. Because of the larger sample of the male artists, the spectrum of difficulties and the tasks needed to resolve them are of greater variation. The central task of creativity for both male and female writers is to find ways to separate out from symbiosis and to establish their own ways of relating to others, to the environment, and to themselves. The separation from the symbiosis with the mother is only the earliest of such series of creative self-definitions, the one which sets almost inescapable precedents and fashions the basic style of an artist's creativity. It appears from these observations, if only in outline, that a special relationship with the parent, or first position in the sibling sequence, assures advantage enough so that later actual hardships encourage rather than quell creative, independent solutions to problems. Then creativity can develop against considerable odds.

Transitional Objects and the Intermediate Area between Mother and Child

In separating from the mother, all humans use some form of a transitional object. The first transitional object, whose precursor is the mother's breast, is, so to speak, a detachable breast, which a child can control as it cannot control the unavailable mother. Its use (indicated by clutching and clinging) appears around the age of six months. It may be a soft object like a blanket, a body part or body position; or it may be a somnolent state. These soothing substitutes of the mother assist the infant to regress to the symbiotic state and to sleep. The second transitional object of the toddler stage is progressive in its use and establishes a never questioned play space between mother and child, in which the child is free to follow his wishes and imaginings. The use of this transitional object is learned at the close of the first and through the second year of life when the child begins to have motor control, object constancy, evocative memory, some capacity to symbolize and play at make-believe.[11] The second transitional object is a real "not me" thing, a plaything (teddy bear, favorite doll, or toy car, a fantasy, etc.), on which the child projects special meanings; it is the precursor of all later *self–invested* tools, instruments, media of expression, by which the individual relates to the cultural world of values, ideas and thoughts. By play with the secondary transitional object, the child enjoys his growing capacities and achieves a sense of control over his environment without any pressure to perform.[12] To distinguish the different functions which transitional phenomena and states have for our authors, we might differentiate between the use of first, *anaclitic* transitional objects and second, *instrumental* transitional objects. The function of anaclitic transitional objects is regressive and soothing; their aim is to achieve forgetfulness, illusion of the mother's presence, and sleep. The function of instrumental transitional objects is to playfully master waking reality in the absence (emotional or physical) of the mother, to assist in the separation from the symbiosis, and to mediate progressively and provisionally between the child and the world of persons and things. So that the transitional object develops to ever greater complexity of playful mastery, the preoedipal parents (both father and mother are important) must accept the transitional object into the parent/child relationship, must be emotionally available to the child and assist in its rewarding use. Hoffmann fixes the origins of Nathanael's sandman fantasy in the already-existing intermediate area within his primary group, the story-telling evenings in his family's living room. Because he needs to allay discomfort caused by his parents' lack of ease, and anger at being sent to bed, Nathanael projects discomfort and anger on the sandman figure provided by the nurse/mother. The technique of containing such imaginings inside the framework of a story which he learned from his parents in the safe play space allows him freely to manipulate and hence control his fearful and thrilling feelings embodied in transitional object, the sandman figure. In successive stages, the fantasy becomes an ever-changing, finer tool for growth, and a rich source of enjoyment.

All transitional objects and phenomena are self-referent; they continue to have a strong emotional investment and remain largely pleasure/unpleasure, primary process oriented. And it is this self-reference which distinguishes them from other tool behaviors whose function is making use of the environment. Self-referent and nonself-referent instrument behaviors stand in complementary relationship to each other and influence each other. The child may take pleasure (self-referent) and gain skills (nonself-referent) employing his body in the mastery of the environment. Transitional instrumental phenomena gradually become enriched in range, quality, and complexity by the development of nonself-referent intelligence, language, thought, skills, i.e., secondary process.[13]

An individual may come to use all kinds of soothing symptomatic behavior (for example, illnesses, compulsions, recurrent fantasies, drugged states) as anaclitic transitional objects. He may likewise transform the pleasure, control and security giving playthings of childhood into complex artifacts. All our authors share a strong need for transitional objects of both kinds. In many of our authors we can observe a close relationship between their symptomatic behavior (i.e., use of anaclitic phenomena) and their art (instrumental phenomena). In the development of artists, as our authors portray it and as we can reconstruct it from their biographies, all manner of difficulties and happy solutions occurred in the use they learned to make of transitional objects. These solutions are basic individualized response patterns to a particular symbiosis. The patterns reflect how the child felt in the symbiosis and how the child learned to handle the transitional object in emerging from the symbiosis. Together these response patterns determine a person's subjective style of employing persons and instrumental transitional objects. Literary style is based on these early response patterns. The vast importance of instrumental transitional objects to the artist derives from the fact that they allow satisfying, progressive, and cathartic externalizations. Our artists used their secondary transitional objects more persistently as links to the maternal world than other persons do; and they had a much greater and lifelong emotional investment in them as their lifelines to the world.

The possible range of meanings and functions of, and the close relationship between, the symbiosis, the two kinds of transitional objects and works of art appears in a practice Stifter reports about himself.[14] At the height of his 1864 psychosomatic illness and severe depression, when suffering from crippling insomnia, anxiety, and oversensitivity of the intestine, he prescribed bedrest and fasting for himself. He stopped all activity, discontinued all correspondence —

even to his friend and publisher, Heckenast. He kept his wife at his bedside for days, made her hold his hand and feed him a simple diet. He gazed at her and gradually gained reassurance from looking fixedly at her face. Then, still secluded in his room and in her presence, he began to write on a particular story and the writing strengthened the calming effect of the motherly presence. This regime finally enabled him after weeks and months to recover and to resume, at least temporarily, his social duties in the world.

Our authors offer a wide array of insights into the range which exists in the use of transitional objects, into their interpersonal origins and developments, and their later manifestations. Most authors know of and describe both kinds of transitional phenomena. Hoffmann's repetitive diary scribblings, Nathanael's solitary recitations to the automaton, Edna's recurrent fantasies, Grillparzer's long, dreamy diddling scales on the piano, Kafka's extensive somnolent trances lying on the sofa are anaclitic phenomena.[15] So are Hoffmann's alcohol usage, Stifter's, Kafka's, and Mörike's reliance on psychosomatic illnesses, and Plath's and Chopin's incapacitation by long depressions. Some of our authors alternate between using their symptoms as anaclitic, transitional objects and using their art as instrumental transitional objects; others use both concurrently and in a mixture of both anaclitic and instrumental functions.

The central question which arises in respect to transitional objects and states is why some of them remain for our artists simply an unchanging thing, habit, state, and why others are transformed into the cultural treasures of humanity. E.T.A. Hoffmann's life gives us an instructive example of the transformation of an invariant, anaclitic fantasy to instrumental use and hence into a work of art. During the stressful years of his young manhood, Hoffmann preferred unapproachable women as fantasy love objects whom he fled once the woman came to love him. When finally forced to settle into a steady professional life, he married a woman whom he did not love, had a child with her and stayed with her. During another stressful period as free-lance artist when he had lost his home, his position and income during the French occupation of Prussia, he again resorted to such a fantasy love, which complemented his already existing alcoholism. The fantasy concerned his thirteen to sixteen year old music student Julia. The many drunken entries about her into his diaries with their few cryptic pseudonyms and invariant phrases over several

years betray by their very form that he used this fantasy anaclitically.[16] Then Julia was promised in a marriage of convenience to a
merchant years her senior; Hoffmann violently protested the marriage; and her family no longer allowed him to teach her and to see
her. He had no control over losing her and *felt* the loss of a love
object for the first time. It was at this point that he transformed the
fantasy into works of fiction. The first of these is his *Don Juan*
(1812) in which Julia appears as the violated muse who comes to
inspire the poet in the hour of her death. Only when Hoffmann felt
anger and grief about Julia could he transform the fantasy into narrative elaboration, and begin to speak about it and work it through. The
inapproachable woman henceforth disappeared from Hoffmann's life,
but continued to inhabit his fiction in various forms. One difference
between the anaclitic transitional object (the fantasy in this case) and
the instrumental transitional object (the fantasy shaped into a narrative) is that the fantasy substitutes for the woman but the narrative
uses and develops the now available feeling response to the woman.

In Hoffmann's early development, we can conclude that his severely
depressed mother was often physically and emotionally unavailable to
him; her internalized image in him (his selfobject) remained archaic;
his earliest feelings towards her were split off, and remained unconscious.[17] Hence, the anaclitic transitional object, her temporary substitute, became a permanent, walled-off fantasy. In his adult life, the
substitute appeared as that fantasy which did not permit him a
mutual love. Simultaneously, the anaclitic fantasy could not, till
Julia's loss, change into an instrumental form. That is why
Hoffmann's writing up to *Don Juan* remained without women figures
— hence very limited. The Julia experience marked a major breakthrough in his literary career. If therefore, the feeling behind split
off anaclitic states, fantasies etc. becomes available to the artist by
life circumstance in transitional periods, split off selfobjects and feelings can be integrated into the mature psyche and symptoms can
become works of art.

Unless a person remains totally autistic or severely addicted, anaclitic transitional objects do not dominate the entire life of a person,
but usually only a circumscribed area of experience in which the
mother was not available to the child. There they remain encapsulated, and produce as non-verbalized signs such invariant defensive
maneuvers as were Kafka's tuberculosis, eating problem, and

somnolence and the host of other such regressive conditions which we observed in all our authors.[18] These states limited and handicapped the creativity and productivity of those authors afflicted by them, just as they crippled their professional lives and curtailed their life span. Hoffmann died of alcoholism related complications at age forty-six; Mörike and Chopin ceased writing prematurely, and Mörike, Stifter, Kafka, and Plath were forced by their illnesses into extensive, unproductive sick leaves, finally into early retirement and/or suicide. The use of the work of art can counteract for an author the regressive pull that anaclitic phenomena exert. Stifter quite literally often wrote himself well.

The Writer's Medium as an Instrumental Transitional Object

A work of art can be used in many ways, ways which were acquired during the early primary group/child relationship and ways which authors often replay in lifelong patterns with later partners (wives, husbands, friends, publishers, institutions, audiences). Stifter's and Hoffmann's cases illustrate well the close relationship between anaclitic and instrumental use of transitional objects. Depending on the particular relationship to the parents, the instrumental transitional object may be abandoned altogether for relationship to other persons (object relationships) and/or for self-invested tool usage (trades, professions); and/or the instrumental transitional object may be kept and developed into an artistic medium. If kept it can become an instrument for mastery or it can develop in a manner that recalls anaclitic usage, namely as a tool to lean against supportive figures. At best the verbal medium serves our authors and their heroes to attain ever greater mastery over the world and the self and to assimilate ever more of the world into the self; at worst, it serves them to destroy themselves and others. Between the two extremes we find various degrees of positive and negative uses of the medium, each of which has its particular stylistic characteristics. Let us look at a few.

The instrumental use of the work of art always involves some form of aggression, power and vents anger.[19] Josephine, for instance, uses her singing/piping to control her audience. They are to recognize her art in exactly the way she prescribes. She persists in her demand; the indifference of the mouse folk only increases her angry, repetitive insistence. She does not care about the casualties at her performances; she only seeks an angry control over her paternal surrogates. Because her art has no other purpose except to tie the mice to her, it remains focussed on melodramatic manipulation. Just so the narrator's style remains defensively intellectualized at the expense of evocative emotional resonance. In fact, in all these cases the instrument has the task of maintaining an angry bond without which the hero cannot live. Hence, the actual use of the instrumental transitional object remains largely anaclitic, and the work of art used for the purpose one-dimensional and repetitive. Such a work has only one theme, namely power; only a few characters, namely oppressor and oppressed; only one purpose, namely manipulation; only a few formal devices to achieve that purpose, such as melodrama, reiteration, exaggeration, and pleonasms (cf. our discussion of the narrator's and Josephine's different, yet related styles). For that one theme and purpose, however, the artist will exploit his finely honed sensitivity and gifts of observation (cf. the discussion of Josephine's and the narrator's insight into the mouse folk, chapter 6).

The anaclitic use of her medium is slightly different for a woman writer like Sylvia Plath. Like male artists, she directed her writing from earliest childhood to the parent of the same sex, her mother. But while the fathers of the writers objected to their son's use of art, Sylvia's mother encouraged it — in fact, she lived through it vicariously.[20] At the same time, the mother did not permit the child to express anger and to acknowledge that she lived through her daughter (cf. the eight year old's symbolic gesture of hiding her poems to the mother under the latter's dinner napkin).[21] To hold on to the mother, Sylvia as an adult continued to write for the mother. Simultaneously, in order not to be stifled by the engulfing mother, and to punish her for her vicarious life, Sylvia wrote of anger, and violence, and satirized her mother's world. But just as Kafka in his writing remained bound to his father (cf. "My writing was all about you")[22] so Sylvia Plath remained bound in angry symbiotic relationship to her mother and the kind of art which that bond allowed.

The parental partners in the symbiotic game can be active contributors as we see from the example of Sylvia's mother, or they can be impervious to it as was Kafka's father. The authors can be unaware of their tie as was Sylvia Plath, misunderstand it as did Kafka, or use their fiction and their heroes to work through it as did Schnitzler and Mann. When it is used in a symbiotic relationship in which aggression was neither tolerated nor acknowledged, the instrumental transitional object appears as the destructive work of art. In these cases, the work functions as a weapon against and as a connecting link to the partner. As the difficulties of authors with their public (their parental surrogates) show, the work can be felt as the vulnerable outer limit of the author's self (e.g., Kafka's warning to Felice not "to touch" the chains which tied him to writing; *LF*, 450). Hence, the work cannot be relinquished and must be held onto because it safeguards the author's ego boundaries (e.g., Stifter's difficulties with relinquishing work for publication). The cases of Kafka's Josephine and of Sylvia Plath herself show that destructive works of art can kill their author.[23]

The close or angry preoedipal tie between artist, work and audience fatally limits the aesthetic effectiveness and range of an artist. Like an anxious gatekeeper, the artist must keep his work away from the public and free interchange.[24] Like the victim of a repetition compulsion, he must return to similar themes, forms, casts of characters, images, etc., and can only develop within its confines. Kafka's reluctance to publish and his imprisonment in the authority struggle theme find their explanation in the work's defensive function. If the confines of the preoedipal tie are very narrow (and if aggression or sexuality cannot be acknowledged, they are likely to be curtailed)[25] the writer's chances for development will be circumscribed and expression dominated by that which cannot be expressed openly.

A still different use of the instrumental transitional object in an anaclitic function appears in Stifter's and his artist's case (cf. Chapter 5). We noted that the symbiosis with his mother was of a precarious nature, traumatically disrupted, and that the early primary group did not tolerate the expression of sexual and aggressive impulses. The church school which the boy attended on his father's death must have provided an environment similar to the maternal symbiotic one, and one to which he responded with the same feelings. The art and poetry instruction which the pubertal boy received there allowed him to maintain himself securely in the symbiosis with the maternal school (he won the poetry prizes when it came to write encomia at the school's anniversaries) and to transform intolerable aggressive and sexual impulses into artistic expression. As Stifter's need for maternal support increased when he got older and was under stress, even the minimal assertion required for instrumental transitional object use was a threat to the security he craved. He therefore learned to negate, mask, transform and neutralize by projection even his symbolic aggressive/sexual impulses. At the same time, the stylistic devices of negation and transformation, namely doubling, paralleling and contrasting, revealing and denying, doing and undoing, frayed his narrative into ever more numerous detailed strands and yielded a security-giving submersion into the flow of the narrative. In this manner, the instrumental transitional object, his art, increasingly became only a means for security and its productions themselves protective shields. Stifter's (and his hero's) life story was literally a flight into the process of generating artifacts. The proliferation of security measures in its turn gave rise to fears of being overwhelmed by these very measures. His artistic and life task therefore became the striking of a delicate balance between the fear of drowning in the abundance of security measures and the fear of not having enough of them.

Art, form, style though they can be used defensively, need not be defenses. What is the early relationship most favorable to acquiring an instrumental transitional object which can be used for personal growth through life's richness and crises and to give satisfaction and enjoyment? Mörike's tale *Mozart on the Way to Prague* provides us with a paradigmatic, utopian case. The progressive use of the instrumental transitional object leads away from the early mother to the oedipal mother, to her substitute, the muse, to the oedipal father, and to wider social relationships. In the tale, the symbiotic relationship therefore appears from the start as a wider social, familial matrix which permits a wide range of expression of emotion. The childlike artist can move into emotionally close relationships with his partners easily and quickly. To be sure, there are dangers because of anger and guilt; but they can be overcome. The relationships themselves provide many media of expression; everyone in the household is musical, there are instruments everywhere, and everyone is willing to participate in Mozart's playing at some times and to listen to it at others. By his art, the artist can profoundly affect his partners and make them respond to his anger, his joy, his fear, his hatred and his love. He can compose for them spontaneously and he can perform work he designed earlier. He can make them participate in his enjoyment of his medium; he can make restitution to them for his anger and gain their approval. They freely accept his gifts, increase his awareness of his own powers, and add their own contributions to his mastery. They allow him to come into relationship with them and to leave them without guilt. They encourage his development and new exploits.

Mörike views the creative process as a continuous exchange between the artist and the world for their mutual enrichment. The artist uses his transitional object, his music, to bring his personal materials (themes, memories, feelings) as well as cultural materials (i.e., the Don Juan theme, the musical forms) into new and expanded, yet familiar relationships. In these relationships, his musical materials are energized and enriched by new and varied meanings, by play with and instruction from older members of his society and contemporaries. In this process the works grow in the same measure as their producer grows in the human relationships. The transitional object maintains and enriches the relationship of all participants and it makes new relationships possible between them. Simultaneously it serves to differentiate its creator from the members of the social matrix. The transitional object of this nature is an instrument of repeated splittings, differentiations and reintegrations of the artist's ego functions in interchange with the world in a potentially endless series. Many of our authors use their works as instruments to free themselves (as did Hoffmann, for example, from such anaclitic instrument users as Nathanael) and to open themselves to new, enriching contacts with their contemporary society. But most of our authors, and especially their heroes, realize only a very narrow segment of their ego potentials in the creative process. The early symbiotic relationship which they experienced left them with too great a need for anaclitic relationships and defenses, with too many ego areas walled off from access to reality and hence from development.

Several of our authors acquired in their early relationships several instrumental transitional objects. From Hoffmann's tale it appears that this doubling occurred because the threat to self integration was so great that one instrument of mastery was not enough. Nathanael derives the impulse to write and the impulse to paint from the death threatening imagery of his nurse's tale. Many of our authors are double and triple talents, (e.g., Hoffmann — music, writing, painting; Stifter, Plath, Mörike — writing and painting; Grillparzer — music and writing). The different arts may become associated with different parent figures and hence come to bear the imprint of that parent's style and relationships with the artist-child (cf. our discussion of

Grillparzer, *op. cit.).* The different arts, however, may also become associated with specific developmental phases and with phase specific parent figures (e.g., Mörike's three different poetic styles, cf. Chapter 4, or Stifter's association of his painting with the oral and his writing with the oedipal parents, cf. Chapter 5).

All through this discussion I have insisted on calling the work of art a transitional object to make it clear that I am here concerned with the affective and self-referent aspects of the use of works of art in maintaining or establishing a relationship to others and to the world. Male and female artists differ in the sex of the persons in relationship to whom they employ their medium. For male writers, the use of the medium itself is sexualized.[26] They feel unconsciously that their use of the (maternal) medium is a threat to their fathers; hence they use the medium as a means to struggle against or to atone to their fathers. For males, the *use* of the medium is likely to be conflicted. Female writers feel no such sexual conflict; they struggle against and for their mothers. For male writers there is a straight line of development from the earliest transitional object, the breast, and the instruments acquired in the mother/child symbiosis to the later supportive and inspiring muse. For women, the developmental line is not as simple because the girl changes from her attachment to the mother to that to the father during the oedipal period. As a consequence, both men and women can initiate her into her art. But if the early mother favors its early use and later curtails it, the transitional object, *the medium itself* may become conflicted. For a woman writer it therefore seems to take a strong counter-pull against maternal figures by a male figure (her "secondary" muse) so that she can overcome her handicap. Our male writers see oral and anal mother figures as the first inspirations, supporters and earliest teachers of their protagonists; they lay the *emotional* foundations for the use of art. The nurse who initiates Hoffmann's Nathanael into the benefits of storytelling finds her ironic, self-consciously Post Freudian equivalent in Adrian's earliest muse and teacher, the dirty stable girl Hanne; her lusty voice introduces him to the art of polyphony. Like their protagonists, all our authors had in their early lives those music loving and storytelling mothers (Büchner, Grillparzer, Mörike, Plath, Mann), aunts (Hoffmann), grandmothers (Schnitzler, Stifter), great-grandmothers (Chopin), or grandfathers (Plath) who awakened and nurtured such similar love in the very small child. The first nurturing muse provides the artist with a key to the world, which remains the most important and, in some cases, the only way of opening the doors to the world without and the world within..

Splitting and Reintegration as Psychological Processes and Stylistic Devices

One mechanism, namely splitting, learned when the 12 to 18 month old child begins to move actively away from the mother, can form symbolic representations, and has evocative memory, aids the separation out of the maternal symbiosis by providing the most important mental function by which the hazards of separation can be overcome. The transitional object helps the child to master the mother's absence, and splitting and its symbolic representation help him to manage conflict with her.[27] Splitting particularizes and therefore limits conflicts. By splitting the mother's image into the good and the bad mother, for instance, the child reduces fears of destroying the mother whom he needs; he keeps the good mother but gets rid of the bad one who opposes his will. Gradually, many different dualities and opposites develop out of the early good/bad, here/there, now/then, now/later splits. The creative person's capacity to visualize and experience the coexistence of opposites in one object, in one place, and at the same time has its genesis in such splitting and the early management of ambivalence.[28] By way of splitting (and such splitting mechanisms as reversal, displacement, or negation) preconscious and unconscious materials become available for ego mastery.

In the mature writer, splits occur not only along the line of presently important dualities but also of all dualities experienced in the individual development (i.e., the oral versus the anal mother, the preoedipal father versus the oedipal father, etc.). We have seen that many of the writers and artists in the transitional periods in which we encountered them project unsettled and new conflicts in split off forms on their media.[29] All our writers and their artist-protagonists have the capacity for extensive and profound splitting. The less the writers have denied or repressed of their development, the more strongly they have felt about the persons significant to them, the greater their emotional investment in the natural, social and intellectual world, the richer, more resonant, and original are the personal potential   sources   for   splitting   and   the   possibilities   for recombinations. Splitting and its projection into the artistic medium *(i.e,* the transitional object) have the function (as they do for the infant) to break up unmanageable problems (i.e., contradictory feelings about one object, event, etc.) into manageable parts. These parts the writer can experiment with, pit against each other, recombine, or transform by eliminating some while integrating others.

The synthesizing function of the ego, the writer's linguistic and symbolic capacity to work through the opposites and to integrate them into new syntheses adequate to his present reality, complements the capacity for splitting. For an author, the two functions work together on a primary and secondary process level through an entire tale, that is, through the entire creative process.[30] The synthesizing function might be described as the capacity to combine many ego functions for a variety of integrative maneuvers. Such central and largely unconscious ego functions as aggression, identity, sexuality and creativity operate together with secondary, largely conscious ego functions such as thinking, imagination, language and affects in the synthesizing function as well as in splitting.[31] Splitting and synthesizing form a continuous dialectical process. Splitting and synthesizing together generate the fabric of fiction (plot, character, locale, imagery, etc.) and its formal elements. We have already commented on the advantages of the novella-form for the evocation of the creative process (cf. Chapter 1). Its emphasis on crisis and conflict allows for the dramatic, particularized representation of splitting, duality and opposites; its well delimited closed form necessitates forceful resolution and emphasizes the need for closure to the creative process. Psychic splitting and integration maneuvers learned in a particular symbiosis have characteristic effects on the writers' individual form and style preferences within the novella tradition. Within the basic creative and narrative processes, the kinds of splits an author attributes to his hero and exhibits himself, and the patterns of reintegration vary widely. A few examples will demonstrate how widely they vary, and what maneuvers of integration occur for what reasons.

As we have seen in our discussion of transitional object use, the different artist figures and writers differ in their capacity to use their ego potentials and hence to use the full capacity to split and to synthesize. But special difficulties concerning integration arise, the greatest for Büchner's Lenz. Being schizophrenic, Lenz has not acquired that minimal ego core (or stable selfobjects and hence stable psychic structures)[32] which a person needs as a basis for integrative maneuvers. His is a chaotic, psychotic, radical splitting of objects, of emotion from sensation, of sensation from perception, of fantasy from reality, etc., which Büchner renders stylistically by the absence of a personal grammatical subject, an experiencing *I,* and by verbless constructions, etc. Lenz can only organize his fragmenting ego around a center external to him, the father figure of Oberlin. As long as Lenz can identify with Oberlin, he can symbolize and resolve internal conflicts in his sermon and his discussion about art. Büchner draws decisive parallels and contrasts between himself and Lenz regarding their unequal capacity to synthesize. His syntactical control, his patterning of images, his narrative sequencing etc. are guided by his desire to understand Lenz's psychology and the origins of his self-fragmentation. At the same time, Büchner differentiates himself from Lenz by his analytical motivation and empathy.

Hoffmann's Nathanael uses several maneuvers of reintegration. His kind of splitting and symbolizing is richer than that of Grillparzer's fiddler, for instance; it reflects a larger range of development all the way up to young adulthood, hence potentials for reintegration are rich. For a time, Nathanael succeeds in resolving his internal conflicts by projecting them into symbols and by re-integrating them into a formalized poem. When this maneuver fails him, he attempts another self-integration and attacks the splits which he has projected on others (his attack on Spalanzani). This is a regressive move, a regression which terminates in his attack on the splits in himself — his suicide. Nathanael's case makes it clear that in deep regression a unifying ego core disappears and hence the capacity for symbolization and form use. Hoffmann himself had enough of an ego core (in those areas not affected by his alcoholism) to create a unifying integration through symbolizations. The sandman object symbol and its accompanying unifying metaphors (i.e., glasses, eyes, dolls etc.), the complex narrative forms, and the use of irony constitute an almost overly formalized system of integration. Like Nathanael, Hoffmann supported a defensive, formalized identity by various fantasies, his drinking and a strong identification with another artist, namely Mozart.[33]

Any kind of splitting necessarily involves destruction, hence guilt. The impulse to make restitution can therefore give a unifying direction towards integration. In Mörike's *Mozart,* the splitting which occurs on the physical level (the orange) or the affective level (the good and bad father) can be undone on a symbolic level (the orange into a song; the wish to murder the father into an opera). Mörike shows a variety of possible splits. He attains their redemption by a change in level of abstraction, by their integration into a cultural tradition, and by acts of restitution. The integration maneuvers which Mörike attributes to Mozart (the various song and style characteristics — cf. Chapter 4, my discussion of Mörike's "registers") were his own. The unifying integrative motivation which he attributes to Mozart (guilt and atonement) likewise was Mörike's own. Mörike shows this motivation to work to a limited extent for Mozart; his atonement is accepted by the father. It is not accepted by the mother figure, a situation which parallels Mörike's own. The integrative mechanism of guilt and atonement did not work well for him, as he remained dependent on guilt producing later symbiotic relationships which first inspired and later stifled his creativity.[34]

The aggressive aspects in splitting dominate the works of Kafka, Schnitzler, Mann, and Sylvia Plath. Their common motivation is a struggle to maintain a symbiotic relationship between child-artist and parent figures in various splittings. Just as the characters assure their self-cohesion through the irresolvable opposition to an adversary, the authors achieve narrative cohesion through the sharply dialectical structuring of the narratives. Juxtaposition between essayistic and narrative styles (Kafka) and counter-pointing of characters (present/past self pitted against split-off mother figures, Plath) are but two of such formal integrative maneuvers. We might generalize from the power motivated works, that unacknowledged and angry power play (by action or works of art) for the sake of self-integration maintains symbiotic but safely distanced relationships; it is destructive to the artist and to those whom he succeeds in involving in his destructive, manipulative art. The distrust of the artist which Kafka and Plath but also Mann and Schnitzler share has its reasons in their similar concern with power play as an integrative modality.

We have seen that such manipulative art comes into existence because of the artist's early deprivation, distance from parent figures, and compensatorily developed intellectualism.[35] Kafka, Plath, Mann and Schnitzler felt that like their artists, they themselves tended to safeguard their self-integration by power play against an adversary. Their awareness of and insight into the dilemma of their characters,

and their analytical stance to them (in characteristic individual variations) represents another, post-Freudian unifying modality of integration. By using the modality of awareness and by working through and
resolving the splittings *by allowing the underlying affect to emerge)*
they differentiate themselves from their creations and substitute for
the psychosocially less advanced modality of power play the higher
and more advanced modality of psychological portrayal and analysis.

A final integrative strategy of the creative process for many of our
authors and for some of their characters, is the possibility of casting
off aspects of the self or of selfobjects no longer adequate to present
circumstances. By splitting, the inadequate part-self can be isolated
and delimited. It is precisely by the distinction they draw between
themselves as successful narrators and their failing protagonist alter
egos that authors define themselves, attempt to assimilate and to
integrate as much as they can of their alter egos, and then cast off
unassimilatable parts. The narrator is after all not identical with the
author. He is that aspect of the author which tells the story, analyzes
the characters and accomplishes his task as an artist. The narrator
is the author's creative self. This aspect is distinct in most authors
from the psychopathological part of the self attributed to the hero.
This is why so many of our authors show the failure and death of
their heroes. It accomplishes and highlights their success as artists.
As we have seen the protagonist (e.g., Mörike's Mozart) or the author
may grow through such works — even if it be in a limited sense —
and gain greater powers of tackling new works, other themes, and of
mastering his present situation in the world (e.g., Hoffmann). In fact,
for our woman authors this need and desire for growth and autonomy
through differentiation from insufficient part selves and objects is the
driving impulse in the use of their art. The desire for differentiation
and autonomy probably organizes the woman writer's creative
endeavor more directly and radically because for social and psychological reasons differentiation and autonomy are harder for her to
attain than for male writers. Kate Chopin's heroine Edna uses her
painting in a bid for autonomy and freedom. In the conflict which
develops over the issues of differentiation (differentiation from husband, lover, mother, role of mother, role of female artist) she fails
and is overcome by the too strong and too regressive mother imago.
But Kate Chopin herself, by her craft and ironic insight, for a time at
least, succeeded in differentiating herself from and mastering that

part of herself which was Edna.

We have seen that our authors vary widely in the kind of splitting which they and their protagonists use; they vary just as widely in the kinds of integrative maneuvers, with their specific stylistic characteristics, which they employ in their art. And they vary widely in the motivations which drive them to creation. Of gravest danger to the artist's survival as a unified self and as a writer is the total absence of a coherent ego core, with its basic personal style. Without this core the writer cannot function and must cling in absolute dependence to another person and his style. Creation, and for that matter emotional (and physical) life can only be maintained if that person is actually present (cf. Lenz's need for Oberlin). It is the tendency toward self-disintegration which makes the writer similar to the schizophrenic. Most writers, however, have received in the early symbiotic relationship with their mothers enough of a specific ego core to be able to tolerate extensive splitting and to achieve reintegration by various integrative maneuvers. Of these, projection of the splits into the artistic medium and their symbolic integration by various symbolic, analytical or formal maneuvers is the most advanced solution. Of the integrative motivations, power play is the most damaging to the writer. Each integrative motivation, however, has its own specific maneuvers and stylistic characteristics. But each maneuver and motivation has also its own payoffs and pitfalls. For instance, immersion in the production of ever new artifacts to find security in change itself, such as Stifter attempted, had the drawback of generating too many artifacts and arousing fears of drowning in the abundance.

The very act of finishing and publishing the completed work constitutes an act of self-integration for the author. By this act, he reestablishes new ego boundaries and ends the state of ego diffusion. We have seen that this final reintegration posed numerous problems for our authors. Writers can close themselves off never to produce again, as Mörike did; they can remain too open to the work after publication and suffer its acceptance (Plath) or its rejection (Chopin) as direct assaults on their ego boundaries; or they can let go and turn to different concerns.

The Rewards and Risks of the Creative Process

In tracing the patterns of splitting and reintegration, we have come to understand some specific motivations for creation and their specific psychic gains. There are however, other rewards which all authors share. As the artist experiences the break-in which initiates his creative process with its break or diffusion of ego boundaries, he becomes open to contact with his immediate social surroundings and open to the feelings of others for him. If, at this point, he receives approving acceptance from others and engages with them in a creative endeavor like Mörike's Mozart, he feels his self-worth and creative capacity energized and enhanced. The enjoyment of his capacities by others reawakens in him the approving glance of his mother/father at his infant display of activity. This original source of his creative energy is restimulated and enhanced by the creative energy that radiates out from his present companions.[36] Another supply of energy comes from his testing himself in and against his medium, which may resist him, accommodate itself to him, and fill him with gratification at his skill and mastery. Mörike's *Mozart* is the most moving instance of the creative process as a social event in which the artist's narcissism is nurtured by the society about him, and enhanced by his success in handling his medium in the tragic and comic vein alike.

A further reward comes during the process itself. The good-enough release from the symbiosis has given the artist's ego functions resiliency to continue to function and to function well under stress. Past psychic energies, as they are released from repression during the process, flood all ego functions, heighten and eroticize them and bring about extreme and gratifying tensions. Kafka described this heightening as "the fire" of these hours.[37] All our writers describe the growth of excitement to almost orgiastic intensity during creation, as it gains a driving force of its own (cf. Kafka's metaphor of the hunt, Hoffmann's of a growing intoxication, or of a raging fire). This fever of the artist's thought, emotion, and concentration is increased by the present awareness of and the narcissistic pleasure in the smooth and seemingly effortless coordination of many ego functions during the creative process. A variant of the primarily phallic erotic gratification (Hoffmann, Kafka, Mann) is the psychosocially earlier, polymorphously erotic joy of feeling immersed in (e.g., Chopin's Edna) or supported by a medium (e.g., Stifter's Friedrich). It is the heightening of the ego functions and the gratification derived from it which authors seek and fear in the creative experience.[38]

The crucial importance of communication with and confirmation by an audience for the artist's narcissistic energy supply during creation appears from the tragic results of their absence. In our tales it is the artist's usual lot to be ignored, abused, exploited, or derogated. Hoffmann's Nathanael receives a rebuff when he reads his poem. Kafka's Josephine sings to deaf ears. Lenz's sermon is grossly misunderstood. Because audiences (readers) represent the early parents to all these artists, the effect of rejection is devastating and leads them to lose their foothold in reality. Our authors share this sensitivity to audiences with their protagonists. The unfavorable public criticism *The Awakening* received affected Kate Chopin so strongly that she curtailed her courageous imagination and eventually gave up writing altogether.[39] We have seen in Sylvia Plath's case that acceptance by an audience of the wrong work can be just as devastating. It is the unavoidable openness of ego boundaries to attack from without and to surprise from within which makes the writer's a hazardous job.

Because they fear the wound to their narcissism, all artists seek protection during the creative process. We have commented on their need for a safe-guarding play space which novella form, symbolic medium, and protective locale may provide. Just as crucial, however, are the helper and mentor figures who guide the artist through periods of creation, reincarnations of the early nurturing muse. They provide precisely that kind of feeding of flagging self-esteem and depleted narcissistic energy which the individual requires. They assist the struggling protagonist with encouragement, challenge, and involvement. The range of helper figures is vast, but once again Mörike's tale provides the purely positive models.

At the country house, where Mozart entertains the gentry, there appear among the figures who represent the parents of early childhood several minor characters who seem to have no other function except to contribute to the general hilarity. On closer look, their characterization and participation is very significant. The cousin of the bride is a poet of sorts who accommodates his talents to Mozart's presence. The poem he composes helps Mozart make good a social blunder. His rivalry with the composer is challenging and friendly; he gives of himself freely and ungrudgingly. The other helper figure is female, the maiden aunt so beloved of children in 19th century households; she is somewhat masculine (she sings in the same range as the men), desexualized yet maternal, friendly and undemanding. The father figure of the tale at times appears also as a helper. As the father of latency, he demands discipline but does so unthreateningly; he sees to the restitution of things broken or lost and rewards the acquisition of formal skills. All these are figures of latency.[40] They assure safe passage through difficulty; unlike the preoedipal and oedipal parents, they are separate and distant enough from the protagonist so as not to be engulfing or overpowering. For both men and women writers, such mentor figures can be males or females.

The importance of such helpers for the successful writer appears most clearly from their failure. If the artist in his creative struggle regresses too far, becomes too vulnerable and elicits from the helper an authoritarian response, he may actually turn into a angry oedipal or preoedipal parent (cf. our discussion of Chopin's *Awakening*). Misunderstanding the artist's temporary unsettledness for immature and obstinate helplessness, the helpers may infantilize the artist, as do Nathanael's friends. In fact, unacknowledged angry behavior by helper figures (cf. our discussion of Mann's Zeitblom and Büchner's Oberlin) is of greater concern to our authors in their fiction than outright betrayal or attack by others. Passive hostility, overprotectiveness, and double binding are the gravest harms the writers fear.

All our authors had such helper figures in their own lives. Hoffmann's friend Hippel was a lifelong confidant, who supplied money and influence and also shared his interests, enthusiasms, and studies.[41] Husbands (Sylvia Plath), professional advisors (Kate Chopin) for women writers, wives or children for male writers (Thomas Mann) may assume this function in practical matters. The wife's function (especially if she was never an object of passion) can alternate between being a good preoedipal mother and a latency helper (cf. Stifter). Some artists use different friends for specific needs and occasions. Thomas Mann, for example, befriended experts in different fields as helpers for specific tasks in his work. Some, like Stifter, for the sake of security, tie themselves to a publisher, whom they experience as much bound to them as a marriage partner.[42] The assistance which such helpers provide can be specific and mundane or it can afford the writer a propitious intellectual and/or emotional ambiance. Even our loneliest writer, Kafka, could not have done without such helpers; he needed Max Brod and Felix Deutsch to provide him with intellectual stimulation, his sister to take care of his mundane affairs, and finally, Robert Klopstock and Dora Diamant to help him die.

Literary art, especially the writing of fiction, demands a long process of involvement in the world, of splitting and differentiation and reintegration over many years and through many developmental periods. It depends on a long learning of many maneuvers, especially stylistic maneuvers. The farther back into early developmental levels a writer is thrown in the creative process (or the farther he attempts to reach back), the more of these early materials he tries to incorporate into his present reality, the more difficult his task of reintegration and the greater the ego strength needed. Such ego strength is gained from a good release from the symbiotic mother; but it needs to be tested, strengthened and matured by much nurturing. The writer gains some such nurturing and strengthening from his participation in and identification with the cultural heritage of his society. Additional strength, however, comes from the mature writer's awareness of his mission to construct a future together with his contemporaries (cf. our discussion of Mörike, Chapter 4).

Since the writer of fiction needs to project the materials of his personal experience into the more complex patterns of the social and cultural world to which he belongs, the achievement of these integrations is a task of maturity. In fact, since abstract operations can only be performed consistently after early puberty (after about age eleven to twelve) and since abstract operations are needed to design such a conscious formal artifice as a fictional plot and characters, all our authors began writing fiction during early or late adolescence. Playing with words, writing poems, preoccupation with puppets, theater, or story telling began much earlier for most (from age five). Hoffmann, Mörike, Mann, Schnitzler, Grillparzer, Chopin, and Plath report extensive reading and their first longer compositions during early puberty.[43] Not only did these writers begin to write early, but they persisted with working on literary projects over many years, for usually ten or more years until their first publication. In general, it seems to take an apprenticeship of ten or more years and a prodigious amount of effort and paper before the writer of fiction achieves an independent voice.[44] From what we have learned about the creative process, the length and complications of the apprenticeship should not surprise us. Thomas Mann in his usual inimitably ironic manner

expressed this long struggle with the creation of fiction best by saying, "that a writer is one to whom writing comes harder than to anybody else."[45]

Summary

This concludes the account of the anatomy of the muse. Each individual creative process derived its initial impetus from a present
conflict which caused earlier conflicts to surface. How the writer
handled the emerging creative crisis depended on five interrelated
factors in his early development, factors which are alike for men and
women. They are: (1) the kind of symbiosis and the kind of release
from the symbiosis he experienced; (2) the kind of transitional object
use he acquired in infant and toddler stages; (3) the kinds of splitting
he learned; (4) the kinds of integrative maneuvers he learned; (5)
encouragement, confirmation, or rejection of early transitional object
use by nurturing and admired persons. An endless number of variations of these five factors are possible in individual development.

All our writers give evidence (and that distinguishes them from
other people) that a very strong early relationship with the mother
was disrupted traumatically in the early stages up to age three; that
they partially substituted an instrumental transitional object for the
mother and henceforth for human relationships; that the early primary group encouraged and approved this substitutive transitional
object use; that the transitional object became an important adaptive
and satisfying tool over long years of practice. Four of the factors
which we discussed importantly shape the basic style characteristic
of an author. Aesthetic form is therefore more importantly rooted in
a writer's early development than even matters of content. Such crucial autobiographical works of an author as the stories we discussed
are a recapitulation of his development. Works of this sort can
advance the writer's development, retard it, or halt it altogether. In
the continuously assimilative and adaptive process which literary
creation is at its best, a writer works over a given personal/cultural
problem by projecting it into his medium, by breaking it down there,
and by recombining it into a new synthesis. He may achieve an
entirely new synthesis (which is unlikely), or he may achieve a synthesis of old patterns and a few new reintegrations. He may be able
to discard some aspects of a problem or an entire problem. This may

enrich him or cripple him. He may offer progressive or symptomatic resolutions. His contemporaries may reward him or may ignore him; they may favor his symptomatic or his progressive resolutions. Whatever the case be, the process itself for him has all or any of the following purposes: 1) to release repressed and unrepressed feeling and to master past traumatic and problematic personal issues; 2) to replenish psychic energy supplies both from the present external and the past internalized sources; and, 3) to acquire a reintegration of ego functions more appropriate to present social, cultural, political, interpersonal, and developmental circumstance.

NOTES

Introduction

[1]The genres of the "artist novel" and "artist novella" have found repeated treatment in the various histories of the German novella and the German novel, and it is not my intent to deal with them here. On artist figures as motifs in novel, novella, and drama, cf. the bibliography in Wilpert, *Reallexikon der Literatur* (Hamburg: Körner, 1959).

[2]Cf. "Arthur Schnitzler's *The Last Letter of a Litterateur:* The Artist as Destroyer," *American Imago*, vol. 34, 3 (1977), 238-276. "Aesthetics, Psychology and Politics in Thomas Mann's *Doctor Faustus*," *Mosaic*, vol. 11, 4 (1978), 1-18. "Grillparzer's *The Poor Fiddler:* The Power of Denial," *American Imago*, vol. 36, 2 (1979), 118-146.

[3]Karl Kroeber, "The Evolution of Literary Study, 1883-1983," *PMLA*, 99, 3(1984), 326-339.

[4]Murray Krieger, "Words about Words about Words: Theory, Criticism, and the Literary Text," *ACADEME*, 70,2 (1984), 17-24.

[5]Charles Altieri in "A Report to the Provinces: Reflections on the Fate of Reading among Behavioral Scientists." *Profession 82: Selected Articles from the Bulletins of the Association of the Departments of English and the Association of Departments of Foreign Languages*, 27-31, finds as do I that social and behavioral scientists are beginning to appreciate the humanist's concern for emotion and its study through subjective narrative.

[6]Sebastian and Herma Goeppert in *Psychoanalyse interdisziplinär* (Munich: Wilhelm Fink Verlag, 1981), give an excellent account of the hermeneutics of literary countertransference.

[7]Cf. *Freud and Man's Soul* (New York: Alfred A. Knopf, 1983).

[8](New York: Farrar, Strauss and Giroux, 1984); also "Freud and the Seduction Theory: A Challenge to the Foundations of Psychoanalysis," *The Atlantic Monthly*, February 1984, 33-53.

[9]Paul Robinson. "Freud's Last Laugh," *The New Republic*, March 12, 1984, 29-33.

[10]"A Difficulty in the Path of Psycho-analysis," *Standard Edition*, vol. XVII, ed. James Strachey (London: Hogarth Press, 1973), 141 ff.

[11]"The Psychoanalyst in the Community of Scholars," in *The Search for the Self*, II, ed. Paul H. Ornstein (New York: International Universities Press, 1978), 685-724. My italics.

Chapter I

[1]Kate Chopin, *The Awakening*, ed. by Margaret Culley (New York: Norton, 1976), 27.

[2]Cf. Harry Slochower's comment on the crucial importance of form as manifestation of the artist's meaning, "Editorial Note," *American Imago*, 36 (1979), 1.

[3] *The Notebooks of Malte Laurids Brigge*, translated by M.D.H. Norton (New York: Norton Co., 1964), 27.

[4]Jay Harris and Jean Harris, *The Roots of Artifice: On the Origin and Development of Literary Creativity* (New York: Human Sciences Press, 1981), 24.

[5]"Die Krise der romantischen Subjektivitat: E.Th.A. Hoffmanns Künstlernovelle 'Der Sandmann' in historischer Perspektive," in *Literaturwissenschaft und Geistesgeschichte: Festschrift für Richard Brinkmann*, ed. by Jürgen Brummack, et al. (Tübingen: Niemeyer Verlag, 1981), 348-370. Author's translation.

[6]On the capacity to imagine the co-existence of opposites, cf. Albert Rothenberg, *The Emerging Goddess* (Chicago: University of Chicago Press, 1979).

[7] Cf. Pinchas Noy, "The Psychoanalytic Theory of Cognitive Development" in *The Psychoanalytic Study of the Child*, 34 (1979), 169-216.

[8] *Op. cit.*, Noy, 172-177.

[9] Cf. Patrick Colm Hogan, "King Lear: Splitting and its Epistemic Agon," *American Imago*, 36 (1979), 1, 32-44, for a similar use of the term.

[10] *Op. cit.*, Hogan, 33.

[11] What I call an integrating device or strategy corresponds to Jaroslav Havelka's "radical subjective ambiguity of imagination." *The Nature of the Creative Process in Art: A Psychological Study* (The Hague: Martinus Nijhoff, 1968), 88-89. I am interested in the ordering capacity of the device and what it tells me about mastery.

[12] The importance of aesthetic form and formal elements has been much stressed in recent psychoanalytic literary and art criticism, especially by Jaroslav Havelka, *The Nature of the Creative Process in Art. Op. cit.*, and Norman N. Holland, *The Dynamics of Literary Response* (New York: Oxford University Press, 1968) and by Harry Slochower, *Mythopoesis* (Detroit: Wayne State University Press, 1970).

[13] Lawrence Kubie, "Impairment of the Freedom to Change with the Acquisition of the Symbolic Process," *The Psychoanalytic Study of the Child*, 29 (1974), 259.

[14] Heinz Kohut, "Creativity and Adolescence: The Effect of Trauma in Freud's Adolescence," *The Psychoanalytic Study of the Child*, 33 (1978), 461.

[15] Cf. Louis A. Gottschalk, "Psychoanalytic Contributions to the Generation of Creativity in Children," *Psychiatry*, 44 (1981), 3, 210-229, adds such other factors as comprehensibility to others, utility, generalizability to other fields, continued outputs, a capacity to stimulate others to originality.

[16] K.R. Eissler, *Goethe: A Psychoanalytic Study 1777—1786* (Detroit: Wayne State University Press, 1963).

[17] Frank Barron, *Creativity and Personal Freedom* (New York: Van Nostrand, 1968).

[18] (Boston: Houghton Mifflin, 1941).

[19] (New York: Random House, 1972).

[20] *Strd. Ed.* IX, 141-154; *Strd. Ed.* XI, 59-138; *Strd. Ed.* XIII, 209-237.

[21] K.R. Eissler's *Talent and Genius: A Psychoanalytic Reply to a Defamation of Freud* (New York: Grove Press, 1971) is the most outstanding treatment of creative heroism.

[22] Cf. Harry Slochower's summary, "The Psychoanalytic Approach: Psychoanalysis and Creativity," in *Essays in Creativity*, ed. by Stanley Rosner and L.E. Abt (Croton on Hudson, New York: North River Press, 1974), 151-190.

[23] Ernst Bloch, *Das Prinzip Hoffnung*, 2 vols. (Frankfurt/Main: Suhrkamp Verlag, 1959). Harry Slochower, *Mythopoesis* (Detroit: Wayne State, 1970).

[24] According to the Homeric hymns, cf. "Hymn to Hermes," in *The Homeric Hymns*, translated by Apostolos Athanassakis (Baltimore: Johns Hopkins, 1976) the new-born Hermes freed himself from his swaddling bands, went and stole the cows of Apollo, killed a turtle, and used the turtleshell and cowhide strings to make an instrument to lure the animals to the cave of his mother. All the attributes of the divine child-artist-inventor appear in this hymn.

[25]Frank Barron, see footnote 17.

[26]A. Altus, "Birth Order and its Sequelae," *Science*, 151 (1966), 44-49.

[27]Freud, *Strd. Ed.*, XVII, 156, "If a man has been his mother's undisputed darling he retains throughout life the triumphant feeling, the confidence in success, which not seldom brings actual success along with it."

[28]The family has been held to be the precondition for creativity by psychoanalytic writers and hence group upbringing looked at askance. Studies such as Bruno Bettelheim's *Children of the Dream* (New York: Macmillan, 1969) well summarize the predominant psychoanalytic attitude to family rearing. A more positive attitude to other than family group rearing practices comes from Charlotte Kahn and Geraldine Pirkowski, "Creativity and Group Rearing," *The Psychoanalytic Study of the Child*, 29 (1974), 231-255.

[29]With the recent move from oedipal to preoedipal issues, the study of creativity has centered on infancy and on factors of psycho-*social* development. Cf. *Gruppendynamik der Kreativität*, ed. by Günter Ammon (Munich: Kindler, 1974).

[30]"Creativeness, Charisma, Group Psychology," in *The Search for the Self*, II, ed. by Paul H. Ornstein (New York: International Universities Press, 1978), 793-843.

[31] Cf. Barron, *Creativity and Personal Freedom, op. cit.*

[32] *Creativity and Personal Freedom, op. cit.*, 214-249. For additional agreement, cf. also, from a psychoanalytic perspective, the recent summary of significant personality characteristics of creative subjects in Charlotte Kahn and Geraldine Pirkowski, *op. cit.* see footnote 28.

[33]D.W. Winnicott, *Playing and Reality* (New York: Basic Books, 1971), and K. Michael Hong's "The Transitional Phenomena: A Theoretical Integration," *The Psychoanalytic Study of the Child*, 33 (1978), 47-79.

[34]T. Wayne Downey, "Transitional Phenomena in the Analysis of Early Adolescent Males," *The Psychoanalytic Study of the Child*, 33 (1978), 19-46.

[35]Bruno Bettelheim, *The Uses of Enchantment* (New York: Vintage Books, 1977), or Stanley H. Cath and Claire Cath, "On the Other Side of Oz: Psychoanalytic Aspects of Fairy Tales," *The Psychoanalytic Study of the Child*, 33 (1978), 621-639.

[36] Cf. C.G. Jung, *Man and his Symbols* (New York: Dell Publishing, 1968).

[37]For a summary, cf. Winfried Kudszus, *Literatur und Schizophrenie* (Tübingen: Niemeyer, 1977).

[38] Cf. Sigmund Freud, *Briefe 1873—1939*, edited by E. and L. Freud (Frankfurt/Main: S. Fischer Verlag, 1960), 405-406, letter to Romain Rolland and its discussion in *Strd. Ed.*, XXI, 57.

[39]Barron, *op. cit.*, chapters 20-21.

[40]"Creativity: Retrospect and Prospect," *Journal of Creative Behavior,* 4(1970), 149-168.

[41] *The Act of Creation* (London: Hutchinson, 1964), especially 87-97.

[42]Ernst Kris, *Psychoanalytic Explorations in Art* (New York: International Universities Press, 1952). Lawrence Kubie, *Neurotic Distortion of the Creative Process* (Lawrence, Kansas: University of Kansas Press, 1958); and "Impairment of the Freedom to Change with the Acquisition of the Symbolic Process," *The Psychoanalytic Study of the Child,* 29 (1974), 257-262.

[43]P. Weissmann, "Theoretical Consideration of Ego Regression and Ego Function in Creativity," *Psychoanalytic Quarterly,* 36 (1967), 1, 26-37.

[44] *Gruppendynamik der Kreativität,* ed. by Günter Ammon (Munich: Kindler, 1974).

[45]Pinchas Noy, "The Psychoanalytic Theory of Cognitive Development," *The Psychoanalytic Study of the Child,* 34 (1979), 169-216.

[46]J. Havelka, *The Nature of the Creative Process in Art op. cit.*

[47]Albert Rothenberg, *The Emerging Goddess* (Chicago: University of Chicago Press, 1979).

[48]Pinchas Noy's definition of primary and secondary processes *(op. cit.,* footnote 7) is helpful here. According to it, the primary and secondary process are "two different forms of adaptation. According to the primary process mode, everything perceived and recalled from memory is sorted out, categorized, and understood in terms of the self and its needs. The object is represented in terms of whether it satisfies, frustrates or threatens; the event, in terms of how it influences or can be influenced by the self ... By the use of the secondary process mode, an individual can categorize and understand the events and phenomena in terms of reality; he can comprehend the inner relations between the various objects on their own; he is able to discern regularities, detect repetitive and similar patterns of order, and derive rules that determine the occurrence of the events." 197-198.

Chapter II

[1]The scholarship on Hoffmann has become extensive over the last few years. Klaus Kanzog in "Zehn Jahre E.T.A. Hoffmann Forschung:E.T.A. Hoffmann Literatur von 1970-1980: "Eine Bibliography," *Mitteilungen der Hoffmann Gesellschaft,* 27 (1981), 55-103 provides a sample. Lothar Köhn in his introduction to *Vieldeutige Welt. Studien zur Struktur der Erzählungen E.T.A. Hoffmanns und zur Entwicklung seines Werkes* (Tübingen:Max Niemeyer Verlag, 1966), summarizes different points of view on the *Sandman.* Köhn presents fine insights into Hoffmann's use of ambiguity and ambivalence in the tale. Peter von Matt, *Die Augen der Automaten:E.T.A. Hoffmanns Imaginationslehre als Prinzip*

seiner Erzählkunst (Tübingen: Niemeyer Verlag, 1971) deals with the artist problematic but misunderstands Nathanael's failure. Unlike German structural, philosophical/aesthetic orientations, the criticism of Anglo-American scholars has inclined to a common-sense psychological interest in Hoffmann's irrationalism, cf. for example Ernst Fedor Hoffmann, "Zu E.T.A. Hoffmann's 'Sandmann'," *Monatshefte*, 54 (1962), 244-252; or Horst Daemmrich, *The Shattered Self: Hoffmann's Tragic Vision* (Detroit: Wayne State University Press, 1973). S.S. Prawer in "Hoffmann's Uncanny Guest: A Reading of 'Der Sandmann'," *German Life and Letters*, 18 (1964/65), 297-308, is the first scholar to consider a possible analytical contribution to interpretation but veers off to a Jungian analysis. Ingrid Aichinger in "E.T.A. Hoffmanns Novelle 'Der Sandmann' und die Interpretation Sigmund Freuds," *ZdPh*, 95 (1976), Sonderheft, is the first to present Freud's insights seriously to a German scholarly audience but does not go beyond Freud. My own 1975 essay on the *Sandman* from a psychoanalytic perspective was concerned with the psychodynamcis of the poet which Freud overlooked. Cf. "E.T.A. Hoffmann's *The Sandman*: The Fictional Psycho-Biography of a Romantic Poet," *American Imago*, XXXII, 3 (1975), 217-239. James McGlathery who appraises Hoffmann as an ironic psychologist of sexuality in *Mysticism and Sexuality in E.T.A. Hoffmann* (Bern: Peter Lang, 1981) also presents valuable background material on life, work and influences. Of the *Wege der Forschung* volume on *E.T.A. Hoffmann* (Darmstadt: Wissenschaftliche Buchgesellschaft, 1976), Klaus Günzel's essay on Hoffmann's development as an author (359-380) is especially helpful. The problem of narrative perspective which has recently moved into the limelight [cf. Silvio Vietta, "Das Automatenmotif und die Technik der Motifschichtung im Erzählwerk E.T.A. Hoffmanns," *Mitteilungen der E.T.A. Hoffmanngesellschaft*, 26 (1980), 25-33; John M. Ellis in "Clara, Nathanael and the Narrator: Interpreting Hoffmann's 'Der Sandmann'," *German Quarterly*, 54 (1981), 1-8] presents few difficulties to the psychoanalytic critic. Since the primary process with which Hoffmann is concerned is by definition multivalent, perspectives and hence interpretations are also.

[2] *St. Ed.* 17, 230.

[3] The meaning of the name was explicated by Freud. The most recent comments on the name occur in Samuel Weber, "The Sideshow, or Remarks on a Canny Moment," *MLN* (1977), 1102-1133, and James McGlathery, *Mysticism and Sexuality* (Bern: Peter Lang, 1981). The novella contains various other *leitmotifs* which contribute to cohesion, psychic depth, and organization. Most striking is the *leitmotif* of the eye, of glance, of eyeglass, of binoculars. Next in frequency is the circle of fire, the symbolization Nathanael uses to describe his imprisonment in his approach/avoidance conflict. Fires and burning are equally frequent; so is the doll imagery and the symbolism of buildings, windows, stairs and other spatial representations, all of which symbolize or are projections of aspects of the hero, e.g., house represents the self.

[4] Quoted from J.T. Bealby's translation in *The Best Tales of Hoffmann*, ed. by E.F. Bleiler (New York: Dover Publications, 1967), 197.

[5] Hoffmann is concerned with Nathanael's growing up. Hence, the oedipal situation involves not only sexual threats and sexual competition, but also extends to child/adult differences in size and experience, the child's struggle with trust/distrust,

dependence/autonomy, omnipotence/competence, the entire complex of generational misunderstandings, disillusionments, and conflicts, which begins in infancy.

[6]With Klara, Nathanael is caught in an approach/avoidance dilemma. If he comes too close to her, he fears loss of self. If he withdraws, fears of alienation, self-fragmentation, and artistic impotence overwhelm him, cf. John Dollard, Neal E. Miller, *Personality and Psychotherapy* (New York: McGraw-Hill Book Company, 1950), XXII, 352ff.

[7]Donald W. Winnicott's first paper "Transitional Objects and Transitional Phenomena," *International Journal of Psychoanalysis*, 34 (1953), 89-97, has found much elaboration. James Hamilton discusses insightfully the ego mastery aspect involved in the use of transitional fantasies, cf. "Transitional Fantasies and the Creative Process," *The Psychoanalytic Study of Society*, 6 (1975), 53-70.

[8]How weakened Nathanael has become appears when he meets Coppola again. He has lost the firmness of purpose he displayed to the eyeglass seller earlier. He is ashamed of his revived panic, "for this childish fear of specters" (202). He discards his fear and along with it the attempt to understand his feelings. In contrast with the first Coppola episode, he is not startled by the discrepancy between his overpowering feelings and what occasions them, the eyeglass seller, and makes no attempt to elucidate the disproportion. Rather, he becomes defensive toward the eyeglass seller, feeling that he has done him an injustice. To "square accounts" (203), Nathanael even buys some binoculars from the man. Yet, we may well ask what Nathanael must make amends for? He has done nothing to the man, only said "as quietly and as calmly as he possibly could... I don't want to buy any weather glasses, my good friend" (202). From his defensiveness, it is clear that Nathanael confuses what he has actually said and done to the eyeglass dealer with what he felt about him --namely fear and aggression (the wish to throw him down the stairs). He makes no attempt to verify the relationship between inner and outer reality as he did by writing of his fears to his beloved and friend. In fact, they have cut him off from such verification. In buying the binoculars, in disregarding the warning laughter of Coppola (the narrator's indication that Nathanael has some inkling of the danger to himself), Nathanael deprives himself of further checks on his cancerous inner urges. Not being able to tell the difference between what he feels and what he actually does, he is unable to control either feeling or action. Most literary critics believe that Nathanael's later violent outbursts constitute his madness. They overlook that we are given an earlier and subtler example here.

[9]The narrator reports Coppelius' appearance from the narrator's standpoint: "a crowd began to gather. In the midst of them towered the lawyer Coppelius" (214). Many critics believe for this reason that Hoffmann attributes objective reality to Coppelius, that it is Hoffmann's intent "das Dämonische in der Welt zu bannen," cf. Wolfgang Kayser, *Das Groteske in Malerei and Dichtung* (1960, rde 107), 139. I do not believe that this is the case. Rather, by having Coppelius appear in external reality, Hoffmann emphasizes that what Coppelius represents, namely fear of castration, self-loss and death, is real and that this fear motivates human behavior.

[10]P. Weissmann in *Dynamics in Psychiatry*, ed. by G.S. Philippoulos (Athens, Basel, New York: S. Karger, 1968), 277.

[11]On the growth of the self through mirroring, cf. Paul Ornstein's summary of Kohut's self psychology: "Phase-appropriate maternal responses of reflecting, echoing, approval, confirmation, and admiration of the greatness and perfection of the grandiose self optimally lead the normal maturational steps of transformation and internalization of archaic grandiosity and exhibitionism toward a capacity for the pursuit of ego-syntonic ambitions, goals and purposes; a capacity for the enjoyment of various functions and activities; and the attainment of a realistic and stable self-esteem, all of which are end-points of this developmental line, i.e., functions of a mature, cohesive self." *The Search for Self: Selected Writings of Heinz Kohut*, Vol. 1, (New York: International Universities Press: 1978), 56-57.

[12]His fascination with these was strong, cf. his interest in the writing of Pinel, cf. Hans Georg Werner, *E.T.A. Hoffmann: Darstellung und Deutung der Wirklichkeit im dichterischen Werk* (Berlin and Weimar: Aufbau Verlag, 1971), 103. His knowledge and observation outstrip the contemporary psychiatric literature.

[13]For a further analysis of the identity of Nathanael/narrator/Hoffmann cf. Maria M. Tatar, "E.T.A. Hoffmann's 'Der Sandmann': Reflection and Romantic Irony," *MLN*, 95, 3 (1980), 585-608. On Hoffmann's use of the narrator as a structural device, cf. Chapter 1.

[14] Cf. Ludwig Marcuse on Freud's reluctance to analyze authors who were close to his thinking. See "Freud's Aesthetics" in *Freud As We Knew Him*, ed. by Hendrik M. Ruitenbeek (Detroit: Wayne State University Press, 1973), 385-411.

[15]For a recent summary of Hoffmann's poetics and the Serapion's principle see Ilse Winter, *Untersuchungen zum Serapiontischen Prinzip E.T.A. Hoffmanns* (The Hague: Mouton, 1976).

[16]Wulf Segebrecht, "Heterogenität und Integration bei E.T.A. Hoffmann," in *Wege der Forschung: E.T.A. Hoffmann* (Darmstadt: Wissenschaftliche Buchgemeinschaft, 1976), 381-397. In the following I am giving a psychological account of what other critics have formulated in terms of a philosophy of composition based on dualism.

[17] *E.T.A. Hoffmann in Aufzeichnungen seiner Freunde und Bekantten*, ed. by Friedrich Schnapp (Munich: Winkler, 1974), 709.

[18]E.T.A. Hoffmann, *Tagebücher* (Munich: Winkler Verlag, 1971), 107. Page references henceforth will be given after diary quotes in the text. Translations are my own.

[19]Heinz Kohut "Preface to *der falsche Weg zum Selbst*, Studien zur Drogenkarriere by Jürgen vom Scheidt," in Vol. II *The Search for the Self*, ed. by Paul H. Ornstein (New York: International Universities Press, 1978), 846. Brackets are mine.

[20]Kohut describes such a merging with a twin in *The Analysis of the Self: A Systematic Approach to the Treatment of Narcissistic Personality Disorders* (New York: International Universities Press, 1971), 193-196.

[21]Coppelius' touching and thereby spoiling the children's food by evoking their disgust has its internal psychosexual explanation. At the same time, Hoffmann's uncle might have been given to such aggressive-regressed behavior. With so much 18-19th century tacit and accepted child abuse, it is hard to tell if such violence was a factual as well as a psychic reality.

[22]The quality of parenting appears from the fate of his brothers. The eldest became a ne'er-do-well; the other did not survive infancy. Unfortunately, the biographical information on Hoffmann is fragmentary and unreliable as it is on most writers of the 19th century. The best is still Harvey W. Hewett-Thayer, *Hoffmann:Author of the Tales* (New York: Octagon Books, 1971) and the reedition of Hans von Müller's edition of letters, diaries and contemporary testimonies, cf. *Briefwechsel, Tagebücher* (Munich: Winkler Verlag, 1967-72).

[23] Cf. Klaus Günzel, "Zu E.T.A. Hoffmanns Entwicklung als Schriftsteller," *Wege der Forschung, op. cit.,* 365f.

[24] He continued drinking (cf. his last order of champange mentioned in his letter of January 12. 1822), and his social indiscretions (speaking in public about the political meaning of his recent poetic work) even into his terminal illness. As his life story demonstrates, his alcohol abuse and dependence fits the criteria of DSM-III for alcoholism. 1) continuous use of alcohol for at least one month; 2) social complications of alcohol use; 3) psychological dependence or pathological patterns of use (binges, blackouts); 4) tolerance or withdrawel symptoms. His illnesses, including his terminal illness and death by a paralysis, are similar to the secondary symptoms of chronic alcoholism --gastritis (repeated from comments of 1803 on in the diary), cirrhosis of the liver (the abdominal hardening he writes about in his 1818 illness, *Letters,* II, 169), neuritis (the "nervous fever" --letter of 16. April 1819, *Letters* II, 343 *ff.* Cf. *Comprehensive Textbook of Psychiatry/III,* 3. edition, vol.II. Ed. by Harold I. Kaplan, et al. (Baltimore: Williams and Wilkins, 1980), 1629 ff. For political aspects, cf. Günzel. Hoffmann became a member of the Immediate Commission which was to give judicial support to strict censorship and repression of political opposition. Hoffmann refused to cooperate with the spy system of the Prussian police state and was himself under investigation when he died.

Chapter III

[1]All references to Büchner's *Lenz* will be quoted from Georg Büchner, *Sämtliche Werke und Briefe,* vol. 1, edited by Werner Lehmann (Hamburg: Christian Wegner Verlag, 1971), 79-101. The translation is my own as Michael Hamburger's in *Leonce and Lena* ——*Lenz* ——*Woyzeck* (Chicago and London: University of Chicago Press, 1972), as well as Carl R. Mueller's in *Complete Plays and Prose* (New York: Hill and Wang, 1963), are not literal enough for my purposes.

[2]Büchner's method of using a historical figure and making him into a figure who exemplifies and by means of whom he analyzes a problem of social-aesthetic reality is discussed insightfully by Albert Meier in "Georg Büchners Ästhetik," *Georg Büchner Jahrbuch*, 2 (1982), 196-208.

[3]The struggle lasted from 1777 till his death in 1792, a chronic schizophrenic. The later stages of the process toward chronicity can be observed in Lenz's correspondence during the late seventies, eighties, into the early nineties. Cf. *Briefe von und an J.M.R. Lenz*, ed. by Karl Freye und Wolfgang Stammler, 2 vols. (Bern: Herbert Lang, 1969). Needless to say, these letters were not available to Büchner. Büchner abbreviates the actual course of schizophrenia and attributes to Lenz an estrangement from reality and a social disintegration which the schizophrenic only reaches after years of torment and rejection.

[4]The Oberlin account Büchner used appears in "J.F. Oberlin: Herr L...Edition des bisher unveröffentlichten Manuskripts. Ein Beitrag zur Lenz-und Büchnerforschung," Hartmut Dedert, *et al.*, *Revue des Langues Vivantes*, 42 (1976), 357-384. Gerhard Peter Knapp in *Georg Büchner: Eine kritische Einführung in die Forschung* (Frankfurt/Main: Athenäum, 1975), and in "Kommentierte Bibliographie zu Georg Büchner," *Text und Kritik. Sonderband Georg Buchner* (1979), 426-455, gives bibliography on Büchner research and on *Lenz*. Thomas Michael Mayer, "Zu einigen Tendenzen der Büchner-Forschung: Ein kritischer Literaturbericht," *Text und Kritik. Sonderband Georg Büchner*, 3 (1981), 265-311, and Reinhold Grimm, "Abschluss und Neubeginn: Vorläufiges zur Büchner-Rezeption und zur Büchner-Forschung heute," *Georg Büchner Jahrbuch*, 2 (1982), 21-40 evaluate and update the research. Maurice B. Benn's *The Drama of Revolt* (Cambridge: Cambridge University Press, 1976) is the best general interpretation available. A considerable literature has grown around the question if the tale is a fragment or if it ends where the Oberlin account ends. My own analysis supports the recent critical contention that the tale is essentially finished as we have it in the copy of Büchner's fiancée.

[5] Cf. Gerhard Irle, *Der psychiatrische Roman* (Stuttgart: Hippokrates Verlag, 1965), who finds the novella a phenomenological scientific description of a schizophrenic break long before Kraepelin.

[6]The sociological-political criticisms are to be found in Cornelie Ueding, *Denken, Sprechen, Handeln* (Bern: Lang, 1976), and Jan Thorn-Prikker, *Revolutionär ohne Revolution: Interpretation der Werke Georg Büchners* (Stuttgart: Klett, Cotta, 1978). The religious criticism is developed by David Richards, *Georg Büchner and the Birth of Modern Drama* (Albany, New York: State University of New York Press, 1977). Finally, Francis Michael Sharp's psychological interpretation from an antipsychiatric perspective focuses upon the Oberlin/Lenz relationship as an example of Büchner's critique of religion and the bourgeoisie, "Büchner's 'Lenz': A Futile Madness," *Psychoanalytische und Psychopathologische Literaturinterpretation*, ed. by Bernd Urban and Winfried Kudszus (Darmstadt: Wissenschaftliche Buchgesellschaft, 1981), 256-279.

[7]Ursula Mahlendorf, "Grillparzer's *The Poor Fiddler:* The Terror of Rejection," *American Imago,* 36, 2, (1979), 118-146.

[8]Stylistic contrasts dominate the entire tale as Peter Hausbek was the first to point out, "'Ruhe' and 'Bewegung.' Versuch einer Stilanalyse von Georg Büchners *Lenz,* " *GRM, N.F.,* 19 (1969), 35-59.

[9]It was Walter Höllerer who called attention to the "erlebte Rede". *Zwischen Klassik und Moderne* (Stuttgart: Klett, 1958), 423. Much speculation has concerned itself with the question how much Büchner identifies with Lenz. My concern is with the stylistic realization of the identification.

[10] *E.g.* an incapacitating sore on Lenz's leg for which he received much attention from Oberlin's wife in Oberlin's account.

[11] Another unchanging presence in the story is the moon. It is full ("The full moon stood in the sky," 85) when Lenz gives his sermon, and it is still full two weeks later when he is brought to Strasbourg ("high, full moon," 101). Even more than the mountains, the celestial image makes it clear that Büchner's descriptions are not naturalistic, but symbolic devices to express states of the psyche and provide commentary by the author. The double function of the moon appears memorably in its use after Lenz's resurrection attempt. The moon's unchanged presence denotes an uncaring universe; it is a heavenly eye, seeing neither human suffering nor human rebellion. But the moon is also the pupil of the eye of a "stupid" heaven upon which Lenz projects anger and impotence ("The sky was a stupid blue eye and the moon stood in it quite ridiculously, dim-wittedly," 94). The final earth and moon images vividly contrast the unchanging, beautiful, unresponsive universe with Lenz's now pitiful condition. The preciousness of the image ("the earth was like a golden chalice over which ran the golden waves of the moon," 101) starkly underlines the darkness and forsakenness of Lenz's fate. The moon is radiating light, but Lenz has ceased to see: "dull fear grew in him *the more the objects were lost in darkness*" (my italics). The mountain and moon represent Oberlin and serve to indicate the changing relations between the two men.

[12]The stylistic investigation concerns me only with respect to the narrator's directing the reader's response. The subtle way in which Büchner achieves this makes him particularly modern. Cf. Gerhard Schaub, "Georg Büchner: *Poeta Rhetor:* Eine Forschungsperspektive," *Georg Büchner Jahrbuch,* 2 (1982), 170-195, especially 184.

[13]In Oberlin's account, Lenz moves into the parsonage during Oberlin's absence and then stays there. Büchner, stressing his status as outsider, has him stay at the schoolhouse. Comparisons with Oberlin's account will be given when they show how Büchner used the source for his own purposes. Cf. Albert Meier, *op. cit.* footnote 2.

[14]Lenz is much too regressed to respond to any specific woman or her memory. What he responds to is his earliest experience of his mother. It is to Büchner's credit that he omitted Oberlin's speculations and the temptation to fabricate an unhappy love story as the reason for Lenz's madness.

[15]The women in Lenz's dramatic works have the same quality of victimized and insubstantial extensions of men. Büchner used the dramas as a source and must have

fashioned Lenz's image of women from them. An important political point of Lenz's plays was protest against the exploitation of women. The political aspect does not cancel the psychological truth of Lenz's experience of women as persons. While the victimized woman was a social and literary reality of the Storm and Stress period, strong women were equally real.

[16]Kohut's theories concerning the archaic self with its need to be mirrored, affirmed by an empathic adult and to have the adult provide the organizing center of the infant's world are more adequate ways of seeing Lenz's regressed relationships to adult figures than Freudian oedipal theory. Cf. Heinz Kohut, *The Restoration of the Self* (New York: International Universities Press, 1977). Further, Kohut in "Creativeness, Charisma, Group Psychology," *The Search for the Self*, vol. II, ed. by Paul H. Ornstein (New York: International Universities Press, 1978), 801, sees creativity energized predominantly from the grandiose self, that is to say from the self that has its origin in the approving, mirroring selfobject (i.e., parent), whose earliest form is the mother. Büchner's description of the relationship to parent figures gives the mirroring/approving function to the father. For Lenz it is the nurturent father who is the source of creativity.

[17] Cf. Günter Ammon, *Handbuch der Dynamischen Psychatrie,* vol. I, "Schizophrenie" (Munich: Reinhardt Verlag, 1979), 364-462.

[18]Oberlin, like many 18th century parsons, had a reputation as a healer, but did not know of Lenz's previous psychotic episodes. He took Lenz in because he was a friend of Kaufmann's and because he hoped for his help with the parish. Only during his trip to Switzerland did he find out about Lenz's previous episodes. He returned early so as to protect his pregnant wife from any kind of shock. Büchner's Madame Oberlin, a major character in the pastor's account, has only a minor role. Unintentionally, Büchner's Oberlin relates as an equal to Lenz at the beginning of his stay, as a concerned equal, a stance which benefits Lenz.

[19]Oberlin gives the name of the child as Friederike and hence connects the incident with Lenz's supposed fixation on Friederike Brion. Büchner omits the name of the child, sensing correctly that the incident is only important in reference to the father symbolism and the search for the father. The addition of the name to Büchner's ms by recent editors misses Büchner's intent.

[20]Büchner understood from the historical Oberlin's account that as far as Oberlin was concerned Lenz's unhappiness was due to his moral profligateness, his disobedience to his father and to womanizing *(Revue des Langues Vivantes, op. cit.,* 374). Büchner uses this information to show what strategies Lenz would likely use to test, pay back, annoy Oberlin.

[21]The beating incident comes almost verbatim from Oberlin's account. Büchner of course understood its significance with its overtones of asking for a blessing from the father. What is amazing to me is that in the criticism of the novella no one has commented on the cruelty of the hoax played on Lenz and on Oberlin's density in delivering the gift.

[22]On the double bind in schizophrenia, cf. Gregory Bateson, "Toward a Theory of Schizophrenia"; "Double Bind" in *Steps to an Ecology of Mind* (San Francisco: Chandler Publishing Company, 1971), 201, 278.

[23]I disagree with H. P. Pütz, who finds that Büchner relies more heavily on Oberlin's diary in the second half of the narrative. The large agreements of the first few pages of the fourth section give way to a total difference in the final four pages. Cf. "Büchners Lenz und seine Quelle. Bericht und Erzählung," *ZfdPh*, 84 (1965), Sonderheft, 1-22. Where Oberlin gives moralizing comments and expresses his fear of the madman, the narrator enters into Lenz's inner experience which he contrasts against the uncomprehending Oberlin and family.

[24]How little consideration the father of the historical Lenz had for his sick son appears from his indifference to his physical and mental illness when he was informed of it by Schlosser *(Briefe,* II, 126) and Lenz. The father did not respond for a year and a half to pleas for help. Only when threatened by the publicity of a public solicitation for funds for Lenz's care did a brother come to get Lenz. When Lenz, on return home, proved unable to maintain steady employment, the rejection continued.

[25] *Lenz* is no less a work of political protest and plea for humanity than is *Woyzeck.* The cruelty against Woyzeck is gross and obvious. From his medical studies at Strasbourg, his knowledge of Pinel's reforms and Jacobi's somatic theories of madness, Büchner cannot but have been struck by Oberlin's total disregard of the fact that Lenz is ill. The same is true of Lenz's friends. The social criticism in addition to the charge of indifference and coldness of heart in Büchner's work has only been noted recently in sociological and Marxist studies, cf. Ueding and Thorn-Prikker, *op. cit.*

[26]After the infant becomes capable of cognitively recognizing differences between himself and the nurturing parent at approximately one year, he still seeks to merge with him/her in symbiosis and to receive the parent's acceptance, goodness, esteem and to participate in his/her mastery of situations, competence, authority. With good enough parenting, the child suffers only gradual and age-appropriate disappointments in his parent's acceptance and authority. These gradual disappointments intrude reality factors upon the child's omnipotence and grandiosity and help build by internalization from the parental self (the selfobject) a reliable sense of the capacity of the self. This selfobject is different from the parent and invested with narcissistic energy. Lenz lacks such a dependable inner structure, his pathology is a psychotic pathology of the self in its earliest beginnings. He seeks external supports from whom he can obtain structure by identification. Büchner knew of the importance of Goethe to the historical Lenz. In identification with Goethe, Lenz must have compensated for his lack of inner structure. When he lost Goethe's support, he sought a center in various friends, Oberlin among them. Cf. John E. Gedo and Arnold Goldberg, *Models of the Mind: A Psychoanalytic Theory* (Chicago: University of Chicago Press, 1973), especially Chapter 11, "A Psychoanalytic Nosology," 156ff.

[27]The only critics to discuss the integrated role of the conversation on art are Thorn-Prikker, *op. cit.* 59-84 and Walter Hinderer, *Über deutsche Literatur und Rede: Historische Interpretationen* (Munich: Fink Verlag, 1981), 182. Thorn-Prikker sees Lenz's madness as deliberate social protest, and the conversation as testimony of his position. Hinderer sees Büchner point to the many latent possibilities which Lenz has for fulfillment. The criticism has made much of Büchner's supposed credo as a realist in this conversation. My concern is with its function in *Lenz* as a total work of art. Thorn-Prikker draws many parallels between Büchner's and Lenz's aesthetics and rejects as I do the notion that Büchner defines a realist's position.

[28]On different meanings of this episode, cf. Hinderer *op. cit.;* Hans-Jürgen Schings, *Der mitleidigste Mensch ist der beste Mensch* (Munich: C.H. Beck, 1980), 68 *ff,* and Heinrich Anz, "'Leiden sey all mein Gewinst.' Zur Aufnahme und Kritik christlicher Leidenstheologie bei Georg Büchner," *Georg Büchner Jahrbuch,* 1 (1981), 160-168.

[29] Cf. *Büchner Kommentar zum dichterischen Werk* by Walter Hinderer (Munich: Winkler Verlag, 1977), 166-167.

[30] Cf. Ottomar Rudolf, *Jacob Michael Reinhold Lenz: Moralist und Aufklärer* (Bad Homburg: Verlag Gehlen, 1970), 252. My translation.

[31] Cf. Büchner Kommentar, 159-160.

[32]Our information about Büchner is even more sketchy than about Lenz as few autobiographical documents of his were transmitted. Büchner's brother edited his letters with the view that Büchner's significance lay in the political views he upheld. Therefore all personal parts of the letters and even all reminiscences are restricted to his political role.

[33]Rudolf *op. cit.* 22-27, convincingly shows that Lenz's father was not the indifferent, fanatical or tyrannical monster that he was made out to be by the Strasbourg circle --e.g., Schlosser *et al.* His educational theories show that he had understanding for his sensitive son as a child. The problem was precisely the father's heavy investment in the son, an investment that could not tolerate any difference from himself. His second son, Lenz was born after several sisters and when his older brother was already at school. The father therefore had time to spend on young Lenz. As the father was very busy with his career, his intense interest probably alternated with neglect.

[34]Her final illness was protracted over several years. Earlier, extensive illnesses are mentioned. Lenz refers to her in his letters to his father and brothers only in formal greetings. His letters to her are not extant.

Chapter IV

[1]Translated by Mary Hottinger in *Nineteenth Century German Tales,* ed. by Angel Flores (Garden City, N. Y.: Doubleday Anchor Books, 1959).

[2]Gerhard Storz, *Eduard Mörike* (Stuttgart: Klett, 1967), 379-381. Other information on biography, cf. Hans-Ulrich Simon, *Mörike—Chronik* (Stuttgart: Metzler, 1981).

[3]Renate von Heydebrand in *Eduard Mörikes Gedichtwerk* (Stuttgart: Metzler, 1972), gives a detailed account of Mörike's aversion to historical writing. She shows that all of his writing, including his narratives, was based on personal, internal event rather than on external fact.

[4]Several of the characters show a marked similarity to Hoffmann's characters and have similar functions. Mörike's Eugenia is the equivalent of Hoffmann's Donna Anna. Eugenia's bridegroom is as ineffective a male as Hoffmann's Don Ottavio. Mörike's interpretation of *Don Juan* agrees with Hoffmann's in that both see the don as a rebel.

[5]Like the Mozart of the tale, Mörike experienced inspiration during carriage rides on journeys, on walks in nature, in company with his friends, and in the solitude of night, Heydebrand, 285 ff. The actual composition of the Mozart novella took from 1847 to 1855, with most of the actual writing being done during the first years of his marriage 1851-1855.

[6]Von Heydebrand in her chapter "Töne und Tonarten" distinguishes between three major "registers." They correspond to the three moods I find, which have their origin in the different developmental stages. "The differentiation between these three registers is based on stylistic influences from three different traditions in German literature after 1800: from folk poetry, from the poetry of antiquity, and from that native poetry of the past centuries which had a deliberate social function" (242, author's translation). Von Heydebrand's folk song register corresponds to my lyrical-idyllic-intimate mood. Note that Zerlina's song is inspired by Italian folk tunes. Heydebrand's classical register corresponds to my tragic-elegiac mood; her poetry with social function to my festive-social mood. This last category includes Mörike's large production of often trivial occasional poems.

[7]Structure and content of the novella have provoked some disagreements among scholars. For a bibliography of the more important points of view cf. Helga Slessarev, *Eduard Mörike* (New York: Twayne Publishers, 1970), and G. Wallis Field, "Silver and Oranges: Notes on Mörike's Mozart-*Novelle,*" *Seminar,* XIV, 4 (1978), 243-254.

[8]I designate those images, figures, incidents, etc. as allegory whose meaning is conscious to and unambiguously intended by the author; for example, the orange tree of the story represents the tree of cultural life. In a symbol, one or several meanings are unconscious, that is to say, none or not all of the meanings are intended by the author. The object symbols of the novella, the opera *Don Giovanni,* as well as the orange, have allegorical as well as symbolic meanings.

[9] Cf. Harry Slochower for a review of the psychoanalytic literature on creativity in *Essays in Creativity,* ed. by Stanley Rosner and Lawrence E. Abt (Croton-

Hudson, New York: North River Press, 1974), 151-190.

[10]On the role of oedipal strivings in the artist and the search for the father, cf. Phyllis Greenacre, *The Quest for the Father* (New York: International Universities Press, 1963). In Mörike's development the role of the father was, as for any artist, a crucial one. My interpretation must needs differ from Greenacre's as the oedipal situation for each child has its unique configurations. Preoedipal stages for Mörike play a larger role than Greenacre would have it. The artist in his quest in this tale has some similarity to the culture hero Harry Slochower describes in his *Mythopoesis: Mythic Patterns in the Literary Classics* (Detroit: Wayne State University Press, 1970). Slochower's tripartite quest structure appears in the tale not as separate chronological events but rather as different ways in which the hero relates to the social world. He fits into, rebels against and restructures the cultural world.

[11]At the next creative moment, the emphasis is once again on the roundness of place --the dining room is circular. During the last creative episode, darkness and night in the role of maternal environments substitute for place designations.

[12]A similar stimulation of the senses is described in the two other incidents. In the festive hall the company is busy with eating, drinking, reciting poetry, viewing an engraving, playing music, singing, and dancing. During the third creative episode, the sensual stimulation is less but the erotic overtones and the intensity of feeling (anger, dread, desire, fear, delight) are high. In the second and third episodes, the sensual stimulation is that of later, more sophisticated developmental stages than the early oral one.

[13] Cf. also Ammon's discussion of the reactivation, in creative states, of the energies internalized from the earliest primary group. Günter Ammon, *Handbuch der Dynamischen Psychiatrie* (Munich: Reinhardt Verlag, 1979), 135-139.

[14] Cf. Herbert Marcuse's excellent discussion of this counter-tradition embodied by the Orpheus and Narcissus figures, *Eros and Civilzation: A Philosophical Inquiry into Freud* (New York: Vintage Books Edition, 1962) specifically 149-154.

[15] Cf. Ammon, *op. cit.* "Creativity is always connected with sexual interests," 135.

[16]Marcuse, 191. His art played this social role for Mörike. He read the completed novella to friends several times (Simon, 227); he planned to have a composer contribute a ficticious Mozart composition and a painter a Mozart portrait to the published novella.

[17]Even in two other lighter episodes of the tale, in the initial coach conversation between Mozart and his wife and in Constance's tale about the household wedding gifts, the father-son theme plays a considerable role. The function of these two excursions concerned with the Mozart household is precisely to show that the composer is not a father figure, even though he has children to whom he wishes to be a father (364-365), and even though he has fantasies about being a model father. It is quite significant that being a father coincides for Mozart with being a gardener. At one point Mozart even takes steps to realize his gardener-householder fantasy by buying garden tools and household wares. Actually, he forgets tools and wares in his busy life as a composer. The roles of father-gardener and of artist are incompatible.

[18]The role of restitution in Mörike's account of the artistic process agrees with Melanie Klein's position. Klein finds that "the desire for perfection, sublimation, is rooted in depressive anxiety about having caused disintegration." Cf. "A Contribution to the Psychogenesis of Manic-depressive States," in *Contributions to Psychoanalysis* (London: The Hogarth Press, 1965), 290. In Mörike's tale the artist causes disintegration to a part of the father's world, his property, his values, his women.

[19]Marcuse, 191-193.

[20]Mörike's life at the time of the tale's writing makes possible an even more optimistic interpretation. He was just married, and fathered two children; for a brief while he was free of his brothers' and sisters' demands for financial and moral support. His literary efforts brought him friendships with other artists, some public acclaim (new editions of his poems, requests for contributions to journals, etc.) and even an audience at literary lectures.

[21]Eugenia, in this view, would be an aspect of woman, namely the terrible mother as seen by Jung and his students, cf. Erich Neumann, *The Great Mother: An Analysis of the Archetype* (Princeton: Princeton University Press, 1972).

[22]There is some argument whether or not Mörike stopped writing entirely. Subsequent to the novella, he did a number of translations, occasional birthday poems and the like, a never completed revision of his novel *Maler Nolten*, and a very few great poems, "Erinna to Sappho" (1863) and "A Visit to a Carthusian Monastery" (1862). Both of these poems deal with the subject of death. We might therefore rather say that except on the subject of death his inspiration left him. For the rest, he was, after all, a professional artist with some established work and thought habits which it must have taken some time to completely eradicate.

[23]"Father, however, in his restless activity, living even at home only for his science, took only the remotest interest in our education. If he influenced us at all, it happened by chance hints or, so to speak, through the loving and serious impression of his person. Conversation with him was rarely expressly instructive and almost never so with the younger children like myself." From "At my Investiture at Cleversulzbach, July 1834," *Sämtliche Werke* (München: Carl Hanser Verlag, 1964), 1201. Author's translation.

[24]Simon, *op. cit.* 89-90.

[25]Von Heydebrand, *op. cit.* 284 ff. "Thoughts and descriptions of the therapeutic effect of art...recur in Mörike's letters and notes...Mörike expects the psychic satisfaction which emanates from any successful activity to a special degree from poetic creativity because the finished work is also intended to have such an effect."

Chapter V

[1]All references to Stifter's letters, works and essays will be to *Sämtliche Werke*, issued by the Bibliothek deutscher Schriftsteller aus Böhmen, Prague-Reichenberg, 1901 ff. Volume number and paging will be given in the text in parenthesis after quotation. All translations are my own.

[2]The two passages of 1863 and 1853 attest to his unchanged classicism.

[3]The large literature on Stifter is evaluated by H. Seidler, "Adalbert Stifter-Forschung 1945-1970," in *Zeitschrift für deutsche Philologie*, 91 (1972), 113-157; 252-285, and updated in "Die Adalbert Stifter-Forschung der siebziger Jahre," *Vasilo*, 30 (1981), 3/4, 89-134. On *Progeny* cf. J. Müller, "Stifters Humor. Zur Struktur der Erzählungen 'Der Waldsteig' und 'Nachkommenschaften,'" in *Vasilo*, II (1962), 1-20; and Margaret Gump, *Adalbert Stifter* (New York: Twayne Publishers, 1974). Gump summarizes the characteristic Stifter scholarship in the German speaking countries up to the late 1960s. On *Progeny* as a turn to the active life cf. Konrad Steffen, *Adalbert Stifter: Deutungen* (Basel: Birkhäuser Verlag, 1955), 187-193.

[4]Most recently Friedbert Aspetsberger, "Stifters Erzählung 'Nachkommenschaften,'" in *Sprachkunst*, 6 (1975), 238-260.

[5]K. K. Polheim, "Die wirkliche Wirklichkeit. Adalbert Stifters 'Nachkommenschaften' und das Problem seiner Kunstanschauung," in *Untersuchungen zur Literatur als Geschichte. Festschrift für Benno von Wiese* (Berlin: Schmidt, 1973), 385-417.

[6]The only recent study on Stifter's depression is Alfred Winterstein's, *Adalbert Stifter: Persönlichkeit und Werk, eine tiefenpsychologische Studie* (Wien: Phoenix Verlag, 1946). The details of the depressive pattern will concern us later. For the time being, it suffices to point out that the exacerbation of the depression during the period 1863-1865 had no apparent cause.

[7]For the novels, the revision process could last 7-9 years. *E.g.* In July 1858 Stifter promised his publisher Heckenast to finish the three volume novel *Witiko*, early in 1860. By November of 1859, he assured Heckenast that he would only need that winter to finish (XIX, 188). He sent a first sample by October 1860 (XIX, 244). During 1861 he sent several sections but by December he was still at work on the fourth chapter of book I. From May 1863 to fall 1864 he interrupted work on *Witiko* altogether. In December 1864, Heckenast finally received the complete first book. Over the next two and a half years, through 1865 - November 1867 Heckenast received section after section, first of ms. then of sometimes almost completely revised proofs of the following two books.

[8]On Stifter as a painter cf. Fritz Novotny, *Adalbert Stifter als Maler* (Wien: Verlag Anton Schroll, 1947); Franz Baumer, "'Musik für das Auge.' Progressive Elemente bei Adalbert Stifter als Maler und Zeichner," *Vasilo*, XXXI (1982), 121-144; Ursula Mahlendorf, "Stifters Absage an die Kunst?" in *Goethezeit: Festschrift für Stuart Atkins* (Bern, Munich: Francke Verlag, 1981), 369-383.

[9]Adalbert Stifter, *Julius: Eine Erzählung*. Text-critical edition by Kurt
Gerhard Fischer (Linz: Oberöstereichischer Landesverlag, 1965). On the similarities between *Julius* and *Progeny* to account for difficulties Stifter has with narrative perspective in *Progeny*, cf. Friedbert Aspetsberger, *op. cit.* 244.

[10]On the significance of first works, cf., Winterstein.

[11]On the transformation of the mother figure into a younger woman and
daughter, cf. Freud, *Std. Ed.*, IX, 7-11.

[12]The Kaspar Hauser case occupied the European press in 1828. All of Stifter's
early work was dominated by his imitation of Jean Paul. But Stifter had good
biographical reasons to identify with this particular Romantic theme.

[13]On the meaning of such punishment fantasies, cf. Winterstein, 13.

[14]Cf. Martin Selge's critique of the literature on the comparison of versions in
Adalbert Stifter: Poesie aus dem Geiste der Naturwissenschaften (Stuttgart:
Kohlhammer, 1976), 72-73 and 113-114.

[15]The wild animal metaphor to represent passion appears as a central theme in
Stifter's novella *Brigitta*.

[16]In this conversation with the landlady, the name Roderer is repeated again and
again with an emphasis which reminds of similar repetitions of names in
Bergkristall. Emphasis on names, in Stifter, serves to imply strong feeling.

[17]His first tale *Der Kondor* (1841) an oedipal flight fantasy.

[18] Cf. Jean-Louis Bandet, "Der Eindringling in das Haus des Vaters," *Austriaca*
(Tübingen: Niemeyer, 1975), 230-246.

[19]On the sense of *déjà vue* and the meaning of references to ancient times as
symbolic of a return to the early mother and the womb, Freud's accounts are
most revelant in *Interpretations of Dreams* and in *The Psychopathology of
Everyday Life, Strd. Ed.*, vols. V, 399, 447 and 478, and VI, 150-151, 265-268.

[20] Cf. Heinz Kohut, *The Restoration of the Self* (New York: International
Universities Press, 1977), 185. Classical analysis attributes a similar role to the
father in the oral phase, cf. James W. Hamilton, "Object Loss, Dreaming and
Creativity: The Poetry of John Keats," in *The Psychoanalytic Study of the
Child*, 24 (1969), 488-531. This early role of the father is different from that
with which the post-oedipal boy identifies. The antiquity of this figure in an
individual's development is expressed by the greater age attributed to him. He is
not threatening as the younger, more active father of the post-oedipal period.
Stifter's father figures (cf. Risach of *Der Nachsommer*,) are all of such grandfatherly dimensions.

[21] *Playing and Reality* (New York: Basic Books, 1971), 47.

[22]Recent critics regard the economic independence of Stifter's heroes as
alienated fantasy, cf. on the role of the "Erbschaftstopos," Rudolf Wildbolz,
Adalbert Stifter (Stuttgart: Kohlhammer, 1976), 117. The transient oral dependence of Stifter's youthful heroes is expressed by the inheritance topos. Older
guide figures like Peter, in harmony with their psychic function in the narratives,
are self-made men. They represent a different phase of human development.

[23]Polheim and other critics have dealt extensively with: (1) the historical meaning of the picture and Stifter's assessment of contemporary art. Friedrich's picture, according to his critics, is better than any contemporary painting, (2) the relationship of this painting to Stifter's own, (3) the renunciation of his own painting in the story. What is striking is the picture's utter annihilation.

[24]The sequence for Peter is exactly that.

[25] Cf. Polheim for a review of the literature. I am concerned with the psychological meaning implied by the emphatic repetition, *wirkliche Wirklichkeit*.

[26]An undercoating takes him five long working days, the painting itself from early spring to December --8-9 months of daily working.

[27]In Stifter's late work, a shift to the present tense marks especially dramatic moments, cf. Hans-Ulrich Rupp, *Stifters Sprache* (Zürich: Juris Druck, 1969), 75.

[28] Cf. Adalbert Stifter's *Jugendbriefe*, ed. by Gustav Wilhelm (Nürnberg: Verlag Hans Carl, 1954), 66-68.

[29]Helga Bleckwenn, "Künstlertum als soziale Rolle: Stifters Berufswahl," *Vasilo*, 28 (1979), 35-42; and "Künstlertum als soziale Rolle, II: Stifters Berufslaufbahn in den vierziger Jahren," *Vasilo*, 30 (1981), 15-45. Bleckwenn shows that Stifter, despite his bestseller status, remained a marginal figure of his age. She observes from a sociological perspective what I find in the psychodynamics. If Stifter could not confess to the role of either painter or writer, he could not participate in literary or political society.

[30] Cf. Michael Kaiser, *Adalbert Stifter: Eine literaturpsychologische Untersuchung* (Bonn: Bouvier Verlag, 1971) gives a detailed picture of the denial of themes in Stifter. He does not look at the interlinked techniques and strategies.

[31]Pinchas Noy, "Form Creation in Art: An Ego Psychological Approach to Creativity," *International Journal of Psychoanalysis* (1978), 229-255, 233.

[32]Stifter used this particular form only three times in his work --in the early *Feldblumen*, *Nachsommer* (1857) and *Progeny*.

[33]Adalbert Stifter, *Jugendbriefe*, op. cit., 70-71.

[34]Stifter does not explain why Susanna's father should be so much older than his own father.

[35]On breaches in narrative perspective, cf. Aspetsberger, *op. cit.*, 245.

[36]The adjustment of Friedrich's timing to that of the Roderers appears in a small incident involving time. Friedrich first meets Susanna by chance in the forest at eleven o'clock. Afterward he sees her several times on the same path and begins to watch with his binoculars in order to meet her on time. She tests him, once by coming early and once late, and he meets her both times. From then on, they come regularly at eleven o'clock, pass in silence, and return to their separate homes. Their time frames have been tested and adjusted to each other. Roderer, without needing to be told, says later: "I knew that you were going the same paths" (292).

[37] Cf. Freud, "Family Romances" (1909), Strd. Ed., vol. IX, 235-244.

[38] Stifter was using the Hohenstauffens in the contemporary *Witiko*. The example provides insight into the fear underlying in Stifter's oedipal situation -- being swallowed by the oral mother. Barbarossa's river is transformed into Friedrich's moor.

[39] Martin Selge, *op. cit.* develops how Stifter, the trained naturalist, used doubling to have the reader participate in natural processes by patient observation of the processes.

[40] Cf. Stifter's use of negation with Freud's in "Negation" (1925), Strd. Ed., vol. XIX, 235.

[41] Stifter criticism has recently given considerable attention to his negative view of history. A thought like, "Der Mensch denkt, Gott lenkt," probably underlies the negating process in the historical narratives. Cf. Michael Kaiser, *op. cit.*, especially chapter 2.2.1.

[42] Cf. Kaiser, *op. cit.*; Wildbolz, *op. cit.*

[43] Cf. George Pickering, *Creative Malady* (New York: Dell Publishing, 1974).

[44] *E.g. Die Mappe meines Urgrossvaters* which exists in widely different versions, accompanying the entire life of the author.

[45] On his financial dependency on his publisher, cf. Klaus Aman, "Stifter und Heckenast: Literarische Produktion zwischen Ästhetik und Ökonomie," *Vasilo*, 27 (1978), 47-58.

[46] The day after sending the story away for publication Stifter reported a dream to his wife, an occurrence rare in itself. "At 4 I put the Roderers into the mail. And then I went to bed and measured all through my dream a painter's canvas of twenty inches" (XX, 149). Note that the painting in the dream has not been begun. The dream wish puts Stifter at the beginning of the process and cancels the finished story.

[47] Cf. Winterstein, 9.

[48] On the clinging of the child even to unsatisfactory or destructive maternal objects (and their real or fantasied substitutes) cf. Michael Balint, *The Basic Fault: Therapeutic Aspects of Regression* (London: Tavistock Publications, 1968), and Heinz Kohut, *The Restoration of the Self* (New York: International Universities Press, 1977).

[49] Adalbert Stifter, *Gesammelte Werke*, vol. XIV, ed. by Konrad Steffen (Basel: Birkhäuser Verlag, 1972), 117-118.

[50] Steffen, *op. cit.* 118-119.

[51] Cf. Freud's discussion of breaking dishes in Goethe's *Poetry and Truth* in Std. Ed., XVII, 145-156.

[52] The young doctor of the first version of the *Journal of My Greatgrandfather*, for example, for expressing his jealousy, loses his bride.

[53]But succoring nature can turn into terror --of moor or of icy landscapes as in *My Greatgrandfather*.

[54]According to Alfred Winterstein, *Adalbert Stifter, op. cit.*, 335, Stifter's depressions follow losses or disturbances in self-esteem. I find that the tenor of his life gets depressed gradually after he assumed office as school inspector, that is to say, under the stress of a responsible, social activity and remained depressed continuously with some exacerbations of the overall depression.

[55]The amount of work involved in maintaining the duration and hence the safety of the process was staggering. Stifter described his working procedure in the following manner: "First the main idea in my mind. 2. Working out detail, still in my head. 3. Plan of detail, sentences, expressions, scenes on individual scraps of paper with pencil (for that I need the most precious hours). 4. Writing the text on paper with ink. 5. Correction of this text after some time with cuts, additions, etc. 6. Correction of the correction after some time, fusing it into the main body of the work. 7. Finished writing in clean copy" (XX, 45). We must add that Stifter corrected and changed much in proof, and worked narratives over for reedition. Steps 4-7 and the emendations in proof constitute several stages of a process over a period of time. Stylistic investigations which only consider *Urfassung* and changes for a later edition (such as those for the *Studien*, for instance) only encompass a small part of the entire process. On the methodological difficulties in studying this kind of composition cf. Martin Selge, *op. cit.*, especially 72 ff.

[56]Winterstein finds that Stifter did not experience a depression after the suicide of his step-daughter Juliana. This is simply not true. Stifter's mood during 1858-1859 was very somber and dominated by thoughts of death. He also lost then two recently discovered nieces (Josephine and Luise Stifter, who were not blood relatives) to tuberculosis.

[57] cf. footnote 7.

[58]The last version of that narrative works through some of the constriction by techniques of denial which totally dominates such late works as *Der Kuss von Sentze*. *Journal*, in describing the young doctor's grief for the loss of his family allows powerful emotions. It appears to find possibility for psychic release in the very denial of life. *Journal* thus is evidence that writing, unlike the completely compulsive painting process, contained the possibility of salvation.

Chapter VI

[1]All references to "Josephine the Singer, or the Mouse Folk" will be to Nahum N. Glatzer's edition of *The Complete Stories* (New York; Schocken Books, 1976), in the Muir translation.

[2]Cf. *Briefe*, 1902-1924, edited by Max Brod (New York: Schocken Books, 1958), 447. Translations will be mine and references included parenthetically in the text with the identification L. References from *Diaries*, 1910-1913, edited by Max Brod, translated by Joseph Kresh (New York: Schocken Books, 1974, 4. ed.) will be quoted as D I. *Diaries* 1914-1923, edited by Max Brod, translated by Martin Greenberg with cooperation of Hannah Arendt (New York: Schocken Books, 1974), as D II. *Letters to Milena*, edited by Willy Haas, translated by Tania and James Stern (New York: Schocken Books, 1953), as LM; *Letter to his Father/Brief an den Vater*, bilingual edition, translated by Ernst Kaiser and Eithne Wilkins (New York: Schocken Books, 1966), as LFa; Gustav Janouch's *Gespräche mit Kafka* will be quoted from *Erweiterte Ausgabe* (Frankfurt: Fischer Verlag, 1968) in my own translation, as Janouch; quotations from *Hochzeitsvorbereitungen auf dem Lande* (New York: Schocken Books, 1953) as H; *Briefe an Felice*, edited by Erich Heller and Jürgen Born (Frankfurt: Fischer Verlag, 1967), as LF.

[3]To Max Brod, July 5, 1922: "What I played at now will happen. I did not buy myself off by writing. I died all my life long and now I will actually die" *(Letters*, 385). On the meaning of his tuberculosis, cf. John S. White's "Psyche and Tuberculosis: The Libido Organization of Franz Kafka," *The Psychoanalytic Study of Society*, IV (1967), 185-251.

[4] Cf. Hartmut Binder in *Kafka Kommentar zu sämtlichen Erzählungen*, (Munich: Winkler Verlag, 1975), 233 for a collation of all biographical materials to *Josephine*. "The Judgment" *(Kommentar*, 123) is the most famous case of the one night story.

[5]Cf. Hartmut Binder on Kafka's position as a Western assimilated Jew and his interest in Jewish nationalism in *Kafka in neuer Sicht* (Stuttgart: Metzler, 1976), 267 ff.; also Christoph Stölzl, *Kafkas böses Böhmen* (Munich: edition text und kritik, 1975); E.T. Beck, *Kafka and the Yiddish Theater* (Madison, Wisconsin: University of Wisconsin Press, 1971), and Arnold J. Band, "Kafka and the Beilies Affair," *Comparative Literature*, XXXII, 2 (1980), 168-183.

[6] *Kommentar*, 324;325;330.

[7]The most important studies of the tale, Heinz Politzer's *Franz Kafka: Parable and Paradox*, 2. ed. (Ithaca, N.Y.: Cornell University Press, 1966), Walter H. Sokel's *Franz Kafka: Tragik und Ironie* (Munich: Langen, 1964), and Wilhelm Emrich's *Franz Kafka* (Frankfurt/Main: Athenäum Verlag, 1958), give various universal interpretations of the artist theme, whereas Binder, *Kommentar*, links the story to the specific biographical situation i.e., Josephine as a latter-day prophet for the national movement.

[8]Stölzl and Binder (see note 5) give the most graphic details of the rampant antisemitism Kafka encountered at the end of WWI in Prague and during the period of inflation in Berlin. However, social unrest with its antisemitic rioting occurred in Bohemia all through Kafka's childhood.

[9]Politzer, Sokel, and Emrich name different aesthetic theories as Kafka's targets; recent criticism has added others, e.g. Margot Norris, "Kafka's Josephine: The Animal as the Negative Site of Narration," *MLN*, 98 (1983), 366-383, the theories of

Conceptual and Dada art. On Kafka's secondary school education in poetics and aesthetics, cf. Hartmut Binder, *Kafka Handbuch*, I (Stuttgart: Kröner Verlag, 1979), 195 ff.; also Heinz Hillmann, *Franz Kafka: Dichtungstheorie und Dichtungsgestalt* (Bonn: Bouvier Verlag, 1973, 2. ed.).

[10]Malcolm Pasley, "Der Schreibakt und das Geschriebene. Zur Frage der Entstehung von Kafkas Texten," in *Franz Kafka: Themen und Probleme*, ed. by Claude David (Göttingen: Vandenhoeck and Ruprecht, 1980), 9-25 insightfully divides Kafka's oeuvre into narratives of dynamic, sequential, interpersonal events and reflections on static, enigmatic themes. He does not see that in *Josephine* Kafka makes the relationship between the two ways of writing his theme.

[11]The Muir translation ("but the latest is that she has disappeared") obscures the shock of our realization that Josephine must have disappeared ("Verschwunden war"), even as the narrator was speaking. Franz Kafka, *Sämtliche Erzählungen*, edited by Paul Raabe (Frankfurt: Fischer Bücherei, 1970), 185. Roy Pascal, *Kafka's Narrators* (Cambridge: Cambridge University Press, 1982), 220, finds the narrator reliable.

[12] *Diaries*, I, 278. Martin Greenberg, *The Terror of Art* (New York: Basic Books, 1965), shows that Kafka's understanding of the internalization in the early story was still quite superficial, 64-65.

[13]The narrator reports *words* from her only once, and then the verbal expression is a pun on her disputed art, piping: "Ich pfeife auf eueren Schutz" (176) ("Your protection isn't worth an old song," 365-366).

[14]Binder, *Kommentar*, 323ff, argues against Josephine's representing Kafka, the artist. and relates her to the young Palestinian Puah Bentovim, Kafka's Hebrew teacher. cf. footnote 7.

[15]"Datierung aller Texte," in *Kafka—Symposium* (Berlin: 1964), 56. On the need for creative bursts, cf. Malcolm Pasley, "Der Schreibakt," *op. cit. and Walter H. Sokel*, "Zur Sprachauffassung und Poetik Franz Kafkas," in *Franz Kafka: Themen und Probleme*, ed. by Claude David (Göttingen: Vandenhoeck and Ruprecht, 1980), 9-25; 26-47.

[16]Joachim Unseld, *Franz Kafka: Ein Schriftstellerleben: Die Geschichte seiner Veröffentlichungen* (Munich: Carl Hanser, 1982), 192.

[17] Cf. Heinz Kohut on narcissistic (nurturance and empathy) disturbances "hidden by seemingly oedipal symptomatology," in "Thoughts on Narcissism and Narcissistic Rage," *The Search for the Self, op. cit.* 625.

[18]On his mother deprivation and its consequences cf. White *op. cit.*, and Calvin S. Hall, Richard E. Lind, *Dreams, Life and Literature: A Study of Franz Kafka* (Chapel Hill: North Carolina Press, 1970).

[19] Cf. Kohut on the narcissistic use of others by artists during creative spells in "Creativeness, Charisma, Group Psychology," in *The Search for the Self, op.cit.* That Kafka needed the women solely to confirm him by admiration, appears also from the fact that all of them saw him as socially or intellectually superior --and

usually both. He had no interest in them as love objects. They were inaccessible to him either by location --Felice lived in Berlin, Milena in Vienna --or by parental objections to marriage --Julie. Further by letters or by telephone, they were his connection to the world of reality --that is nurturers.

[20] The look of Kafka's notebooks and diaries and the ms of the work confirm that his creative impulse came in longer and shorter bursts. Finished work shows little correction and emendation. Each sentence, once completed, seemed perfect to him (D I, 45). Likewise Josephine. She admires every note she emits. When the beginning of a work did not carry him through of its own momentum, he stopped working on it and began a new one. Cf. Pasley, "Schreibakt," op. cit.

[21] The passage appears almost a summing up of the famous conversation of Adrian Leverkühn and his alter ego in Chapter 23 of Thomas Mann's Doctor Faustus (1948). The parallelism is one of problem and age.

[22] Norris, in "The Animal as the Negative Site of Narration," MLN, op. cit. finds the matrix erased even in the very narrating. Pascal, in Kafka's Narrators, op. cit. with his appreciation of the linguistic and perspectival play of the tale considers it positively and her story "the triumph of art" (232).

[23] In terms of Kafka's biography this would mean that Kafka was not homosexual and that he remained regressed in a rather undifferentiated polymorphous sexual state. As an artist, this would give him the capacity to erotize all his processes; visual, auditory, kinaesthetic processes just as much as thinking, imagining, remembering. His sensuous, physical response to language, for instance, would be due to this lack of differentiation. Cf. "I read sentences of Goethe's as though my whole body were running down the stresses" (D I, 233).

[24] White in his essay on Kafka's tuberculosis likewise speaks of "the magic attraction of death," and of "the tuberculosis...a protective agent.... a maternal substitute filling the everlasting need for being nursed by the mother" (248).

[25] Mice in both the Jewish and the German tradition have positive and negative connotations. In the Talmud, the mouse appears as demonic and divine, cf. Frazer, The Golden Bough: A Study of Magic and Religion (New York: The Macmillan Company, 1962), 381. For pfeifen of mice cf. line 2147 of Faust.

[26] On the matter of his stay at Zürau as a sign of not wanting to get well and on his ambivalence about the illness cf. L, 168, 180. About recommended stays in Switzerland, L 165, or in the South, L 197.

[27] There is no specific documented evidence that Kafka was familiar with 2 Alphabet of Ben Sira 24a and 34a or the Perek Shirah, in which the singing mouse appears according to Dov Neumann's Motif Index of Talmudic—Midrashic Literature (Bloomington, Indiana: Indiana University Press, 1954). Kafka might have come across the folktale of the singing animals in paradise during his 1917 occupation with the paradise myth and during his study of Hebrew and Jewish folk literature in 1923-1924.

[28]Though Kafka was acquainted with some of Freud's writings, it is doubtful if he knew the 1923 essay *The Ego and the Id*. Since the father problem had occupied him all his life, the split into the three parts of the self is probably an independent assessment of his own psychic situation. At the outbreak of his illness Kafka occupied himself especially intensively with psychoanalytic theory as it was developed to 1917 (cf. L, 168). Binder *(Kafka in neuer Sicht,* 533 ff) maintains that by 1918 Kafka rejected all psychological explanations of his illness. I think that Kafka then rejected formalized psychological systems and their explanations. He probably neither could nor would stop trying to understand himself in diaries, letters and work. The superego Kafka describes as the mouse folk is not the kind of superego which results from the resolution of the male oedipal conflict. Hall and Lind in *Dreams,* 86-87 come to a similar conclusion. They find that Kafka's dreams show a passivity, a predominance of shame over guilt, a dislike of his own body, a lack of castration fear, a presence of penis envy, all of which are characteristic of the preoedipal child or of the female resolution of the oedipal conflict.

[29]On the mouse folk as Kafka's view of Western Jewry, cf. Binder, Kommentar, 332.

[30]The title of the story: "Josephine the Singer, or the Mouse folk"and the arguments over the balance metaphor of the title (cf. Binder, *Sicht,* 124-125; Politzer, 308 ff, Emrich, 200) have obscured the narrator as figure. Roy Pascal, *Kafka's Narrators, op. cit.* 217 ff. details a serious, reliable historian's role for him.

[31]Binder, in *Kafka in neuer Sicht,* 8-34, especially 8-17 finds that Kafka was incapable of philosophical thought, of the ego function of abstract thinking (of Piaget's operations) and warns against interpreting any of Kafka's metaphors in a general sense. If such a general sense is assumed by the reader, contradictions in readings automatically arise because Kafka was bound to the concrete, autobiographical situation and would be unable to notice contradictions. While the metaphoric power of the work is its outstanding feature --the strength of his primary process is obvious -- the primary process is controlled by the secondary process and the philosophical content of the work deliberate. In the narrator, Kafka created a character who understood the almost total absence of the secondary ego functions in Josephine and the mouse folk. By *creating* the narrator, Kafka shows the strength of his secondary process.

[32]Binder *Kommentar,* 324 ff. equates Josephine's art with art in general, as does Politzer. Sokel, alive to the Nietzschean and Dionysian overtones of the narrative, 514 ff, deals more adequately with Josephine's being a musician, with the theme of power and of primary process associated with music since Schopenhauer in the German literary tradition.

[33] Cf. Janouch, 83. This remark resembles some of Thomas Mann's in *Doctor Faustus*.

[34] Cf. The diaries and letters on increases in such sensitivity during periods of personal crisis, July 1922, L, 388 ff. On the hyperaesthesia, cf. John S. White, "Psyche and Tuberculosis," *op. cit.* 188.

[35] Cf. "as a consequence of the density of population every noise once overcome is followed by a new one still to be overcome and thus on in an infinite series" (L, 388).

[36]"Kafka's Poetics of the Inner Self," in *From Kafka to Dada to Brecht and Beyond*, ed. by Reinhold Grimm *et al* (Madison, Wisconsin: University of Wisconsin Press, 1982), 19.

[37]My translation, *Sämtliche Erzählungen*, 185. The Muir translation obscures Kafka's simplicity.

[38] Cf. Schnitzler's almost contemporaneous "leap into ethics," (my "Arthur Schnitzler's *The Last Letter of a Litterateur:* the Artist as Destroyer," *American Imago*, 34,3 (1977), 238-276) and Adrian Leverkühn's fashioning of new musical values (my "Aesthetics, Psychology and Politics in Thomas Mann's *Doctor Faustus*," *Mosaic*, XI, 4 (1978), 1-18). For many modern authors, the matter of values is central to the artist's dilemma.

[39]Phyllis Greenacre, "Woman as Artist," *Psychoanalytic Quarterly*, 29 (1960), 208-227.

[40] Cf. my "Franz Grillparzer's *The Poor Fiddler:* The Terror of Rejection," *American Imago*, 36,2 (1979), 118-146.

Chapter VII

[1]The text will be quoted from *Kate Chopin: The Awakening. An Authoritative Text. Contexts. Criticism*. Edited by Margaret Culley (New York: Norton, 1976). This edition also provides a fine sampling of the most important criticism of the work, of its contexts, and of contemporary reaction to it.

[2]Harry Slochower, *Mythopoesis: Mythic Patterns in the Literary Classics* (Detroit: Wayne State University Press, 1970), cf. Introduction, 22 ff.

[3]Chopin's novella is the earliest in which a woman portrays herself as a woman artist. I found no examples of the woman artist story in German literature up to Christa Wolf's *A Model Childhood*, (1976). When I speak of women writers, I speak of Western women writers. Linda Huff, *A Portrait of the Artist as a Young Woman: The Writer as Heroine in American Literature* (New York: Frederick Ungar, 1983), though citing a few earlier but artiscaly poorer examples, also finds the woman artist story rare.

[4]On the female oedipal situation, cf. Juliet Mitchel's *Psychoanalysis and Feminism* (New York: Vintage Books, 1975), Part I. Despite its simplified approach the book is helpful. On very early gender differentiation and its effect on later development cf. Herman Roiphe and Eleanor Galenson, *Infantile Origins of Sexual Identy* (New York: International Universities Press, 1981).

[5]George Sand's invention of a protective god figure finds its equivalent in the father gods of Lou Andreas Salomé, cf. *Frau Lou: Nietzsche's Wayward Disciple*, by Rudolph Binion (Princeton: Princeton University Press, 1968). In Willa Cather's novella "Flavia's Artists," (1904), the industrialist husband of the mother figure Flavia plays the fatherly muse to the story's young heroine. In Kate Chopin's own life, her Austrian physician, Dr. Kolbenheyer, fulfilled the role of the fatherly muse, encouraging her to follow a writing career. Some feminists, Huff *op. cit.* dispute the male muse, seeing men as enemies to female self-development.

[6](Princeton: Princeton University Press, 1977), 61. Unfortunately, exact life histories of women writers are even more difficult to ascertain than they are for male writers. Of the 86 women writers I checked, the professions of their fathers were given for 55; they were all in either intellectual professions, or in occupations which allowed for intellectual interests. The implication made by the biographers was that the father provided the intellectual orientation and, before the availability of advanced education for women, the formal training of the women writers. In eleven cases out of the 86, the biographers state specifically that the relationship to the father was close. In most of the other biographies such closeness is implied. The mother's role in the life of the writer is remarked on in 15 cases; it is a complex relationship in all fifteen. Anne Sutherland Harris and Linda Nochlin in *Women Artists: 1550—1950, Los Angeles County Museum of Art* (New York: Alfred Knopf, 1976), point to a similar role of the father for women painters, whose painter fathers till the advent of the 20th century provided the only access to the craft. Ellen Moers, in *Literary Women* (New York: Doubleday, 1976) while also interested in the father's role, comments on the conflict with the mother --and increasingly on conflicts with brothers. Matina S. Horner, "Femininity and Successful Achievement: A Basic Inconsistency," in *Feminine Personality and Conflict*, ed. by J.M. Bardwick *et al.* (Bermont, Cal.: Brooks/Cole Publishing, 1970), 45-74 summarizes the research on woman's internalized achievement restraints.

[7]Elaine Showalter, *A Literature of Their Own*, 22.

[8]The criticism dealing with *The Awakening* stressed the Flaubertian influence on the work (which is there) and hence overlooked that of German Romanticism. Kate Chopin read German with ease and, during her excellent high school education, read such authors as Goethe and E.T.A. Hoffmann in the original. Dr. Kolbenheyer, who was Austrian and who rekindled her intellectual interests after her husband's death, must have reawakened the early familiarity with German literature. He, in any case, introduced her to Schopenhauer and, no doubt, Nietzsche.

[9]Critical studies of the novella concentrate on Edna's male relationships and see her death in terms of them and/or the social situation. Cynthia Griffin Wolff's "Thanatos and Eros," in *Kate Chopin: The Awakening, op. cit.*, 206-217, delineates well Edna's regressive development and like Anne Goodwyn Jones' excellent *Tomorrow is Another Day: Women Writers in the South, 1859—1936* (Baton Rouge: Louisiana State University Press, 1981) sees the other two women as alternative portraits to Edna. Wolff, neglecting the artist theme, belongs to the critics who regard Edna a failure, while Huff (*op. cit.*) and Jones find her a serious artist who, because of the incompatability of mother and artist roles, sacrifices herself (!) for her

children.

[10]Culley's edition misprints this passage which we have corrected following page 908 of *The Complete Works of Kate Chopin*, II, ed. by Per Seyersted (Baton Rouge: Louisiana State University Press, 1969).

[11]In his biography of Kate Chopin, Per Seyersted mentions the influence of Schopenhauer and Wagner but not of German romanticism, cf. *Kate Chopin: A Critical Biography* (Baton Rouge: Louisiana State University Press, 1969). The effect of Mademoiselle Reisz's music on Edna recalls Schopenhauer's theories, e.g., "She saw no pictures of solitude, of hope, of longing, or of despair. But the very passions themselves were aroused" (Chopin, 27). Schopenhauer: "music...expresses...the inner nature, the in-itself of all phenomena,...not...this or that particular and definite joy,...sorrow, or pain, ... but joy, sorrow, pain, ...themselves." *The World as Will and Idea*, Vol. 1, translated by R.B. Haldane and J. Kemp (New York: Routledge & Kegan, 1948), 338. The artist's yearning to escape suffering temporarily in his submersion in artistic work is Schopenhauerian. In making Edna a painter Kate Chopin goes her own way. The influence of Wagner is not merely indicated by Mademoiselle Reisz' use of the Isolde motif but it is structural. Kate Chopin, a few years before Thomas Mann, adopts the *leitmotif* to literature in repeating throughout the novella key sentences (e.g., "the voice of the sea"), images (the bird image), and phrases which characterize (e.g., Mademoiselle Reisz' bunch of violets). The Nietzsche influence appears in the theme of transcendence, self-liberation through art, and rebirth; with bridge, bird, serpent imagery the *Awakening* reflects *Zarathustra*.

[12]Chopin gives a consistent political social allegory. The three males Edna associates with represent important social trends of the times. Mr. Pontellier, off to New York and Wall Street represents the new successful south; Robert with his business quest to Mexico is the unsuccessful new south; Arobin, the dandy, is the decadent south. It is precisely these consistently worked out details (of which we have given only a few examples) which demonstrate the high quality of her craftmanship.

[13]Per Seyersted, *Kate Chopin: A Critical Biography, op. cit.* 48-49.

[14]Her output up to the publication of *The Awakening* steadily increased in quantity and frank sensuousness (e.g. "The Storm"). Following the uproar over the novel, she "never talked to her close friends about the issue; she simply wrote less fiction, and wrote less surely." Jones, *op. cit.*, 139.

[15]Huff, *op. cit.*, 3-10, deriving a stereotyped male artist from Maurice Beebe, *Ivory Towers and Sacred Founts: The Artist Hero in Fiction from Goethe to Joyce* (New York: New York State University Press, 1964) who is "sensitive, dreamy, passive," finds that the women artist by contrast is active, stalwart, spirited, and fearless. Both critics overlook that male and female artist figures when creating are active and self assertive, when failing at their tasks become passive, tormeted, lost.

Chapter VIII

[1] *The Bell Jar*, a Bantam book with biographical notes by Lois Ames (New York: Bantam Books, 1976) 21st printing.

[2] Cf. D.W. Winnicott, *Playing and Reality, op. cit.* We have seen the origins of the transitional object described by Hoffmann in the *Sandman* (cf. chapter 2). For the role of the transitional object in Plath, cf. Shelley Orgel, "Sylvia Plath: Fusion with the Victim and Suicide," *Psychoanalytic Quarterly*, 43 (1975), 262-287.

[3] George Stade, "Introduction," *A Closer Look at Ariel: A Memory of Sylvia Plath*, by Nancy Hunter Steiner (New York: Harper and Row, 1972).

[4] Cf. A. Alvarez in *The Savage God* (New York: Random House, 1972) on the "poet as martyr to poetry" interpretation.

[5] Sylvia Plath, *Letters Home: Correspondence 1950—1963*, edited by Aurelia Schober Plath, (Toronto: Bantam Books, 1977). References to letters will be given to this edition with page numbers following the quotations.

[6] *The Bell Jar*, "Afterword," Lois Ames, 209.

[7] Murray M. Schwartz and Christopher Bollas, "The absence at the center: Sylvia Plath and suicide, in *Sylvia Plath: New Views on the Poetry*, ed. by Gary Lane (Baltimore: Johns Hopkins Press, 1979), find Sylvia's key problem related to "a failure in the early months of her life to find herself consistently reflected in the human environment" (196). Esther's experiences here and elsewhere in the novel confirm that.

[8] This refusal to learn German is usually related to Sylvia's rebellion against her father. Sylvia learned other subjects related to her father's career (e.g., college biology, bee-keeping) very easily. The criticism of the novel avoids the question of the mother world. Proceeding as it does from Plath's own references to her Electra complex and the poem *Daddy*, most critics seek traces of the father and a father world of violence in the book. The satirical thrust and the exile tradition to which the book belongs have not received comment. The criticism and a bibliography are conveniently summarized in *The Art of Sylvia Plath: A Symposium*, ed. by Charles Newman (Bloomington, Indiana: Indiana University Press, 1970).

[9] My objection is to the abuse of shock. The psychiatrist administering it has made no attempt to break through her depression by relating to her unique situation and to her. He employs shock as a purely mechanical, punitive tool. Dr. Nolan, her later psychiatrist, employs shock treatment too, with beneficial effect. She prepares Esther, administers it under anaesthesia, and combines it with supportive psychotherapy to help Esther integrate herself.

[10] Cf. Heinz Kohut, *The Restoration of the Self* (New York: International Universities Press, 1977), 30-32.

[11] *The Colossus and Other Poems* (New York: Alfred Knopf, 1971), 58-59.

[12] *Ariel* (New York: Harper and Row Publishers, 1966), 81.

[13] *Ariel*, 82.

[14] *Ariel*, 84.

[15] Bruno Bettelheim, *The Uses of Enchantment* (New York: Vintage Books, 1977), 244, 257ff.

[16] David Holbrook, *Sylvia Plath: Poetry and Existence* (London: The Athlone Press, 1976).

Chapter IX

[1] On the role of the ego boundaries in creativity and pathology, cf. Günter Ammon, *Handbuch der Dynamischen Psychatrie* (Munich: Reinhardt, 1979), 135 ff. and Ammon, *Gruppendynamik der Kreativität* (Munich: Kindler, 1974).

[2] On student life as a transitional period, cf. Erik Erikson, *Young Man Luther: A Study in Psychoanalysis and History* (London: Faber and Faber, 1959).

[3] Cf. Pinchas Noy's definition of the primary process, chapter 1, footnote 48.

[4] Cf. the discussion of the uncanny in Chapter 2, of the mystical in Chapter 1.

[5] Cf. Ammon, *Gruppendynamik der Kreativität, op. cit*, 12-35, provides a framework for the discussion of the relationship between the nature of the mother/child symbiosis and its effects on creativity.

[6] On the definition of the infant's waking behavior during the first months as play cf. Jean Piaget, *Play, Dreams and Imitation in Childhood* (New York: Norton, 1962), 90.

[7] Jerome S. Bruner in "The Ontogenesis of Speech Acts," *Journal of Child Language*, 2(1975), 1-19, gives a summary of the research from the speech act perspective on preverbal learning and the development of the formal structures of language. On specific communication structures in the interactions of twelve-week old infants with their mothers (e.g. differences in male/female speechact dyadic mother/infant interactions), cf. M. Lewis and Roy Freedle, "Mother-Infant Dyad: The Cradle of Meaning," in *Communication and Affect*, by Patricia Pliner, *et al.* (New York: Academic Press, 1973), 127-155.

[8] Joel Shor and Jean Sanville, *Illusion in Loving: A Psychoanalytic Approach to the Evolution of Intimacy and Autonomy* (Los Angeles: Double Helix Press, 1978), especially in "Rethinking Female-Male Development," 141-157. Also Nancy Chodorow's *The Reproduction of Mothering: Psychoanalysis and the Sociology of Gender* (Berkeley: University of California Press, 1978), 99-110, for clinical material on preodipal mother/child gender differences and the early sexualization of

the mother/son relationship.

[9]Our information about the mother/child symbiosis for the authors is reconstructed from their later reports on their parents in letters and autobiographical documents, and by inference from the entire family situation and its likely climate. First-born were Grillparzer, Büchner, Stifter, Schnitzler, Kafka, Plath. Middle or last-born children, Hoffmann, Mörike, Mann, had siblings at least three years, usually considerably older, or were first children of second marriages (Chopin) and therefore had special positions in the family constellation. According to A. Altus, "Birth order and its Sequelae," *Science*, 151 (1966), 44-49, first-born children receive most attention, hence are most creative; they are followed by last-born children.

[10]On parental death and creativity, cf. Mark Kanzer, "Writers and the Early Loss of Parents," *Journal Hillside Hospital*, 2 (1953), 148-151. Parental loss as a "primary Pathway to Creativity and Eminence" was researched statistically by J. Marvin Eisenstadt, "Parental Loss and Genius," *American Psychologist*, 33(1978), 211-223. In keeping with the degree of stress in these families, the incidence of mental illness in them is high. Hoffmann's mother was a recluse, an uncle eccentric, his brother a sociopath. One of Mörike's brothers was a suicide, two were sociopaths. Grillparzer's mother and youngest brother were suicides; two remaining brothers were schizophrenic and borderline. Mann's two younger sisters committed suicide. Among our authors, the degree of physical and mental pathology is also high.

[11] Cf. Piaget, *Play, Dreams and Imitation, op. cit.*, 161-168.

[12] Cf. Fred Bush, "Dimensions of the First Transitional Object," *The Psychoanalytic Study of the Child*, 29 (1974), 215-229. K. Michael Hong, "Transitional Phenomena: A Theoretical Integration," *The Psychoanalytic Study of the Child*, 33 (1978), 47-79 distinguishes between primary transitional objects, which include all kinds of transitional phenomena of self-soothing (Winnicott's fantasies and dissociated states, *op. cit.* 26-37), and secondary transitional objects. While Bush sees the transitional object become independent of the mother, I find that the transitional object with artists retains a link with maternal figures.

[13] Cf. Pinchas Noy, Chapter 1, footnote 7. In especially creative persons, the coordination between primary and secondary process, that is between the two hemispheres, is especially well developed.

[14] Cf. Adabert Stifter, *Letters*, 180 ff, *op. cit.*, Chapter 5, footnote 1.

[15]Kafka says in the *Letter to his Father*, "There were years in which I lazed away more time on the sofa in full health than you did in your entire lifetime" (43). Mörike, Mann, Plath, Chopin, Grillparzer and Schnitzler all describe somnolent periods, emptily repetitive actions and fantasies in creative lulls.

[16]The overt reason for using pseudonyms for the girl was to hide his infatuation from his wife. The covert reason lies in the symbol, the butterfly=death, and the acronym, *Ktch*, which stands for Kleist's somnambulist, love-driven Käthchen von Heilbronn. Both symbols refer to Hoffmann's unavailable (dead) early mother. He had an inkling that his obsession for Julia referred to an earlier figure in his life ("Ktch could be viewed as only a mask," January 19, 1812). The secrecy, the cryptic

symbols suggestive of death and love are reminiscent of Abraham and Torok's "intrapsychic vault"..."for losses that cannot ...be acknowledged as losses." Cf. Nicolas Abraham and Maria Torok, "Introjection --Incorporation: Mourning or Melancholia," *Psychoanalysis in France,* ed. by Serge Lebovici and Daniel Widlöcher, New York: International Universities Press, 1980), 8.

[17] Cf. Kohut's discussion of the substitution of drug states for the "selfobject that failed" of the drug addict, "Preface" to "Der Falsche Weg zum Selbst, Studien zur Drogenkarriere by Jürgen vom Scheidt," in *The Search for the Self,* Vol. II, *op. cit.* 846ff. Hoffmann's fantasy functioned like a drug --in fact, he used it together with a drug, alcohol. Only preconscious ideation is creative because it is accessible to emotion, hence modifiable.

[18]The psychosomatic illnesses used anaclitically have the same regressive character as anaclitic fantasies do; however, they show that maternal care was given to the child in physical illness; cf. Günter Ammon, *Psychoanalysis and Psychosomatics,* translated by S. H. Ray (New York: Springer, 1979). On its role in Kafka, cf. Kafka chapter, cf. also the Stifter, Mörike chapters, and the Mann essay, *op. cit.*

[19]I am using the term aggression as that assertion of the self which is needed for growth. Aggression becomes or destructive only when the natural self-assertion of the child is thwarted. cf. Günter Ammon, *Handbuch, op. cit.,* 208.

[20] Cf. the mother's revealing comments about her own frustrated intellectual and literary ambitions in her introduction to her daughter's *Letters Home: Correspondence 1950—1963,* ed. by Aurelia Schober Plath (Toronto: Bantam, 1977).

[21] Cf. Lois Ames, "Notes towards a Biography", 157 in *The Art of Sylvia Plath: A Symposium,* ed. by Charles Newman (Bloomington, Indiana: Indiana University Press, 1970).

[22] *Letter to his Father, op. cit.,* 10.

[23]Impressive examples of destructive works of art are provided by Schnitzler in his *Last Letter,* cf. my discussion in *Imago, op.cit.* and Thomas Mann in *Dr. Faustus,* cf. discussion in *Mosaic, op.cit.*

[24]In terms of Günter Ammon's ego psychology, such a work of art fills a "hole in the ego;" it is a defense vitally needed to keep an ego intact. *Handbuch, op. cit.,* 86.

[25]Günter Ammon's conceptualization of a number of interdependent central and secondary ego functions is helpful here. Cf. *Handbuch, op. cit.,* 95ff. If the child, for instance, is not permitted to express aggression, and cannot acknowledge that it cannot assert itself, all other ego functions are curtailed, such as autonomy, creativity, sexuality, identity, ego boundaries, but also secondary ego functions like language, thinking, imagining. The degrees of handicap depend on the extent to which and the areas of life in which the preoedipal parents prohibit aggression. For Kafka, for instance, parental prohibition extended to having a personal family life. His claim in the *Letter to his Father* that he could not think or speak in the father's presence, reflects the prohibitions against self-assertion.

[26] Cf. Chodorow *op. cit.* on the preoedipal sexualization of the mother/son relationship, footnote 8.

[27] Henri Parens, "Developmental Considerations of Ambivalence," *The Psychoanalytic Study of the Child*, 34 (1979), 385-419. Parens outlines the several subphases in the child's striving for autonomy and separation from the symbiosis and their relationship to ambivalence and symbolization. Mark Kanzer, Maud Bodkin, and Patrick Colm Hogan discuss a similar use of splitting in *Twentieth Century Interpretations of King Lear*, ed., J. Adelman (Englewood: Prentice Hall, 1972).

[28] Albert Rothenberg, *The Emerging Goddess* (Chicago: University of Chicago Press, 1979).

[29] On the similarities of the artist with the paranoid psychopath, in regard to the use of the mechanism of projection, cf. K.R. Eissler, "Remarks on an Aspect of Creativity," *American Imago*, 35 (1978), 1-2, 59-76.

[30] I do not see the two functions of splitting and integrating as two phases of the creative process, nor as shifts in psychic levels, as does Kris in his differentiation between inspiration and elaboration. Kris, *Psychoanalytic Explorations in Art, op. cit.*, 59-60.

[31] Cf. Günter Ammon, *Handbuch, op. cit.* 135 ff. In Havelka's terms, we can describe splitting and synthesizing as a concurrent symbolic and imaginative process. Havelka, *The Nature of the Creative Process in Art*, (The Hague: Nijhoff, 1968), 77 ff.

[32] Cf. Kohut, *The Restoration of the Self* (New York: International Universities Press, 1977).

[33] Cf. Chapter 2. Hoffmann's work as a lawyer and official, like his artistic work, constituted a non-defensive identity.

[34] We might remember that Mörike was dependent on some actual distance from symbiotic relationships (during his student days, in intervals between his mother's death and marriage, or in between employment) to be able to create. The *acceptance* of the gift of atonement which Mozart experiences seems to have been denied to Mörike --for one, because his father was dead, and for another, because the source of his greatest guilt must have been his mother and his incomplete separation from her.

[35] For Plath and Kafka, the maternal deprivation and compensatory attention to intellectual development and to illness are well documented. The compensatory intellectualization reflects general middle class orientation towards education as a means to power and was probably accentuated by Kafka's Jewish minority status, and the immigrant academician status of Plath's parents. Mann's hero, Adrian (and probably Mann) has the same intellectualism. Its origins lie in his birth rank.

[36] Cf. Günter Ammon, *Gruppendynamik und Kreativität op. cit.*, 12-36.

[37] Mann's Adrian and Kafka describe these states most eloquently, possibly because of their guilt feelings over the eroticizing of all ego functions. Cf. my Kafka chapter.

[38]In our treatment of Mörike, Kafka, and Mann's hero, we have observed the many aspects of sexual gratification, fusion, merging through creation and the guilt/fear dilemmas which this may cause.

[39]Grillparzer was similarly silenced. The fear of disapproval had crippled his musical talent from the start and made it an autistic defense. Curiously enough, his literary talent, after he gave up publishing, took a similar turn to autism: For the last twenty years of his life, Grillparzer translated Spanish drama --for himself.

[40] Cf. K.R. Eissler's *op. cit.* description of Freud's use of Fliess which is quite similar to the ideal portrait of the helper. Cf. also the discussions of such figures by Heinz Kohut in *The Search for the Self. op. cit.*, 682ff.

[41]How demanding an artist can be of such helper figures appears from Hitzig's remarks about E.T.A. Hoffmann: "He prized old friends beyond anything... and demanded a similar devotion from them. They were to have no other gods beside him; he considered it a felony if they got married, lived with their children," etc. *E.T.A. Hoffmanns Tagebücher, op. cit.,* LVII.

[42] Cf. Stifter's remark to his publisher Heckenast, "I am married to Heckenast," *op. cit.* 17, 178. The piecemeal sending of work, the repeated requests (and grants) of advances on work not yet executed, all these strategies kept Stifter firmly bound to the publisher-friend through his writing career.

[43]As poetics and exercises in verse form were subjects in schools till the beginning of this century, most of our writers got practice in these disciplines in formal training, which reinforced earlier personal interest. Unfortunately, the data on early interests during the 19th century are relatively scant as biographical information, especially on the early years of the writer, was considered irrelevant, hence transmitted only in romanticized generalizations. How many story telling mothers and puppet theaters have their origin in Goethe's *Truth and Fiction* rather than in the life of the writer is hard to estimate. For 20th century authors we have good evidence through journals, autobiographies and family letters (except for Kafka) on extensive literary activity by age 12-13. Schnitzler had written 25 plays by age thirteen. Cf. *Eine Jugend in Wien: Eine Autobiographie,* (Vienna: Molden, 1968) 46-47.

[44]The only exception seems to be Georg Büchner, for whom, except for a few poems for a family occasions at fourteen in the period style, there exists not a line before he displayed his genius in *Danton's Death*. In view of the evidence for all writers, the absence of an apprenticeship is highly unlikely. After all, even Goethe who began writing his first verse at age six, took ten years until he wrote his first creditable plays.

[45] *Stories of Three Decades,* (New York: A.A. Knopf, 1936), 158.

GLOSSARY

Introduction to Glossary

Theories of the psyche and their conceptual frameworks based as they are on observation and empathy, are analogies or models of actual processes of the mind. They help us understand the different processes of the mind, their developmental aspects and their individual manifestations only imprecisely like superimposed grids. At this point, no one theory suffices to explain the creative process. I have found it necessary to supplement psychoanalytic Freudian theory with the theories of development of Erikson, with the psychology of the self of Kohut, with observations on preoedipal development of Balint, Mahler or Spitz, with the dynamic ego psychology of Ammon, with Piaget's cognitive-developmental psychology, with theories of play of Winnicott, of perception, etc. to grasp the phenomenon from as many aspects as possible. The following glossary is designed to guide the reader in the meaning of major terms used in this book in the hope that they will not be read in their non-technical and often judgmental senses. I am painfully aware that these brief definitions, by necessity of space, simplify concepts and terminologies which have had even within   the   psychoanalytic   movement   itself   intricate,   often contradictory meanings and a complex history.

For a wider understanding of the complexity of definitions, see: L. Laplanche, J.-B. Pontalis, *Vocabulaire de la Psychanalyse* (Paris: Presses Universitaires de France, 1959); Nandor Fodor, Frank Gaynor, *Freud: Dictionary of Psychoanalysis* (New York: Philosophical Library, 1950) Leland E. Hinsie, Robert Jean Campbell, *Psychiatric Dictionary,* 4. ed. (New York: Oxford University Press, 1970); and John E. Gedo, Arnold Goldberg, *Models of the Mind: A Psychoanalytic Theory* (Chicago: University of Chicago Press, 1973).

acting out behavior
   the symptomatic expression of unconscious conflictual tensions; in psychoanalysis, symptomatic behavior outside the therapeutic context; in psychiatry usually synonymous with antisocial behavior.

allegory
   a technique of fiction writing in which narrated events unambiguously, consciously and continuously refer to another simultaneous structure of events or ideas; contrasted to symbolism where the narrative structure has many, or at least one, unconscious meanings.

anaclitic
   emotionally dependent in an infantile manner, e.g., anaclitic transitional object, a transitional object which has the function to substitute for the symbiotic mother.

approach–avoidance conflict/fear–need dilemma
   a conflict between a need/wish to perform an action and the fear of doing so. A person caught in a fear/need dilemma feels impelled to perform an action but once its realization is imminent feels an equally strong urge to withdraw from it. The closer the realization, the greater the fear of performing it. A person caught in an (usually unconscious or partly conscious) approach/avoidance conflict feels frustrated, stalled and cannot move; develops anxiety, somatic complaints,

archaic self
structures of the psyche which reflect the experience of the earliest stages of the mother/child symbiosis.

autistic, autism
a state of existence withdrawn from human contact by rigid defenses such as denial, self-stimulation, mutism or compulsions, in which all psychic processes are concentrated on the self.

basic fault
Balint's concept of a wound to the psyche acquired in a traumatic symbiosis.

bonding
early in development, a lasting, strong, irrational attachment to a person/thing/action.

censor
the repressive function of the ego which prevents ego-alien unconscious materials from direct expression.

character disorder
deficit in ego development or flaw in self development because of faulty early preoedipal mother/child symbiosis which results in deficient/flawed/destructive adult character traits.

condensation
the fusion of many unconscious elements into one image.

countertransference
in the relationship between therapist/patient, the emotional needs, expectations with which the therapist unconsciously responds to the patient. Within the psychoanalytic situation, the countertransference allows the therapist to identify temporarily with the patient and to gain insight into the productions which emerge from the patient's unconscious. For the countertransference to be helpful, the therapist has to be conscious of his needs, conflicts, emotions. In literary analysis the unconscious expectations, feelings, etc. with which the interpreter responds to the underlying dynamics of a

text/author.

denial
an unconscious form of screening oneself from an inner or outer reality, thought, or feeling by averting attention, avoiding or failing to perceive.

derepression
to make accessible to consciousness.

developmental phases
developmental psychologies distinguish between circumscribed periods of the life span during which the organism has an optimal physiological/psychological readiness to learn phase related tasks and have phase appropriate experiences (e.g., the infant has to have the capacity to distinguish body sensations and have sphincter control, before he is ready for toilet training). Developmental periods are designated by either the predominant issue involved (preoedipal, 0-3/ oedipal, 3-6), or the predominant body zone involved (Freudian oral, anal, phallic, genital), or by the predominant experience mode (Erikson's trust [oral], autonomy [anal] etc.), or by predominant operations (Piaget's sensorimotor period, preoperational thought, concrete operations, operations). Each phase in the various psychologies from observation is assigned definite, sequential subphases (e.g., Mahler's four subphases of the separation-individuation process, i.e., preoedipal development: differentiation and development of body image; practicing; rapprochement; consolidation of individuality).

Dingsymbol
object symbol in a novella; a condensation of conscious and unconscious meanings of a narrative into a major symbol which has the structural function to unify the different strands and levels of narration.

displacement
unconscious mechanism whereby one repression gives its affective component to another repression.

dissociative function of the ego
the capacity of the ego to split off and deal separately with incongruous components of a whole; e.g., to split off the good from the bad mother.

double bind
interaction in families of schizophrenics which contains habitually incongruent and entrapping messages; e.g., a parent punishes a child but, on a different level of communication, prevents the child from acknowledging the punishment and from escaping it.

discrepancy experience
a breaking of the inner or outer ego boundaries, flooding of the ego with primary process materials or perceptions.

ego
that part of the psyche which interacts with the environment and with internalizations for the sake of the organism's survival.

ego boundary
an operation of the ego which distinguishes what is real from what is unreal. The inner ego boundary is a boundary toward the repressed unconscious. The outer boundary is that to external stimuli.

ego function
an operation of the ego which follows a developmentally structured course or pattern. Central ego functions (Ammon) are identity, ego autonomy, sexuality, body feeling, fear, ego boundaries, etc. Secondary ego functions are thinking, affect, remembering, dreaming, repression, denying, fantasy.

ego ideal
the positive pole of the superego, an ideal that is appropriate to one's capacities.

ego mastery
  the capacity of any/all the ego functions to cope successfully with a
  given reality situation or internal conflict.

egosyntonic
felt as compatible with the ego's values and capacities.

empathy
  capacity to put oneself in the psychological framework of another
  person; in self psychology, the analyst's (or parents') proper feeling
  for and response to the patient's (child's) particular needs and feelings.

externalization
  the conversion of psychic contents into manifest forms, e.g., a
  psychosomatic symptom is an externalization of an inner conflict.

family romance
  the fantasy of the child that he is the offspring of exalted parents
  and that the actual parents are not his real parents. The family
  romance fantasy reflects two different developmental stages in per-
  ceiving the parents, an early grandiose one and a later disillusioned
  one.

fantasy
  an ego process by which usually unconscious, repressed wishes are
  gratified indirectly in the fabrication of an imagined situation.

fusion
  the wish and fantasied experience of merging with the oral mother
  in a symbiosis. Cf. oceanic state.

grandiose exhibitionist image of the self
  in self psychology, that aspect of the self which desires unlimited
  approval and pleasure. The grandiose self has its origins in the
  mother's loving approval of the infant; because of the inevitable
  shortcomings of maternal care, the grandiosity of this self aspect is
  inevitably disappointed. With good enough maternal care and
  without traumatization, the grandiose self's grandiosity and pleasure

seeking are gradually integrated into egosyntonic ambitions, enjoyment, and self-esteem.

idealized parent imago

in self psychology, that aspect of the self which desires competency, perfection; it has its origins in the preoedipal child's including himself in the parent's power and competency. According to Kohut, the grandiose self and the idealized parent imago are the two poles of the self, formed by gradual steps from earliest interactions with parenting persons, which have a distinct development separate from ego functions and object relationships. In the narcissistic character disorders, these two functions of the self are disordered.

identification

process of obtaining ego strength from unconsciously identifying with another, significant person; internalizing another as a selfobject. Identifications are based on early parental models and are an early way of learning.

internalization

the taking into the self and making part of oneself by extended social learning (consciously or preconsciously) the values, behaviors and attitudes of meaningful persons and/or the culture. The values and behaviors which have been internalized are habitual, automatic, and pre- or unconscious.

interpsychic

interpersonal psychic relationship, processes based on the interrelationship between two or more persons.

introject, introjection

term used about superego formation. Parental attitudes, commands, prohibitions ingested into oneself in a process of unconscious or preconscious identification by the oedipal child, kept for life, and generalized to all interpersonal situations. Introjects are harsh, demanding, categorical, dictatorial, relentless, not accessible to questioning and modification. Internalization is the more general concept; introject is the more specific superego referent.

latency

the years between five to about twelve years of age, after the resolution of the oedipal conflict and before puberty.

libidinal development

the development of the sexual drive through the oral, anal, phallic and genital phases.

mirroring

term of self psychology; means that the empathic adult (therapist) understands, and by word and action, acknowledges and confirms the child's/patient's feelings and needs, especially unconscious/not acknowledged feelings and needs. Through being mirrored phase-appropriately, the child/patient learns to heed, express feelings and needs and to bring his emotional responses and the realities of his particular situation into correlation.

narcissism

a central ego function (Ammon) or the libidinal investment of the self (Kohut). For both Ammon and Kohut the concept has a positive meaning as it does for Herbert Marcuse.

narrative perspective

the perspective from which a story is told, e.g., the all-knowing narrative perspective of the author or the limited one of a character involved in the action.

narrative structure

the patterns (e.g., paralleling and contrasting, doubling) and sequences, the points of view, etc. in which a story is told.

novella

a prose narrative, with one central character, of compact structure, of abundant symbolism organized around one central symbol, dealing with one central, surprising, extraordinary event in the life of a small cast of ordinary people. Written in plain style, the novella emphasizes event over character and shows the intrusion of a power higher than the individual (fate/psychological law/irrational force) into the individual's life.

object
> that which is required for libidinal need gratification, e.g., the earliest object is the mother.

object constancy
> tendency for responses to the object of perception to remain the same regardless of distance or mood; capacity to remember what is absent.

oceanic states
> ecstatic feeling of being merged into a supportive, all-satisfying matrix, mystical states. For Freud, the origin of this experience is the infant's blissful feeling at the mother's breast.

omnipotence of thought
> the belief of the young child that its wishes will always be granted; hence, in adults the unconscious residual thought of unlimited power and competence.

operations
> the functioning of a faculty, especially the intellectual functions of deductive and inductive thinking, planning, deliberating, etc. (Piaget). Concrete operations refer to the capacity to form active non-egocentric schemas or to think through a problem using concrete evidence; abstract operations refers to the ability to deal with a problem without concrete examples.

performance principle
> in Western societies, the judgement of the goodness of a thing, person or action by its success or achievement.

phallic stage
> period of psychosexual development (3-7 years of age) when the penis and clitoris are in the center of interest, stage of boisterous outer directedness.

play space
   the never challenged intermediate space between mother and infant
   in which the infant manipulates, plays with the first not-me object
   onto which he projects needs/feelings/desires.

pleasure principle
   the principle by which the id operates, namely by the criteria of
   immediate gratification of pleasure and avoidance of displeasure.

polymorphous perverse sexuality
   the nonspecific and diffuse eroticism over the infant's entire body.

preconscious
   not immediately available but easily recalled to consciousness.

preoperations
   stage of cognitive development (2-7 years of age) before concrete
   and abstract operations can be performed; preoperational thought
   follows sensorimotor stage (0-2); beginning of language and symbolic
   play, internalization of actions into thoughts.

primary group
   the infant's first social environment of caretakers, of mother, father
   and any other regular caretaker.

primary process
   processes of the id; in Freudian thought, pleasure oriented, not
   modifiable by the reality principle, hence regressed, archaic,
   illusory, timeless, without negation. Its representations are imagis-
   tic and predominantly visual and subject to the mechanisms of condensation, replacement, reversal, etc. It is the mode of dream, hallucination, psychotic states. In recent analytic thinking, the primary process has to be reevaluated as a separate, emotional way of
   knowing equal in importance to the secondary process of thinking
   and reasoning. The primary process has its own course of development and growth (as the complexity of our dreams shows, there is
   increase in richness, diversity). In the primary process mode, a
   person perceives, recalls, sorts out, understands everything as it
   affects the self, its needs, desires, emotions. Hence an object is

represented in terms of whether it satisfies, pleases, frustrates, threatens or can be influenced by the self.

primal scene
the child's witnessing of the parents' sexual intercourse and misunderstanding it as frightening violence.

projection
an unconscious defensive psychic mechanism by which one's own unacknowledged and unacceptable feelings are attributed to another person.

psychic function
a mental activity viewed as an instrument of adaptation.

psychic mechanism
an unconscious mental response or habitual response pattern, e.g., repression, projection, reversal, denial, etc.

psychic structure
internalized, relatively stable pathways along which mental processes work; internalized stable relationships to the self and to significant others.

psychological dynamics
the interactions of psychological processes with each other and with the psychical environment.

psychosis
a state of being severely mentally disturbed, withdrawn, with distorted perception of reality, exaggerated or inappropriate affect, disturbed thinking, delusions and regressed behavior.

psychosocial development
the child's psychological development in the social world from the oral state to adulthood.

reality principle
the principle by which the ego operates, namely to achieve satisfaction and need fulfillment in accordance with the demands of one's environment.

reality testing
ego function which verifies the adequateness and appropriateness of responses to the environment.

repetition compulsion
unconscious tendency to repeat maladaptive, infantile behaviors even if they are unpleasant for unconscious punitive or security gains.

return of the repressed
the return to consciousness of an idea or set of ideas which had been repressed in the unconscious.

reversal
reversal of an instinct from active to passive, e.g., sadism to masochism, or a reversal of the object, e.g., self to others, or a reversal of the content, e.g., love to hate.

secondary process
according to the secondary process mode of the ego a person can order and understand events and phenomena in terms of reality; he can grasp their inner relationships, observe regularities and various patterns of order. He can formulate rules to regulate occurrences; linear, cause and effect oriented thought, organization of memory and of perception as opposed to the global mode of the primary process.

screen memory
protective, usually pleasant memory behind which hides an unacceptable, repressed, potentially disruptive recollection.

self
In Kohut's self psychology, the self is a bipolar psychic structure formed by the two functions of the self, the grandiose-exhibitionist self and the idealized parent imago. The self originates in the confluence of the parents' expectations of the child and the child's capacities as they prove themselves in the environment; the self provides the person with a continuous sense of being the same. Ammon's concept of the ego largely overlaps with Kohut's self but breaks down the psychic functions into a different, more detailed array of ego functions.

selfobject
in Kohut's psychology the earliest internalized objects, i.e., the parents. The selfobject is experienced as part of the self.

sensorimotor development
in Piaget's psychology, the earliest developmental stage during which sense perception and motor activity are coordinated and schemas are learned.

splitting
early psychic mechanism of the ego to deal with ambivalence by splitting the object into opposites; hence extended, the splitting of conflicted functions, actions, etc. into manageable parts.

symbol
metaphor, figure, incident with an array of major and minor meanings at least one of which is unconscious.

symbolic representation (symbolic processing)
(Piaget) symbolic representation becomes possible when the 12 months and older child when forming images can distinguish between signifier and signified and can evoke the signifier as a gratifying substitute for the signified; primary process mode of self-referent thinking.

symbiosis

the earliest relationship between mother and infant when the child experiences himself as part of the mother.

synaesthesia

a subjective substitution of one sense impression for another, or the simultaneous experience of several sense impressions; e.g., "sound touched me," Grillparzer. Synaesthetic experience occurs during heightened or unusual states of consciousness.

synthetic function of the ego

capacity of the ego to integrate experience, information, functions by establishing a unity of context (Kris); integrative function of the ego.

transference

in the relationship with the therapist the patient experiences towards the therapist the strong emotions, vital expectations and wishes he experienced in childhood toward his primary group and its members. The working through of such transference feelings constitutes psychoanalytic therapy. When an author has his protagonist act to another character in an extreme or unusual manner (e.g., Lenz' relationship to Oberlin, Nathanael's to the eyeglass dealer), a transference relationship is at stake and unconscious motivations are the driving force.

transitional object

first transitional object --(anaclitic transitional object) a soft thing like a blanket or sheet which soothes the infant to sleep in the absence of the mother, hence regressive in its function. Second transitional object --(instrumental transitional object) a particularly loved toy which substitutes for the mother and assists the child in playfully exploring the world, hence progressive in its function.

transitional fantasy

a fantasy which has the same function as does the transitional object.

SELECTED BIBLIOGRAPHY

Abt, L.E. and S. Prosner, eds. *Essays in Creativity.* Croton-on-Hudson, New York: North River Press, 1974.

Abt, L.E. and B.L. Weissman, eds. *Acting Out: Theoretical and Clinical Aspects.* New York: Grune and Stratton, 1965.

Aichinger, Ingrid. "E.T.A. Hoffmanns Novelle 'Der Sandmann' und die Interpretation Sigmund Freuds." *ZdPh,* 95 (1976, Sonderheft).

Aird, Eileen. *Sylvia Plath : Her Life and Work.* New York: Harper and Row, 1973.

Altus, A. "Birth Order and its Sequelae." *Science,* 151 (1966), 44-49.

Alvarez, A. *The Savage God.* New York: Random House, 1972.

Aman, Klaus. "Stifter und Heckenast: Literarische Produktion zwischen Asthetik und Okonomie." *Vasilo,* 27 (1978), 47-58.

Ammon, Günter, ed. *Gruppendynamik der Kreativität*. Munich: Kindler, 1974.

Ammon, Günter. *Handbuch der Dynamischen Psychatrie*. vol. I. Munich: Reinhardt, 1979.

Ammon, Günter, *Psychoanalysis and Psychosomatics*. New York: Springer, 1979.

Arieti, Silvano. *Creativity: The Magic Synthesis*. New York: Basic Books, 1976.

Arieti, Silvano. *The Intrapsychic Self: Feeling, Cognition, and Creativity in Health and Mental Illness*. New York: Basic Books, 1967.

Aspetsberger, Friedbert. "Stifters Erzählung 'Nachkommenschaften.'" *Sprachkunst,* 6 (1975), 238-260.

Balint, Michael. *The Basic Fault: Therapeutic Aspects of Regression*. London: Tavistock, 1968.

Band, Arnold, J. "Kafka and the Beiliss Affair." *Comparative Literature,* 32,2 (1980), 168-183.

Bandet, Jean-Louis. "Der Eindringling in das Haus des Vaters." *Austriaca*. Tübingen: Niemeyer, 1975, 230-246.

Barron, Frank. *Creativity and Personal Freedom*. New York: Van Nostrand, 1968.

Bateson, Gregory. "Toward a Theory of Schizophrenia," and "Double Bind." In *Steps to an Ecology of Mind*. San Francisco: Chandler, 1971.

Baumer, Franz. "'Musik für das Auge.' Progressive Elemente bei Adalbert Stifter als Maler und Zeichner." *Vasilo,* 31 (1982), 121-144.

Beck, E.T. *Kafka and the Yiddish Theater*. Madison: University of Wisconsin Press, 1971.

Beebe, Maurice. *Ivory Towers and Sacred Founts: The Artist Hero in Fiction from Goethe to Joyce*. New York: New York State University Press, 1964.

Benn, Maurice B. *The Drama of Revolt*. Cambridge: Cambridge University Press, 1976.

Bettelheim, Bruno. *Children of the Dream*. New York: Macmillan, 1969.

Bettelheim, Bruno. *The Uses of Enchantment*. New York: Vintage, 1977.

Binder, Hartmut. *Kafka–Handbuch*. 2 vols., Stuttgart: Kröner, 1979.

Binder, Hartmut. "Kafkas Hebräischstudien. Ein biographischinterpretatorischer Versuch." *Jahrbuch der deutschen Schillergesellschaft*, 11 (1967), 527-556.

Binder, Hartmut. *Kafka in neuer Sicht*. Stuttgart: Metzler, 1976.

Binder, Hartmut. *Kafka Kommentar zu sämtlichen Erzählungen*. Munich: Winkler, 1975.

Bleckwenn, Helga. "Künstlertum als soziale Rolle: Stifters Berufswahl." *Vasilo*, 28 (1979), 35-42.

Bleckwenn, Helga. "Künstlertum als soziale Rolle II: Stifters Berufslaufbahn in den vierziger Jahren." *Vasilo*, 30 (1981), 15-45.

Bleiler, E.F., ed. *The Best Tales of Hoffmann*. Trans. J.T. Bealby. New York: Dover, 1967.

Bodkin, Maud. "On Splitting in Characterization." *Twentieth Century Interpretations of King Lear*. Ed. J. Adelman. Englewood: Prentice Hall, 1972.

Bruner, Jerome S. "The ontogenesis of speech acts." *Journal of Child Language,* 2 (1975), 1-19.

Büchner, Georg. *Complete Plays and Prose.* Trans. Carl R. Mueller. New York: Hill and Wang, 1963.

Büchner, Georg. *Sämtliche Werke und Briefe.* Ed. Werner Lehmann. Hamburg: Wegner, 1971.

Bush, Fred. "Dimensions of the First Transitional Object". *The Psychoanalytic Study of the Child,* 29 (1974), 215-229.

Butscher, Edward, ed. *Sylvia Plath: The Woman and the Work.* New York: Dodd, Mead and Company, 1977.

Cath, Stanley H., and Claire Cath. "On the Other Side of Oz: Psychoanalytic Aspects of Fairy Tales." *The Psychoanalytic Study of the Child,* 33 (1978), 621-639.

Chodorow, Nancy. *The Reproduction of Mothering: Psychoanalysis and the Sociology of Gender.* Berkeley: University of California Press, 1978.

Chopin, Kate. *The Awakening. An Authoritative Text. Contexts. Criticism.* Ed., Margaret Culley. New York: Norton, 1976.

Daemmrich, Horst S. *The Shattered Self: Hoffmann's Tragic Vision.* Detroit: Wayne State University Press, 1973.

Dollard, John, and Neal E. Miller. *Personality and Psychotherapy.* New York: McGraw-Hill, 1950.

Ehrenzweig, A. *The Hidden Order in Art: A Study in the Psychology of Artistic Imagination.* Berkeley: University of California Press, 1967.

Ehrenzweig, A. *The Psychoanalysis of Artistic Vision and Hearing: An Introduction to a Theory of Unconscious Perception.* New York: Julian Press, 1953.

Eissler, K.R. "Creativity and Adolescence: The Effect of Trauma in Freud's Adolescence." *The Psychoanalytic Study of the Child,* 33 (1978), 461-517.

Eissler, K.R. "Notes on the Environment of a Genius." *Psychoanalytic Study of the Child,* 14 (1959), 267-313.

Eissler, K.R. "Psychopathology and Creativity." *American Imago,* 24, 1-2 (1967), 35-81.

Eissler, K.R. *Talent and Genius: A Psychoanalytic Reply to a Defamation of Freud.* New York: Grove, 1971.

Ellis, John M. *Narration in the German Novella: Theory and Interpretation.* Cambridge: Cambridge University Press, 1974.

Ellis, John M. "Clara, Nathanael and the Narrator: Interpreting Hoffmann's *Der Sandmann.*" *German Quarterly,* 54 (1981), 1-18.

Emrich, Wilhelm. *Franz Kafka.* Frankfurt: Athenäum, 1958.

Enzinger, Moritz. *Adalbert Stifters Studienjahre (1818–1830).* Innsbruck: Ostereichische Verlagsanstalt, 1950.

Erikson, Erik H. *Insight and Responsibility: Lectures on the Ethical Implications of Psychoanalytic Insight.* New York: W.W. Norton, 1964.

Erikson, Erik H. *Toys and Reasons: Stages in the Ritualization of Experience.* New York: W.W. Norton, 1977.

Field, Wallis G. "Silver and Oranges: Notes on Mörike's Mozart-Novelle." *Seminar,* XIV, 4 (1978), 243-254.

Fraiberg, Selma. "Kafka and the Dream." *Art and Psychoanalysis.* Ed. Wendell Phillips. New York: Criterion Press, 1957.

Freud S. *Briefe 1873–1939.* Eds. E. and L. Freud. Frankfurt: Fischer, 1960.

Freud, S. *The Standard Edition of the Complete Psychological Works of Sigmund Freud.* Vols. 1-24. London: Hogarth Press, 1968.

Freye, Karl and Wolfgang Stammler, eds. *Briefe von und an J.M.R. Lenz.* 2. edition. Bern: Lang, 1969.

Fryer, Judith. *The Faces of Eve: Women in the Nineteenth Century Novel.* New York: Oxford University Press, 1976.

Gedo, John E., and Arnold Goldberg. *Models of the Mind: A Psychoanalytic Theory.* Chicago: University of Chicago Press, 1973.

Greenacre, Phyllis. "The Childhood Development of the Artist: Libidinal Phase Development and Giftedness." *Psychoanalytic Study of the Child,* 12 (1957), 47-72.

Greenacre, P. "The Family Romance of the Artist." *Psychoanalytic Study of the Child,* 12 (1957), 9-43.

Greenacre, Phyllis. *The Quest for the Father.* New York: International Universities Press, 1963.

Greenacre, P. "The Relation of the Imposter to the Artist." *The Psychoanalytic Study of the Child,* 13 (1958), 521-540.

Greenacre, P. "A Study of the Nature of Inspiration." *Journal of the American Psychoanalytic Association,* 12 (1964), 6-31.

Greenacre, P. "Woman as Artist." *Psychoanalytic Quarterly,* 29 (1960), 208-227.

Greenberg, Martin. *The Terror of Art.* New York: Basic Books, 1965.

Guilford, J.R. "Creativity: Retrospect and Prospect." *Journal of Creative Behavior,* 4 (1970), 149-168.

Gump, Margaret. *Adalbert Stifter*. New York: Twayne, 1974.

Gunvaldsen, K.M. "Franz Kafka and Psychoanalysis." *University of Toronto Quarterly*, 32 (1963), 266-281.

Hamilton, James "Object Loss, Dreaming and Creativity: The Poetry of John Keats." *The Psychoanalytic Study of the Child*, 24 (1969), 488-531.

Hamilton, James. "Transitional Fantasies and the Creative Process." *The Psychoanalytic Study of Society*, 6 (1975), 53-70.

Harris, Anne Sutherland and Linda Nochlin. *Women Artists: 1550–1950*. New York: Knopf, 1976.

Hartmann, H. "Notes on a Theory of Sublimation." *Psychoanalytic Study of the Child*, 10 (1955), 9-29.

Hausbek, Peter. "'Ruhe' und 'Bewegung'. Versuch einer Stilanalyse von Georg Büchners *Lenz*." *GRM, N.F.* 19 (1969), 35-59.

Hauser, Ronald. *Georg Büchner*. New York: Twayne, 1974.

Havelka, J. *The Nature of the Creative Process in Art: A Psychological Study*. The Hague: Martinus Nijhoff, 1968.

Hewett-Thayer, Harvey W. *Hoffmann: Author of the Tales*. New York: Octagon Books, 1971.

Heydebrand, Renate von. *Eduard Mörikes Gedichtwerk*. Stuttgart: Metzler, 1972.

Hillmann, Heinz. *Franz Kafka: Dichtungstheorie und Dichtungsgestalt*. 2. edition. Bonn: Bouvier, 1973.

Hinderer, Walter. *Büchner Kommentar zum dichterischen Werk*. Munich: Winkler, 1977.

Hinderer Walter. *Über deutsche Literatur und Rede: Historische Interpretationen.* Munich: Fink, 1981.

Hoffmann, Ernst Fedor. "Zu E.T.A. Hoffmanns 'Sandmann.'" *Monatshefte,* 54 (1962), 244-252.

Hoffmann, E.T.A. *Briefwechsel.* 2 vols. Munich: Winkler, 1967.

Hoffmann, E.T.A. *Sämtliche Werke.* Ed. by Walter Müller-Seidel. Munich: Winkler, 1960-65.

Hoffmann, E.T.A. *Tagebücher.* Munich: Winkler, 1971.

Hogan, Patrick Colm. "King Lear: Splitting and its Epistemic Agon." *American Imago,* 36 (1979), 32-44.

Holbrook, David. *Sylvia Plath: Poetry and Existence.* London: University of London, Athlone Press, 1976.

Holland, Norman N. *The Dynamics of Literary Response.* New York: Oxford University Press, 1968.

Hong, Michael. "The Transitional Phenomona: A Theoretical Integration." *The Psychoanalytic Study of the Child,* 33 (1978), 47-79.

Huff, Linda. *A Portrait of the Artist as a Young Woman: The Writer as Heroine in American Literature.* New York: Frederick Ungar, 1983.

Irle, Gerhard. *Der psychiatrische Roman.* Stuttgart: Hippokrates, 1965.

Janouch, Gustav. *Gespräche mit Kafka.* Frankfurt: Fischer, 1968.

Jones, Anne Goodwyn. *Tomorrow is Another Day: Women Writers in the South, 1859–1936.* Baton Rouge: Louisiana State University Press, 1981.

Jungmair, Otto. *Adalbert Stifters Linzer Jahre.* Nürnberg: Verlag Hans Carl, 1958.

Kafka, Franz. *Briefe.* Ed. Max Brod. New York: Schocken, 1958.

Kafka, Franz. *Briefe an Felice.* Eds. Erich Heller and Jürgen Born. Frankfurt: Fischer, 1967.

Kafka, Franz. *The Complete Stories.* New York: Schocken, 1976.

Kafka, Franz. *Diaries.* Ed. Max Brod. 4th edition. New York: Schocken, 1974.

Kafka, Franz. *Letter to his Father/ Brief an den Vater.* Tr. Ernst Kaiser and Eithne Wilkins. New York: Schocken, 1966.

Kafka, Franz. *Letters to Milena.* Ed. Willy Haas. New York: Schocken, 1953.

Kafka, Franz. *Sämtliche Erzählungen.* Ed. Paul Raabe. Frankfurt: Fischer, 1970.

Kahn, Charlotte and Geraldine Pirkowski. "Creativity and Group Rearing." *The Psychoanalytic Study of the Child,* 29 (1974), 231-255.

Kaiser, Michael. *Adalbert Stifter: Eine literaturpsychologische Untersuchung.* Bonn: Bouvier, 1971.

Kanzer, M. ed. *The Unconscious Today: Essays in Honor of Max Schur.* New York: International Universities Press, 1971.

Kanzer, Mark. "Writers and the early loss of parents." *Journal Hillside Hospital,* 2 (1953), 148-151.

Kanzog, Klaus. "Zehn Jahre E.T.A. Hoffmann Forschung: E.T.A. Hoffmann Literatur von 1970-1980: Eine Bibliographie." *Mitteilungen der E.T.A. Hoffmann Gesellschaft,* 27 (1981), 55-103.

Kestenberg, Judith. *Children and Parents: Psychoanalytic Studies in Development*. New York: Jason Aronson, 1975.

Klein, Melanie. "A Contribution to the Psychogenesis of Manic-depressive States." In *Contributions to Psychoanalysis*. London: Hogarth, 1965.

Kleinschmidt, Hans J. "The Angry Act: The Role of Aggression in Creativity." *American Imago*, 24, 1-2 (1967), 98-128.

Köhn, Lothar. *Vieldeutige Welt: Studien zur Struktur der Erzählungen E.T.A. Hoffmanns und zur Entwicklung seines Werkes*. Tübingen: Niemeyer, 1966.

Knapp, Gerhard Peter. *Georg Büchner: Eine kritische Einführung in die Forschung*. Frankfurt: Athenäum, 1975.

Koestler, Arthur. *The Act of Creation*. London: Hutchinson, 1964.

Kohut. Heinz. *The Restoration of the Self*. New York: International Universities Press, 1977.

Kohut, Heinz. *The Search for the Self*. 2 vols. Ed. Paul H. Ornstein. New York: International Universities Press, 1978.

Kris, Ernst. *Psychoanalytic Explorations in Art*. New York: International Universities Press, 1952.

Kubie, Lawrence S. *Neurotic Distortion of the Creative Process*. Lawrence, Kansas: University of Kansas Press, 1958.

Kubie, Lawrence S. "Impairment of the Freedom to Change with the Acquisition of the Symbolic Process." *Psychoanalytic Study of the Child*, 29 (1974), 257-262.

Kudszus, Winfried, ed. *Schizophrenie: Theorie und Interpretation eines Grenzgebietes*. Tübingen: Niemeyer, 1977.

Kudszus, Winfried and Bernd Urban, eds. *Psychoanalytische und Psychopathologische Literaturinterpretationen.* Darmstadt: Wissenschaffliche Buchgesellschaft, 1981.

Lane, Gary, ed. *Sylvia Plath: New Views on the Poetry.* Baltimore: John Hopkins University Press, 1979.

Laing, R.D. *The Divided Self: A Study of Sanity and Madness.* London: Tavistock Publishing, 1960.

Laing, R.D. *The Politics of Experience.* New York: Pantheon Books, 1967.

Lester, David. *Why People Kill Themselves: A Summary of Research Findings on Suicidal Behavior.* Diss., Springfield, Ill., 1972.

Lewis, M. and Roy Freedle. "Mother-Infant Dyad: The Cradle of Meaning." *Communication and Affect.* Ed. by Patricia Pliner, Lester Kranes, Thomas Allaway. New York: Academic Press, 1973, 127-155.

Lindauer, Martin. *The Psychological Study of Literature: Limitations, Possibilities and Accomplishments.* Chicago: Nelson-Hall, 1974.

Mahlendorf, Ursula. "Stifters Absage an die Kunst?" *Goethezeit: Festschrift für Stuart Atkins.* Bern, Munich: Francke Verlag, 1981, 369-383.

Marcuse, Herbert. *Eros and Civilization: A Philosophical Inquiry into Freud.* New York: Vintage, 1962.

Matt, Peter von. *Die Augen der Automaten: E.T.A. Hoffmanns Imaginationslehre als Prinzip seiner Erzählkunst.* Tübingen: Niemeyer, 1971.

Matt, Peter von. "Die gemalte Geliebte. Zur Problematik von Einbildungskraft und Selbsterkenntnis im erzählenden Werk E.T.A.

Hoffmanns." *GRM,* 21 (1971), 395-412.

Mayer, Thomas Michael. "Zu einigen Tendenzen der Büchner-Forschung: Ein kritischer Literaturbericht." *Text und Kritik. Sonderband Georg Büchner,* 3 (1981), 265-311.

McGlathery, James M. *Mysticism and Sexuality: E.T.A. Hoffmann.* Las Vegas, Bern, Frankfurt/Main: Peter Lang, 1981.

Meier, Albert. "Georg Büchners Ästhetik." *Georg Büchner Jahrbuch,* 2 (1982), 196-208.

Milner, Marion. *On Not Being Able to Paint.* 2. ed. New York: International Universities Press, 1967,

Mitchel, Juliet. *Psychoanalysis and Feminism.* New York: Vintage Books, 1975.

Moers, Ellen. *Literary Women.* New York: Doubleday, 1976.

Mörike, Eduard. *Mozart on the Way to Prague.* Tr. Mary Hottinger. In *Nineteenth Century German Tales.* Ed. Angel Flores. Garden City: Doubleday, Anchor, 1959.

Mörike, Eduard. *Werke und Briefe.* Ed. by H.-H. Krummacher *et al.* Stuttgart: Klett, 1967.

Moses, H. "Form and Content." *Psychoanalytic Study of the Child,* 23 (1968), 204-223.

Müller, Hans von. *E.T.A. Hoffmann: Briefwechsel, Tagebücher.* 3 vols. Munich: Winkler Verlag, 1967-72.

Müller, J. "Stifters Humor. Zur Struktur der Erzählungen 'Der Waldsteig' und 'Nachkommenschaften.'" *Adalbert Stifter Institut des Landes Oberösterrich: Vierteljahrsschrift,* 11 (1962), 1-20.

Neumann, Erich. *Art and the Creative Unconscious.* Bollingen Series, LXI. New York: Pantheon, 1959.

Newman, Charles, ed. *The Art of Sylvia Plath: A Symposium.* Bloomington, Indiana: Indiana University Press, 1970.

Niederland, W. "Clinical Aspects of Creativity." *American Imago,* 24 (1967), 6-24.

Niederland, W. "Some Ontogenetic Determinants in Symbol Formation." *The Psychoanalytic Study of Society,* 3 (1964), 98-110.

Norris, Margot. "Kafka's Josephine: The Animal as the Negative Site of Narration," *MLN,* 98 (1983), 366-383.

Novotny, Fritz. *Adalbert Stifter als Maler.* 3 edition. Vienna: Schroll, 1947.

Noy, Pinchas. "Form Creation in Art: An Ego Psychological Approach to Creativity." *International Journal of Psychoanalysis,* 59 (1978), 229-255.

Noy, Pinchas. "The Psychoanalytic Theory of Cognitive Development." *Psychoanalytic Study of the Child,* 34 (1979), 169-216.

Orgel, Shelley. "Sylvia Plath: Fusion with the Victim and Suicide." *Psychoanalytic Quarterly,* 43 (1975), 262-287.

Pascal, Roy. *Kafka's Narrators: A Study of his Stories and Sketches.* Cambridge: Cambridge University Press, 1982.

Pasley, Malcolm. "Der Schreibakt und das Geschriebene. Zur Frage der Entstehung von Kafkas Texten." *Franz Kafka: Themen und Probleme.* Ed. by Claude David. Göttingen: Vandenhoeck and Ruprecht, 1980, 9-25.

Phillipson, M. *Outline of Jungian Aesthetics.* Evanston, Ill.: Northwestern University Press, 1963.

Plath, Sylvia. *The Bell Jar.* 21. ed. New York: Bantam, 1976.

Plath, Sylvia. *Letters Home: Correspondence 1950–1963.* Ed. Aurelia Schober Plath. Toronto: Bantam, 1977.

Polheim, K.K. "Die wirkliche Wirklichkeit. Adalbert Stifters 'Nachkommenschaften' und das Problem seiner Kunstanschauung." In *Untersuchungen zur Literatur als Geschichte. Festschrift für Benno von Wiese.* Berlin: Schmidt, 1973.

Politzer, Heinz. *Franz Kafka: Parable and Paradox.* 2. ed. Ithaca: Cornell University Press, 1966.

Prang, Helmut, ed. *E.T.A. Hoffmann. Wege der Forschung.* Darmstadt: Wissenschaftliche Buchgesellschaft, 1976.

Prawer, S.S. "Hoffmann's Uncanny Guest: A Reading of 'Der Sandmann.'" *German Life and Letters,* 18 (1964-65), 297-308.

Putz, H.P. "Büchners *Lenz* und seine Quelle. Bericht und Erzählung." *ZfdPh,* 84 (1965), Sonderheft, 1-22.

Reiss, Hans. "Kafka on the Writer's Task." *MLR,* 66 (1970), 13-24.

Richards, David. *Georg Büchner and the Birth of Modern Drama.* Albany: State University of New York Press, 1977.

Rothenberg, Albert, and Carl R. Hausman. "Creativity: A Survey and Critique of Major Investigations." *Psychoanalysis and Contemporary Science, 3 (1974), 70–97.*

Rothenberg, Albert. *The Emerging Goddess.* Chicago: University of Chicago Press, 1979.

Ruitenbeek, Hendrik M., ed. *Freud As We Knew Him.* Detroit: Wayne State University Press, 1973.

Ruitenbeek, Hendrik M., ed. *The Literary Imagination: Psychoanalysis and the Genius of the Writer.* Chicago: Quandrangle Books, 1965.

Rupp, Hans-Ulrich. *Stifters Sprache.* Zürich: Juris, 1969.

Schings, Hans-Jürgen. *Der mitleidigste Mensch ist der beste Mensch.* Munich: Beck, 1980.

Schmidt, Jochen. "E.T.A. Hoffmanns 'Der Sandmann' in historischer Perspektive." In *Literaturwissenschaft und Geistesgeschichte: Festschrift für Richard Brinkmann.* Tübingen: Niemeyer Verlag, 1982, 349-370.

Segebrecht, Wulf. "E.T.A. Hoffmanns Auffassung vom Dichteramt und Dichterberuf." *JDSG,* 2 (1967), 62-138.

Seidler, H. "Adalbert Stifter-Forschung 1945-1970." *Zeitschrift für deutsche Philologie,* 91 (1972), 113-157; 252-285.

Seidler, H. "Die Adalbert Stifter Forschung der siebziger Jahre." *Vasilo,* 30 (1981), 89-134.

Selge, Martin. *Adalbert Stifter: Poesie aus dem Geiste der Naturwissenschaften.* Stuttgart: Kohlhammer, 1976.

Seyersted, P. *Kate Chopin: A Critical Biography.* Baton Rouge: Louisiana State University Press, 1969.

Sharp, Francis Michael. "Büchner's 'Lenz': A Futile Madness." *Psychoanalytische und Psychopathologische Literaturinterpretationen.* Ed. by Bernd Urban and Winfried Kudszus. Darmstadt: Wissenschaftliche Buchgesellschaft, 1981, 256-279.

Shor, Joel and Jean Sanville. *Illusion in Loving: A Psychoanalytic Approach to the Evolution of Intimacy and Autonomy.* Los Angeles: Double Helix Press, 1978.

Showalter, Elaine. *A Literature of Their Own.* Princeton: Princeton University Press, 1977.

Simon, Hans-Ulrich. *Mörike—Chronik.* Stuttgart: Metzler, 1981.

Slessarev, Helga. *Eduard Mörike*. New York: Twayne, 1970.

Slochower, H. "Genius, Psychopathology and Creativity." *American Imago*, 24 (1967), 1-2.

Slochower, H. *Mythopoesis: Mythic Patterns in the Literary Classics*. Detroit: Wayne State University Press, 1970.

Slochower, H. "Psychoanalysis and Literature." In *Progress in Clinical Psychology*. Eds. L.E. Abt and B.F. Riess. New York: Grune and Stratton, 1960.

Slochower, H. "Symbolism and the Creative Process in Art." *American Imago*, 22 (1965), 1-2.

Sokel, Walter H. *Franz Kafka: Tragik und Ironie: Zur Struktur seiner Kunst*. Munich: A. Langen, 1964.

Sokel, Walter H. "Kafka's Poetics of the Inner Self." *From Kafka to Dada to Brecht and Beyond*. Ed. by Reinhold Grimm, Peter Spycher, Richard A. Zipser. Madison, Wisconsin: University of Wisconsin Press, 1982, 7-21.

Stade, George. "Introduction." In *A Closer Look at Ariel: A Memory of Sylvia Plath*. By Nancy Hunter Steiner. New York: Harper and Row, 1972.

Steffen, Konrad. *Adalbert Stifter: Deutungen*. Basel: Birkhäuser, 1955.

Stifter, Adalbert. *Jugendbriefe*. Ed. Gustav Wilhelm. Nürnberg: Carl, 1954.

Stifter, Adalbert. *Julius: eine Erzählung. Text—kritische Ausgabe*. Ed. Kurt Gerhard Fischer. Linz: Oberöstereichischer Landesverlag, 1965.

Stifter, Adalbert. *Sämtliche Werke*. Prague-Reichenberg: Bibliothek deutscher Schriftsteller aus Böhmen, 1901 ff.

Stölzl, Christoph. *Kafkas böses Böhmen.* Munich: edition text und kritik, 1975.

Storr, Anthony. *The Dynamics of Creation.* New York: Atheneum, 1972.

Storz, Gerhard. *Eduard Mörike.* Stuttgart: Klett, 1967.

Tartar, Maria M. "E.T.A. Hoffmann's 'Der Sandmann': Reflection and Romantic Irony." *MLN,* 95 (1980), 585-608.

Thorn-Prikker, Jan. *Revolutionär ohne Revolution: Interpretation der Werke Georg Büchners.* Stuttgart: Klett, Cotta, 1978.

Ueding, Cornelie. *Denken. Sprechen. Handeln.* Bern: Lang, 1976.

Unseld, Joachim. *Franz Kafka: Ein Schriftstellerleben: Die Geschichte seiner Veröffentlichungen.* Munich: Carl Hanser, 1982.

Vietta, Silvio. "Das Automatenmotif und die Technik der Motifschichtung im Erzählwerk E.T.A. Hoffmanns." *Mitteilungen der E.T.A. Hoffmann Gesellschaft,* 26 (1980), 25-33.

Wilson, Edmund. *The Wound and the Bow.* Boston: Houghton Mifflin, 1947.

Weber, Samuel. "The Sideshow, or Remarks on a Canny Moment." *MLN* (1977), 1102-1133.

Weissmann, P. "Theoretical Consideration of Ego Regression and Ego Function in Creativity." *Psychoanalytic Quarterly,* 36 (1967), 26-37.

Werner, Hans Georg. *E.T.A. Hoffmann: Darstellung und Deutung der Wirklichkeit im dichterischen Werk.* Berlin: Aufbau Verlag, 1971.

White, John S. "Georg Büchner or the Suffering through the Father." *American Imago,* 9 (1952), 365-427.

White, John S. "Psyche and Tuberculosis: The Libido Organization of Franz Kafka." *The Psychoanalytic Study of Society,* 4 (1967), 185-251.

White, John S. and Calvin S. Hall, *et al. Dreams, Life and Literature: A study of Franz Kafka.* Stuttgart: Kohlhammer, 1976.

Wildbolz, Rudolf. *Adalbert Stifter.* Stuttgart: Kohlhammer, 1976.

Winnicott, D.W. *Playing and Reality.* New York: Basic Books, 1971.

Winnicott, D. W. "Transitional Objects and Transitional Phenomena." *International Journal of Psychoanalysis,* 34 (1953), 89-97.

Winter, Ilse. *Untersuchungen zum serapiontischen Prinzip E.T.A. Hoffmanns.* The Hague: Mouton, 1976.

Winterstein, Alfred. *Adalbert Stifter: Persönlichkeit und Werk, eine tiefenpsychologische Studie.* Vienna: Phoenix, 1946.

INDEX